**MODERN
JEWISH
HISTORY**

*Robert Mandel,
series editor*

TRANSCENDING
DARKNESS

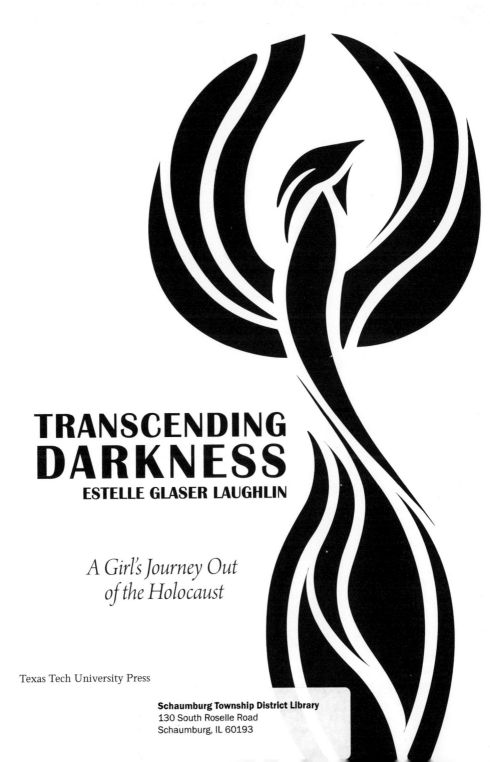

TRANSCENDING
DARKNESS
ESTELLE GLASER LAUGHLIN

*A Girl's Journey Out
of the Holocaust*

Texas Tech University Press

Copyright © 2012 by Estelle Glaser Laughlin

Unless otherwise indicated, all photographs from the author's personal collection.

This book is typeset in Monotype Perrywood. The paper used in this book meets the minimum requirements of ANSI/NISO Z39.48-1992 (R1997). ∞

Designed by Kasey McBeath

Cover illustration by Anna Coventry-Arredondo

Library of Congress Cataloging-in-Publication Data

Laughlin, Estelle.
    Transcending darkness : a girl's journey out of the Holocaust / Estelle Glaser Laughlin.
       p. cm. — (Modern Jewish history)
    Summary: "The memoir of Holocaust survivor Estelle Glaser Laughlin, published sixty-four years after her liberation from the Nazis"--Provided by publisher.
    ISBN 978-0-89672-767-0 (hardcover : alk. paper) — ISBN 978-0-89672-800-4 (e-book)
1. Laughlin, Estelle. 2. Jews—Poland—Warsaw—Biography. 3. Holocaust, Jewish (1939-1945)—Poland—Personal narratives. 4. Jewish children in the Holocaust—Poland—Biography. 5. Majdanek (Concentration camp) 6. World War, 1939-1945—Conscript labor—Europe, Eastern. 7. Holocaust survivors—United States—Biography. I. Title.
    DS134.72.L394A3 2012
    940.53'18092--dc23
      [B]   2012031150

Printed in the United States of America
12 13 14 15 16 17 18 19 20 / 9 8 7 6 5 4 3 2 1

Texas Tech University Press
Box 41037 | Lubbock, Texas 79409-1037 USA | 800.832.4042
ttup@ttu.edu | www.ttupress.org

To my children and grandchildren, in many ways my teachers; to Fredka's progeny; and to the Lamed Vav Zaddikim, upon whom the survival of a civilized world depends

Contents

Part II: *Liberation*

Illustrations

Preface

I t is strange how the legends and songs we hear in childhood stay with us to give us hope and inspiration. My favorite myth is of the phoenix that rose from the ashes and winged its way aloft whispering, "Immortality." Like the mythical phoenix, my mother, sister, and I rose from the ashes of the death camps to start life again. Our rebirth was rooted in the cultural values that shaped and maintained the Jewish people over the ages.

Sixty-four years have passed since my liberation from the concentration camp. I no longer can remember where I last put my glasses, yet I remember—clear as light—scenes that turned my sunny childhood into an inferno and killed nearly everyone I loved. I ask myself, *How did my mother, my sister, and I survive? How did we survive whole, with love, compassion, and joy for life?* Without this human core, survival would have little meaning. These existential questions loom larger in my mind now at the winter of my life, the time of repose and reflection—hence my memoir.

Dredging up the darkness of my past was painful. However, wisdom is seldom gained without tears. Seeing the child I was through the eyes of the woman I am now, I find a strong, resilient, and wise girl. While surrounded by suffering and deprivation, she recalls the good of her prewar past and the good people in her community, casting them as hopeful signs that there were and would always be righteous people. What is special about that girl is that she finds a way to preserve goodness in spite of the evil that rages around her. She brings her own light into the darkness. This is what sustains her and sustains my memoir. Without that, one is overwhelmed with the horror and is left drained of hope for humanity.

I dedicate my memoir to all the wonderful children whose voices were silenced in the Holocaust and to all the children who are in harm's way in our time.

Acknowledgments

With all the gratitude I can summon, I thank my friend Don Montagna for inspiring me to write my memoir, for reading my manuscript, and for his guidance.

My gratitude and affection go to Anna Gillis, Helen Shaw, Rima Schulkin, and friends in my writers' circle—Sally Carson, Barbara Brill, Sara Stone, and Bob Elkins—for their insightful feedback. Thanks also to Miriam Cutler for her generous help with selecting photos and coding them electronically.

My thanks to Merril Leffler and to Dr. Robert Mandel, director of Texas Tech University Press, for their faith in my manuscript and for their efforts to see it published.

I wish I could find a way to properly acknowledge my sons, Steven, Andy, and Bob, and my nieces, Fern and Stephanie, for their inspiration and encouragement.

I owe a special debt of gratitude to my grandchildren, Lauren, Eric, Matthew, Alex, Twain, Nina, and Emmarose, for their eager interest in my story, their questions, and their recognition of the love and courage that shines through people even in the worst times—and, for their appreciation of their own good fortune. Their enthusiasm and wisdom were my inspirations.

Lastly, my deep gratitude to my late husband, Chuck, who nurtured all my personal endeavors.

Chronology of Upheavals that Led to World War II

The upheavals that led to the invasion of my country, Poland, and to World War II began in Germany with the birth of the Nazi Party in 1919. The party started as a gang of unemployed soldiers and became the legal government by 1933, in only fourteen years.

In 1929, the year I was born, the demise of Weimar democracy began with the collapse of the existing government.

In 1932, when I was three years old and had all a child could need—love and a secure home—Hitler received 37 percent of the presidential vote.

In January 1933, President von Hindenburg appointed Hitler Chancellor of Germany. Within months of Hitler's appointment, the Dachau concentration camp was created.

In February, the Reichstag building went up in flames.

In 1934, when my sister and I played peacefully under the protective wings of our community, another newsflash shocked my community: President Hindenburg died. Hitler combined the offices of Reich chancellor and president, declaring himself Reichsführer (leader of the Reich).

In 1935, Hitler announced the Nuremberg Laws, which stripped Jews of their civil rights as German citizens, and Jews were defined as a separate race. This law forbade marriages or sexual relations between Jews and Germans.

Of course, children my age did not understand the complexities or horrors of these events, which were feverishly discussed at home, on the streets, and on the air. But we clearly understood that somewhere on our planet windows of Jewish stores were being shattered, Jewish books went up in flames, people were arrested for no reason, and a terrible man named Hitler stomped the earth. I do not know what other children felt when their ears were filled with the news of violence. I, a Jewish child, felt danger pointing at me from a mysterious place.

In 1936, Berlin hosted the Olympics. Jesse Owens, the African-American track star, was the undisputed hero in the land of "Aryan superiority." I doubt that I paid much attention to this great event, but my teenaged cousins hooted with joy. So did all the adults around me. I am not sure if this is an authentic memory, or if I heard it enough times to remember it as my own.

In March 1938, as part of Hitler's quest for uniting all German-speaking people and for *lebensraum* (living space), Germany took over Austria with the overwhelming approval of the Austrian people.

In October 1938, Germany occupied the northwestern area of Czechoslovakia, called the Sudetenland, and no countries protested these violations of the 1919 Treaty of Versailles.

Still more horrendous events continued to unfold.

On November 9, 1938, German Prime Minister Joseph Goebbels initiated the Kristallnacht (Night of the Broken Glass), a free-for-all against the Jews, during which synagogues were set on fire, Jewish businesses and homes were looted, many Jews were killed, and many were arrested and sent to concentration camps to be tormented. Within days, Jews were forced to transfer their businesses to Aryan hands, and Jewish children were expelled from public schools.

What do I remember of the news that unsettled my community when I was nine years old? I clearly remember newspaper caricatures of Neville Chamberlain shaking hands with Hitler and holding an umbrella in his other hand, and the bitter reactions of the adults. I remember the shock I saw on my parents' faces when the radios shouted the news: "Germany occupied the Sudetenland!" And I have not forgotten the shudder of fear I heard in people's voices when they talked about German forces concentrated at the Polish border.

On September 1, 1939, Hitler began the invasion of Poland, officially starting World War II.

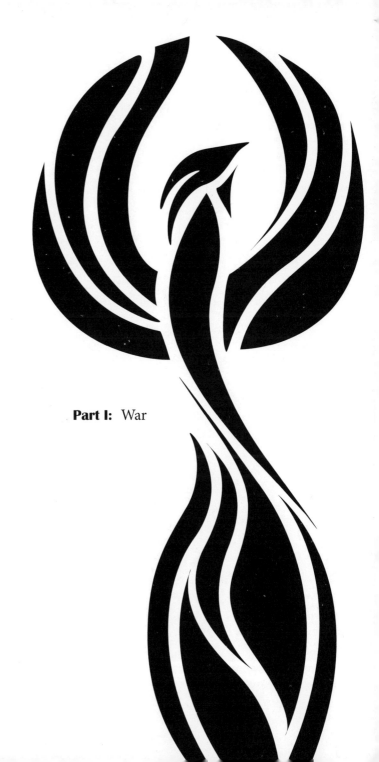

Part I: War

Tata, Fredka, and me, Warsaw, 1938.

1 *Strong! United! Ready!*

The morning of September 1, 1939, was serene. Tata came into the living room in a dapper suit, a hat in his hand, kissed my mother, sister, and me, and left the house to visit his clients on Królewska Street, in the heart of Warsaw. Sometime on that day a deafening explosion shook the earth. Then, silence—as if all the air had been sucked out of the universe. Just as suddenly, screaming air-raid sirens set the city aquiver. Stunned, Mama turned on the radio and we heard, "Attention. Attention. Poland is under attack! German warplanes dropped bombs on Warsaw!"

My gosh! *Is Tata safe? Are we safe without him?* I shuddered.

Unable to contain our fears, Mama, Fredka, and I took posts at a window with a view of the wrought iron gate at the far end of our courtyard, and waited for Tata to come home. As soon as he stepped into the arched entrance, we bolted to the front door to barrage him with hugs and questions. "Tata, Tata, what is happening? Was it a real bomb?"

"Oh yes, it was! I saw the devastation."

"What did you see, Tata?"

"It was awful. And so sudden. I heard a loud rumble of airplanes. I stopped and looked up. Everyone in the street did the same. In a split second, planes dove out of the sky. Then boooom! Bombs were falling and buildings exploded before our eyes. Everyone stood frozen in place. Shocked. So helpless! The bombers took off with the same lightning speed, air-raid sirens began to shriek, and I rushed home to you."

Perhaps we should have expected the attack. For endless months, our radios had blared German threats to annex Poland's only port city, Gdynia. Slogans—"*Silni! Zwarci! Gotowi!*" (Strong! United! Ready!)—screamed from banners draped across the city. Air-raid sirens screeched to drill us for a possible attack. Still, war remained unimaginable until the first bomb fell on Warsaw. Even then, the true brutality of war remained distant.

For me, the real blight of war began on that night. In an instant, I, at the age of ten, and Fredka, eleven and a half, stopped being carefree children and began to carry the tragic burdens of life.

That night I was awakened by a fierce rumble of airplanes. Before I could lift my head from the pillow, brilliant, hissing beams of light illuminated the sky: "Hisss! Hisss!" like wicked winds. A barrage of explosions convulsed the earth. Moments later, terrified people, still in bedclothes, babies in their arms, were running from their houses in search of safety. Some carried small bundles of valuables. Many grabbed the nearest object without thinking. No one really knew where to run.

Imagining greater danger to be on the higher floor, we rushed downstairs to my best friend Janka's house—as if we would rather be covered by the warm earth than be crushed by collapsing buildings.

What ensued that night was beyond my imagination. The heavens opened with blinding blasts of lights, erasing the star-incrusted darkness and making every building a clear target. Then, roaring flocks of Messerschmitts and Stukas swooped down, dropping bombs around us, destroying one house after another, and killing people with every burst. Gargantuan detonations shook the planet, and flames licked neighboring buildings. Quivering with fright, we sat huddled close together, seeking comfort in each other's presence. When the explosions paused, I was not quite sure if I was still alive.

For the next four weeks, bombs rained on our heads. The thunder of detonations, the rumble of collapsing buildings, staccato pops of antiaircraft guns firing from rooftops, cries of panic, plumes of smoke, and the smell of burning flesh were interminable.

My world turned to chaos. Even when the bombardments paused, no one went to work or to school. Always we turned our ears to the radio, hearing urgent calls. "Let us rise up and defend our city! Be on the watch for spies! Beware of German nationals sneaking up on rooftops to send flashlight signals to enemy planes!"

People barricaded the streets with stacks of furniture in hope of stopping the advance of German tanks. A blackout cloaked the city in fearful darkness. My city seemed to stop breathing. Yet this was merely the prelude to events soon to come.

In the silence of one predawn, after hours of pounding detonations, frantic screams of a woman woke me up. "Danger! Danger! Germans are coming! They are killing all the men! Wake up and run!"

I jumped out of bed, flung the blacked-out window open, and looked down at the petite silhouette of my Aunt Malka—barely visible in the last glow of the moon—rushing across the courtyard toward our stairwell, screaming, "Danger!" Startled neighbors in nightdresses leaned out of windows and over balcony railings and called down, "What is going on? What is happening?"

Aunt Malka had sprinted the nearly three miles from Pawia Street—through the fearsome darkness—to arrive at our door, sweat pouring down her cheeks, eyes wide with terror, yelling, "German troops are advancing on our land! They are killing every Polish male they find." She turned to Tata, "Samek, hurry! Get dressed. Run! You must save yourself!"

Aunt Malka was so flustered. Though we could not grasp the whole situation, we got the message loud and clear that we were being invaded and that we were in grave danger.

We turned on the radio. "Attention! Attention!" a voice blared with authority. "This is an official government announcement. German forces are sweeping our land. Attention soldiers! Lay down your arms. All men leave your posts and run home. Run for safety or you will be slaughtered." This order was repeated over and over, along with vivid descriptions of men being butchered.

My mind whirled with horror. *They might kill Tata! My gosh, how will we live without him?* Everything within me constricted. We all talked at once.

Tata announced, "I am not leaving. I am staying here. I won't leave you! No!"

Fredka and I cried, "Tata, run. Please. They will kill you." I was afraid of my own words. I was horrified that he would be killed if he stayed and just as terrified that he would abandon us.

Mama looked limp, her face lifeless. She pleaded, "What can we do? What will I do without you? No, you must run! You must save yourself! Please! Go! Now!"

Tata left us. What else could he do? All the men in our building left. All the men on our street suddenly vanished. There were hardly any men left in the city. They were fleeing toward the Russian border. They ran without a plan or a clear direction, as from a raging fire.

Heartbreaking laments spilled from windows into the courtyards and streets of Warsaw. Mama, trying to be brave for our sake, held back her tears. Fredka and I too tried to protect Mama and did not cry, but I could not stop myself from shivering.

Within hours, as if sobered by the rising day, we learned that the night broadcast was a hoax to provoke panic. A group of Germans had taken over major radio stations and in perfect Polish impersonated known government figures.

A ray of hope returned. We walked to a window and spent tedious hours staring at the street gate, waiting for Tata to return. A day or two passed. A few men came back, but not Tata. Luszek, our neighbor's young son, came home. So did his golden retriever. In his master's absence, the dog had vanished and no one could find him. As soon as Luszek came home, the dog came back from nowhere looking haggard but happy. Still no sign of Tata.

With Tata gone, all color faded from life. Mama, Fredka, and I felt lost in our house. Nothing looked familiar. We could not find a comfortable corner to rest. Unable to cope with the loss, Mama filled a couple of valises with clothes and said, "We are going to Aunt Malka. We will stay there till Tata comes back."

I tucked under my arm the wooden chess game that Tata gave me on my tenth birthday, and I took hold of other parcels that Mama let me carry. Mama, Fredka, and Justina, our maid, lifted their bundles, and together we walked to Aunt Malka's ground-floor apartment on Pawia Street. Justina went right back to wait for Tata to return and to let him know where to find us.

There was despair in my aunt's house. Josek and Dudek, my two handsome, grown-up cousins, were gone. Only Uncle Boris decided that he could not outrun the German army and had stayed home. Josek's bride, Tecia, came to stay with Aunt Malka. I adored Tecia for her beauty and attentiveness. Even though I was much younger, she took time to talk with me and give me hope that things might turn out all right in the end.

All guests slept on cots in the living room. I slept with Tata's chess game under my pillow. When the detonations shook us out of sleep, we left our cots—trembling all over as though an earthquake were passing through our bodies—and we huddled close together, terrified to let go of each other.

During the day, we enjoyed short pauses between raids—like sips of sanity. Fredka and I would run down to the courtyard to play with other children. We romped boisterously and noisily, enjoying the temporary freedom, but we never strayed far from the door. The adults remained cooped up inside the house with grim faces.

One quiet dawn, I felt Tata sitting down, ever so softly, on my cot, bending over me to kiss my face. Stirred, I called out, "Tata!" and reached for him.

Instead of Tata, Tecia responded, "Oh, I am so sorry, I startled you. Did you dream of your father?"

"Yes, I felt him. He was so real."

"You never know," Tecia tried to cheer me. "Maybe he is on his way home. He may even come home today."

The image of that morning stayed with me all day. Dreamily, I pulled a chair to a window, sat down, rested my arms on my chess set, and stared into the courtyard. Children called to me, "Estusia, come out and play." I remained in my solitude, hugging the box, talking to no one, and feeling the tugging nearness of Tata.

Just as dusk began to fall, Tata's face looked up at me from the courtyard. I saw his gaunt cheeks, his blond curls forming a widow's peak on his wide forehead, his steady eyes looking up at me. Tata had come home!

With Tata back, Mama, Fredka, and I went home. Dudek and Josek returned a few days later. Bit by bit we were learning to live with terror. The abnormal, when constant, seems normal.

It took only eight days for the well-disciplined and highly mechanized German forces to sweep through my country and reach the suburbs of Warsaw. We were under siege. Our government fled to Rumania, taking their families with them, and from there they fled to England. Everyone talked about their escape, and I wondered, *What will we do without them?* The leaders were gone, but the people in my city continued to obey their commands to fight for country and honor. Only Warsaw held the line of defense for four long weeks.

In the final days of battle, the German army circled the city and barraged us with incendiary bombs and explosives. They destroyed the water works and electrical systems. We were without food and without water for drinking and for extinguishing the raging fires.

Then came a proclamation: "Armistice! Poland has fallen."

Mama lamented, "Beautiful Warsaw, queen of Polish cities, is in ruins!"

When the bombardment ceased, we went in search of friends and food, but I found it frightful to go into the streets. Hundreds of houses had been destroyed by fire or reduced to heaps of rubble. It was difficult to walk among the still-smoldering ruins. Bodies of people were being pulled out from the wreckage. And after all the horrors we had endured, we waited with dread for Hitler's army to enter our streets.

2 *Invasion*

The Wehrmacht marched into Warsaw on the first of October. The thunder of their boots against cobblestones, the clang of their rifles, arms swinging in unison as if pulled fanatically by one thread, still haunt my dreams. The day was dark with anguish. Holding Mama's hand, I joined the dismal crowd of people standing back on sidewalks to witness our fate.

Immediately, my life changed beyond belief. My once-peaceful streets were soon patrolled by Nazi soldiers in clicking boots and war helmets, with rifles cocked, ready to fire. Like common thieves they entered my neighbors' homes and helped themselves to whatever they wanted. Officers with scissors shamelessly chased after Jews to cut off their beards. We were afraid to utter a word of protest, lest we and our neighbors would pay with our lives.

One unforgettable day, I heard a mournful sigh rise from our courtyard. I rushed out onto the balcony and faced a ring of astonished faces staring down from rows of windows. I followed their gaze and saw Mr. Frenkel, our neighborhood aristocrat, crossing the courtyard. Half his beard was gone! One cheek was startlingly bare and crimson. Disgraceful hands of barbarians had bruised the gentle face of our noblest neighbor. I looked into his grave face and felt myself falling with him, with all my people, into a bottomless abyss. Never before was my soul so wounded, never before had I cried as deeply, as silently, as acrimoniously as at that moment. Mama whispered, "Where is God?"

Each day brought a new calamity. Street megaphones blasted orders and threats to kill us if we did not immediately surrender furs, paintings, jewelry, and currency to pay for the war that we, Jews, were crazily accused of starting. Bravely, my parents and everyone I knew hid what they could. Seeing my people resist cruel mandates gave me heart.

We were forbidden to walk about the streets between nine at night and five in the morning. The curfew silence hung outside my blacked-out windows like a harbinger of danger. The night no longer sparkled with city lights, and laughter no longer made the darkness sing.

We had limited use of water, no radios or newspaper, no electricity, no telephones. We could not reach friends, even in an emergency. We lived in a state of darkness, cut off from the world and everything that was taking place in it.

At night, when the streets were as silent as death, Mama lit the wick on a ball-shaped carbide lantern. A small orb of light formed around the table while the rest of the room was in semidarkness. The tiny flame flickered like a leaf in a hurricane and made our eyes smart. To see fine details, we had to sit close to the light and inhale the putrid odor of carbide. Still, the darkness did not keep us from reading, mending our clothes, or playing. I felt a precarious safety—like hiding in a cave from a pack of wolves—sitting with Mama, Tata, and Fredka within that small circle of light. Sometimes I would imagine the Nazi soldiers who slept in the distance being swallowed into eternal darkness and leaving us to find our way back to our happy lives.

They closed our schools. Bored children got into mischief and drove parents to distraction. After weeks of negotiations, the Judenrat (Jewish Council) obtained permission to open supervised *Ogródki* (playgrounds). Everyone was grateful. The kids, tired of being cooped up, dashed to the playgrounds like alcoholics to bars.

Our counselors, unemployed teachers, taught us spirited Yiddish songs filled with funny animal sounds and amusing characters. Our laughter flowed like warm honey; our fears drowned in the joy of play and make-believe. During quiet time, our guardians told us wonderful Yiddish folktales; they encouraged us to think, use good judgment, and not lose trust.

Our happiness did not last long. After several months, the Germans ordered the Jewish Council to close our short-lived paradise. With nothing to do, Fredka and I spent hours at home. When we became restless, we joined children in the courtyard in self-organized games. Our exuberant voices vibrated throughout the building complex. We made up skits and games in which we slew the Nazi criminals. We bounced balls against the walls of the building and played hide-and-seek, galloping up and down long flights of stairs located in the four corners of the yard. Parents smiled with contentment to see their children playing happily, while those who yearned for quiet greeted us with long faces. For pranks, we rang doorbells in neighboring houses, and bolted down the stairs before the doors opened.

We played boisterously, but were never free of fear or duty. We always kept watch for German soldiers entering the street or building. When we spotted a German uniform in the distance, we scattered home with shrapnel speed to warn and help our parents hide all contraband, white bread and books among them. We children were conscientious sentries—attentive, sharp, and swift.

Another indignity separated us from the city population. We were forbidden to leave our house without wearing a white armband ten centimeters wide with a Jewish star, as if my religion were a disgrace. When Mama adjusted the armband on my sleeve, she would say, "Wait till the world hears about this. The Nazis will be shamed for their disgraceful behavior." Mama's faith in humanity and justice never ceased.

The First Loss

Tens of thousands of young people without means of sustenance, with no present or future, decided to flee for their lives to the Führer's friend, Soviet Russia. Sometime in the late fall of 1939, my three eldest cousins, Aunt Malka's sons, Dudek and Josek, and Josek's bride, Tecia, joined the fleeing throngs. With my cousins gone, my aunt's house on Pawia Street felt empty and dark with sorrow. Everyone in my family was stricken with grief.

It did not take long for rumors to reach us that the fleeing masses had been assaulted and robbed on the way by the border guards who knew that Jewish lives were public property. Aunt Malka searched out those who turned back to ask if by chance they had met her two sons and her daughter-in-law on their way. Those who had seen them passing on the road had no clue about my cousins' fate. It saddened me to see grief etched in my aunt's wan face. She grew thinner each time I saw her, as if she were turning into her own shadow.

My three wonderful cousins were gone, but memories linger. I still remember, clear as light, Josek and Tecia in their first home before the outbreak of war. It was soon after their wedding and the occasion was special—the first family dinner at their own place. We sat around a lavishly decked table with my two aunts, uncles, and my beloved five cousins— all beaming with the specialness of the moment. Toasts were raised to the young couple, and the sound of joyful prattling filled the room.

Josek, tall, blond, and dashingly handsome, and the willowy Tecia were as beautiful as a picture standing next to each other holding hands—love glinting in their smiles. Tecia's comely face was as round and smooth as a freshly picked apple. I loved the pretty way she braided her silky brown hair and wound it around her head like a garland. In my nine-year-old eyes, their small home and the occasion were magically romantic.

My cousins remain frozen in time, as I saw them last—young, bright, exuberant— impossible to imagine dead. Dead people are buried.

My cousin Josek and his
bride, Tecia, Warsaw,
1938.

3 *Ghetto and Moral Resistance*

A new decree panicked the community. Even non-Jews would have to abandon their homes; churches and businesses would have to relocate. Children asked their parents, "What is a ghetto? What will happen to us?" Then we went back to our world of make-believe, with hearts too heavy, and wondered, *How come insane people are allowed to make laws and run the world?*

The day the formation of a Jewish quarter was announced, turmoil hit the city. Both Jews and Christians were in a frenzy to find new homes. Justina, our Ukrainian maid, packed her belongings in two valises, tucked the money my parents gave her into her bra to keep it safe, and left our house. We hugged, our eyes filled with tears, but I felt relieved that I would no longer have to worry that she might denounce us to the German soldiers she dated on her days off.

On the day all Jews had to move into the ghetto, thousands of hungry, cold, overwhelmed, evicted people flooded our streets searching for apartments. By law, no one was permitted to remove furniture, but the streets were full of defiant people pushing carts loaded with household goods. Nowolipki Street, where we lived, and Muranowska and Pawia, where Aunt Hannah and Aunt Malka lived, remained in the Jewish sector. In the ghetto, if you had an apartment, you had everything; without one, you had nothing.

Warsaw Ghetto wall, 1940. Courtesy United States Holocaust Memorial Museum.

Some of my new friends who had been forced into the ghetto were Jewish children born into Christianity, children of mixed marriages, and even third-generation Christians. In some instances, Poles tipped off the Nazis about some irregularities in the family trees of their coreligionists. And that was not all. More nightmarish decrees followed and stretched my belief of grown-ups' propensity for cruelty.

In the spring of 1940, the Judenrat was ordered to build, at its own expense, a thick wall all around the ghetto. I was horrified. *We will be walled in! Imprisoned!*

In no time the brick barrier rose tall to block my horizon. It had twenty-two hellish guarded gates. When a gate swung open, I felt an irresistible temptation to steal a glance at freedom on the other side. At the same time, a shudder of fear went through me and warned me to keep far away. The menacing wall zigzagged, closing off some streets and bisecting others. Chlodna Street was split into three parts and divided by two walls. To keep the Jews and Christians from meeting, the Nazis ordered the Judenrat to construct a bridge about two stories high with steps leading up and down the same street. When I followed Mama across the bridge, she held my hand tightly and cautioned, "Don't look at them. Don't let them notice you." I struggled to heed her warnings and become invisible, but I could not resist my curiosity to check out the faces of our tormentors. I was astounded. *How could people with human faces be so beastly?*

They named our ghetto-prison *"Totkasten"* (Death Crate) and packed our streets with refugees driven out of surrounding areas. Some 400,000 Jewish people were forced to live in a 1.3 square mile area. Thirty percent of the city's population squeezed into less than 3 percent of its space. The deportees came with harrowing stories of mass murders. I would ask, "Mama, Tata, will the Germans do the same to us?" My parents tried to soothe my fears. "Don't fret. Go play. We will look out for you." But they could not hide the blight.

Most evacuees came on foot and without a penny, sometimes without shoes on their feet. German soldiers had driven them out of their beds before dawn, and they had left everything they owned. Talented musicians gave moving performances at street corners. Passersby stopped to listen, and then left feeling guilty for not having money to place in the collection hats.

A skinny, ragged, gifted boy, with dreamy dark eyes, only a couple of years older than I, stole my heart. He always stood at the same street corner, a violin resting under his chin, eyes lost in a dream world, a bow in one hand lovingly stroking the strings and making the violin play so beautifully—no one could pass without stopping to listen. He soon became the talk of the ghetto. I often went out of my way to hear him play my favorite piece, Mendelssohn's Violin Concerto. Then I would place my sandwich in his collection plate and feel ashamed that it was all I could give him in return for what he gave me.

Little tots, no older than three, with bare feet and knees, standing dumbly in the streets yammering, and frozen corpses of children on doorsteps moved my deepest sympathy. They made me fear, *Will that happen to me?* People covered the dead bodies with posters saying, "Our Children Must Live—A Child Is the Holiest Thing."

In spite of the odds against us, the people I knew fought back, even if they had no guns. They struggled against inhumane ordinances, against hunger and death, and to live according to the dictates of their conscience, no matter the cost. The valor of the people in my community gave me hope and the will to persist. Yet, some people now ask me, "Why didn't you fight back?"

Quickly, people marshaled forces and instituted a far-reaching Self-Aid Center to help the needy. Every apartment building formed a committee, and everyone had to contribute, even the misers. Every building established a kitchen to feed the starving. People contributed money and food, and took turns cooking. We children helped stir the big kettles. I felt reassured to see kindness during a time when brutality raged all around me.

Tata's generosity was my greatest inspiration. He served tirelessly on several courtyard committees and contributed money generously—never allowing his name to appear on donors' lists. "Tata, why do you refuse to have your name listed? My friends' fathers are on the list," I pressed him.

"You give because it is the right thing to do. If you expect to be paid back, you call that making a deal." I revered Tata for his humility and kindness as much as I loved him for his playfulness and steadfastness with Fredka and me.

All children over ten had a public duty in our apartment complex. Fredka and I joined a clandestine dance class to put on shows to raise money for an orphanage headed by Dr. Janusz Korczak, the beloved children's author. Every day, we skipped down our stairwell and sprinted across the courtyard and up one flight of stairs to our dance teacher's living room. As soon as a mother-volunteer sat down at the piano to play, we fell silent and took our positions in line. We rose tall on our toes to follow our teacher's instructions.

Our undercover dance productions depended on the goodwill of many neighbors. Parents invited us to their homes and gathered us around tables piled high with bright sheets of crepe paper, scissors, glue, and string. They taught us to drape the fine paper to make tutus and form flowers with petals, as beautiful as real ones. We pasted the flowers on our costumes and stuck them into our hair. We wrapped the tutus around our small waists and felt like magic fairies. It is still a mystery to me where the parents found the troves of material.

The public performance, stirring on many levels, was the climax. Parents helped assemble a simple stage in some dark hall. They illuminated the stage area with carbide lamps wrapped in colored crepe paper for special effects. We took turns sitting with an adult at a table to collect money for tickets, to usher people to their seats, and to distribute the programs we had designed. The enthusiastic guests filled the place, careful not to call public attention to our crime. Then the door closed and shut out the unfriendly world. The audience settled down, we stepped out on the stage, and life became magical. I remember the joy of dancing, the sweet feeling of hearing applause, and the pleasure of being personally praised by the teacher and parents after the performance. Most of all, I remember the evening my beloved author, Dr. Janusz Korczak, and his children from his orphanage attended the performance. I remember clearly the children's faces swollen with hunger, their ashen complexions, and distended bellies. I was as much stirred by the love they expressed toward their surrogate father as I was by their suffering. And the love Dr. Korczak demonstrated toward his children, all thirty of them, moved me beyond words. His gaunt face; the deep-set, kind, and penetrating eyes; the protective tilt of his body toward his children; the elegant motions of his hands; and his soft voice as he spoke on behalf of his children followed me to the darkest corners of my young life, and still nurture my soul. Soon after, Dr. Korczak crossed my path one more time—the last and most unforgettable time.

Smugglers and Informers

I often thought, with deep envy, of the fortunate children outside the ghetto wall who sauntered into stores with displays of fresh breads, pungent kielbasa, fruit, and vegetables as I used to do. *Will I ever again see shop windows with food that look like gardens in bloom? Or windows displaying toys and clothes that spawn dreams in your head? What if I never will?*

Shopping in the ghetto was a subversive act punishable by death. Only the baker in our street remained busy officially baking rationed bread and selling a variety of baked goods under the table. Few stores stayed open and licensed by the Judenrat. Our streets looked sorrowful with all the shuttered store windows.

Sometimes, Mama let me go shopping with her to tiny, secret, one-room stores in neighbors' apartments or to vendors who brought out all kinds of smuggled products into the streets, even luxuries like butter, sugar, chicken, and chocolate. Almost at once, long lines formed to snap them up at high prices. Each vendor charged as much as he or she wanted, and even rotting foods were grabbed quickly. In spite of the fear and limited choice of goods, I liked to go shopping with Mama and looked forward to getting a treat.

I did not need to ask where the limited food and other essentials came from. It was common knowledge that smuggling became an occupation for both Jews and Christians. Even Nazis participated and greedily lined their pockets with bribes from desperate people threatened by imposed starvation. I knew that smugglers traded through holes and cracks in the ghetto walls, and they navigated tunnels and cellars under buildings along the wall. Some children my age became good at sneaking the contraband across the brick divide, and kept their families from starving to death. Of course, many were caught and shot on the spot, leaving liver-colored stains along the wall.

Most people were destitute, depending on the meager rations of two-and-a half kilos of black bread per month. But the lucky ones who traded on the black market, and those who provided such essential services as treating the sick, had some source of income.

Clandestine restaurants, theaters, cafés, and places where couples could dance made money too.

Thanks to Tata's marketable skills as a jeweler and the fact that gold becomes the most reliable currency during wars, we were spared from starvation and freezing, but not without grave risk. While Tata worked secretly in his workshop in our apartment, Mama, Fredka, and I took turns standing guard at my parents' bedroom window with a strategic view of the entire courtyard.

When I stood watch, like a sentry on the ready, I kept my eyes glued to the front gate where we could see immediately anyone entering our courtyard. My uppermost concerns were looking out for German soldiers and being ready to dart into Tata's room to help him hide any trace of his work. However, seeing an unfamiliar Jew entering the courtyard also required caution and, sometimes, quick action. A stranger could have been a beggar—Tata never turned a beggar away. Or he might have been an informer threatening to report us if Tata did not bribe him.

Once, a suspicious-looking man walked slowly and deliberately across the courtyard toward our stairwell. I yelled to Fredka and Mama, who quickly ran to help Tata clear his workbench and make it look Sabbath clean. I kept my post at the window, reporting the man's progress toward our stairwell. By the time the stranger walked up the two flights of steps and rapped on our door, Fredka and I had cleared out of the living room while Mama, a dust rag in her hand, calmly opened the door and said politely, "*Dzień dobry*" (hello). The stranger asked to speak to Tata.

In the next room, Fredka and I pressed our ears to the door to hear if our parents were safe with the stranger. First we heard the intruder's dark voice. We could not make out what he was saying, but it filled us with dread. Then we heard the sound of Tata's voice, polite and steady as always, but stern. Finally all the voices blended harmoniously. More murmurs and the man left.

We flung the door open and fell into our parents' arms. "What happened? Who is he? Are we safe, Mama, Tata?" Fredka and I asked breathlessly.

"Everything is okay. We are all safe," my parents reassured.

"What did he want?" we pressed.

"Let's first make sure that he does not return," Mama cautioned.

Together, we rushed to the window to watch the trespasser cross the courtyard and out the front gate. Then we sat down to listen to Mama tell, and retell, how cleverly and bravely Tata dealt with the blackmailing lout. "He threatened to report us to the Germans if Tata did not give him a ridiculous bribe. You should have seen how cool Tata stayed! He said, 'Don't threaten me. I have no reason to be afraid.' Calmly, Tata reached into his pocket and took out a few złoty and said, 'Times are difficult and I assume you are in need, or else you would not be here. Take it and do not ever show up here again.'"

Jewish collaborators were rare. For the most part, we felt safe among our neighbors and relied heavily on mutual support. We could even count on Jewish policemen to alert us to danger. A policeman would whisper in the ear of a Jew on Muranowska Street, "A German patrol is cruising in the streets and grabbing Jews for forced labor." Or, "Germans just shot a Jew on Zamenhofa Street." The news traveled with lightning speed from ear to ear until the warning buzzed throughout the ghetto. We had to allow for a modicum of distortions, but on the whole the system kept us alert to danger—and jittery.

Books, Theaters, and Underground Tutors When There Was No Bread

To own a book was an act of defiance punishable by death, and many defied. Tata had his beloved secret stash of books by Sholem Ash, Sholem Aleichem, and Isaac Leib Peretz, and he read them to us generously. At night, windows blinded with black covers to keep our existence secret, in a dim room illuminated by a flickering carbide lamp, my family sat locked in an invisible embrace—warm in a frozen universe. Tata's voice flowed with swaddling comfort, conveying nuances that brought remote worlds to life. Fictitious shtetls became real and immediate, and the heroes as familiar as best friends—their joys and fears as authentic to me as my own. Our room was a tiny capsule of paradise separating us from deadly curfew-quiet outside our windows.

Sometimes, Tata read to us stories by brave ghetto authors who sat in cold, dark rooms to write. Tata read to us only works by Yiddish authors. I think he wanted us to appreciate our identity.

Each day, carts rolled down my street collecting the dead, as if the deceased were no more than litter. The common sight of corpses still remained foreign, ghoulish, and repulsive to me. It terrified me to see the loneliness and irrelevance of human life. I tried to look away when I stepped into the street, but my eyes betrayed me. I looked. A silent scream of abhorrence rose in my throat. *People must not die like this—without parents, sisters, aunts, uncles, cousins, and friends to comfort them and cry bitter tears. My God! I do not want to die this way. I do not want Mama or Tata or Fredka to be lost like this.*

The more hideous and dangerous life grew, the more people turned to books, music, and other forms of escape. I saw my first operetta, the *Czardas Queen*, with Fredka and friends in the ghetto. I fell in love with the heroes, the scenery, the schmaltzy love songs, and the Gypsy costumes—as bright as splashes of spring flowers in Łazienki Park before the war.

With our Christian neighbors gone, the red church and the adjoining drab-gray nunnery across the street from our house remained silent and forsaken. Even the voluptuous shrubs and stately trees on the broad churchyard lawn lost their green splendor and appeared as starved for love and care as the rest of the ghetto—until a group of unemployed actors moved into the nunnery and created a secret repertory theater. They breathed life into the comatose building. Doors flung open discreetly and voices seeped out through the cracks in sealed windows. The outside walls remained bare and anonymous. Neither neon lights nor billboards betrayed the covert activities inside.

Tata actively supported this subversive project. Reading books and going to the theater were the only diversions Tata allowed himself. "Talent and beauty must be revered. They touch the best that is in us," he told me with deep conviction.

I loved to eavesdrop on my parents' conversations about the plays and resident actors. Many of them had starred on the Polish stage and films before the war. One of the performers, known for tragicomic roles on the Polish screen, was a frequent guest at our house—until she was grabbed from the street and never heard from again. No one stayed long in my life back then. Her name escapes me, but I clearly remember her tall, slim, graceful figure and oblong face so captivatingly expressive.

Fredka and I tingled with pleasure when Tata took us to see a play at the nunnery. We put on our prettiest, but subdued, dresses—mindful not to attract uninvited attention. Holding Tata's hand tightly, we crossed our sad street to enter the tiny theater and experience a brief miracle. I did not fully grasp the complexities of the plots or the biting humor. Nevertheless, I was magically transported to make-believe places and inside the hearts of imaginary people. Of course, when I was eleven or twelve, and still in my home, I did not yet understand the lasting value of those experiences. Nor did I yet know that when you lose everything, memories become your possessions.

Mama too loved the theater and appreciated beauty, but during this perilous time, her mind focused mostly on practical ways to survive. She pressed us, "Eat, eat." Food was important to Mama. She packed it into us as one packs provisions against an imminent disaster. She was on a rampage to destroy every typhus germ that might have found its

Nowolipki Street before the war. The second building on the left was the nunnery where the secret theater was located during the occupation. This street became part of the Warsaw Ghetto, or Jewish sector.

way to our house. She scrubbed and cleaned every nook and cranny. She aired the house and bedding in the brisk morning air. She washed every food item touched by a human hand, even a rare bite of chocolate.

When I gave my sandwich to a beggar on my way to the Ogródek, Mama admonished sharply, "You should not have done it. You have to take care of yourself first. Who knows if we will have bread tomorrow?"

On the other hand, Tata called me aside and said, "You did the right thing giving your lunch to someone hungrier than you. You skipped only one meal. Can you imagine how many that beggar had missed and how hungry he must be?" He quickly reassured me that Mama's advice came from love and concern. Tata's gentle messages led me to the conclusion that I must be respectful because Mama always meant well, but was not always right.

Mama taught me to steel myself to survive. Tata taught me that stepping outside your own skin and thinking of others is essential to surviving and remaining whole. Perhaps Tata would have lived longer if he had had more of Mama's feistiness. Perhaps her childhood shtetl in Vitebsk, Byelorussia, and the barbarity of the Cossacks who chased her out of her native land, had taught her as much about survival as the rippling fields of golden rye had taught her to love beauty.

Tata avoided leaving the house. He only went out on urgent matters—to meet with business associates, to make arrangements for our tutoring, and to carry food to my destitute Aunt Malka and Uncle Boris on Pawia Street. My aunt and uncle stayed cooped up and alone in their dim, ground-floor apartment and mourned their children who had fled to Russia.

The first thing I did when I returned home from my tutor's or friend's house was to look for Tata. I usually found him sitting in his favorite corner near the tile stove in the living room, always with a book in his hand. I was so relieved to see him! Ghetto children took nothing for granted, not even finding their parents alive when they came home.

Tata was our pillar, the center of our lives. Yet I feared more for his life than I feared for anyone else's. Often, I trailed behind him from room to room like his shadow, afraid to let him out of my sight. I even followed him to the bathroom door, sat down on the floor to wait for him, and then continued at his side. I was so afraid that if I left him out of sight, I might never find him again. In spite of Tata's aversion to stepping out into the streets where brutality ruled, Tata was the one who took Fredka and me to doctors for checkups and held my hand when I sat in the dentist's chair and wept with fear; and Tata was the one who found tutors for us.

Mama would sometimes question him, "What is the point of sending the children to tutors? We don't know if we will survive the day. I think it's madness."

Tata's response always was, "Maybe the secret school is the only normal childhood experience we will ever be able to give them. They must have tutors, no matter the risk."

All over the ghetto parents hired tutors for their children. Their motto was, "The good of the child takes precedence over everything." Some children met their instructors in tiny, cold rooms, for an hour or two, in groups of two or four to share the expense. Not all parents had ready cash to pay and had to sell personal items of clothing or household articles; many sacrificed their meager food rations to pay. And not all parents were able to provide tutors for their children. Too many were homeless, destitute, and barely able to stay alive.

We ghetto children also took an active part in resisting brutality. We sneaked our books and notebooks under our clothes and marched right past the brutal faces of Nazi soldiers who patrolled our streets. We knew perfectly well that if we were caught, we, or our parents, or our teacher, or all of us could be shot. We did not give ourselves particular credit for our daring. We just knew it was the right thing to do. But each step we took was, indeed, a supreme act of courage and an assertion of human worth.

Fredka and I attended a tiny clandestine school run by four brave unemployed teachers who lived on a small, abandoned estate near Karmelicka Street, a ten-minute walk from our home. We called it the *Ogródek* (Little Garden) to cover up its subversive existence. A Christian family used to live on that estate before the formation of the ghetto. The estate was dotted with flowers and shrubs for playing hide-and-seek, and had an open field for ball games. The place was at most two or three acres, but I saw it as being very big.

In my heart, the Ogródek was a paradisiacal place, synonymous with love, freedom, and harmony. This was the only place in the ghetto where I could run until I was out of breath, throw a ball as far as my aim could reach, and dream with a book, or paper and pencil, in my hand. Still, we always had to be on the lookout for German soldiers entering through the gate, and we had to be ready to hide all traces of books and pencils, pronto.

The estate lay hidden behind a fence of tall hedges. I could hardly wait to unlatch the wooden gate, run up the stairs to the door of the cream-colored house, and enter the bare room where Mrs. Marisia waited for her students. Not a single picture hung on the walls, not a scrap of carpet lay on the hardwood floor, and no clutter of teaching materials was in sight. Just two rows of wooden tables and chairs stood in the center facing the teacher's desk. As soon as my friends arrived, we freed our notebooks from their hiding places underneath our garments, and the whole house seemed to wake up from a deep sleep. Fredka, in the next room with the older children, was as happy as I.

Everything about Mrs. Marisia was unforgettable: her flaming red hair; her expressive green eyes that looked right into us, and understood, and sparkled with enthusiasm; her voice that held us like an embrace and made us see things inside our heads, or see old things in a new way.

I loved Mrs. Marisia for playing beautiful records to help us think and imagine things that were invisible and for sharing contraband books that she loved, but above all I loved her when she gathered us under a shady tree, leaned against its trunk, and painted word pictures of scenes around us. Her voice rang with pathos as if she were uncovering secrets that lay before us. She encouraged us to take turns putting words to what we saw. I was amazed at the details that suddenly jumped into existence. All fears seemed to melt with the joy of the moment.

Later, when the Ogródek was wiped off the face of the earth, Mrs. Marisia remained one of my ghetto heroes. I cherished her for the faith in goodness she inspired in me at a time when my world was in utter darkness.

When we flew out of Mrs. Marisia's classroom, Mrs. Posner—a statuesque botanist with smiling eyes and love of nature and children—waited for us among the few secret flower beds to teach us about plant life. I liked her for helping us grow our very own gardens on tiny plots of earth, where we hoed, raked, and planted cabbages, beans, and whatever seeds we could find. Every day we weeded, watered, and checked to see if the longed-for miracle had occurred—if a seedling had broken through the loosened soil. I was as proud as a parent when my beans grew to be as tall as I. I remember one full growing season.

I cannot leave out Dr. Posner—a slender, distinguished-looking historian with sad eyes—so utterly out of place in the world we lived in. He often strolled in the garden, hands folded behind his back, his face a mask of deep thought. When he would pass us on his solitary walks, he would reach out to pat our heads. I liked the feel of his touch. It was sad and tender.

I attended this fragile paradise for about one-and-a-half years, until the end of 1941—the last year we remained rooted in our home. That year I could still count on seeing life stir behind every neighbor's windowpane, and I could be reasonably confident that if I called someone's name, his or her face would pop out and smile down at me. It was the last year I frolicked with all my courtyard friends, Janka, Felusia, Mata, Lusia, Benio, and others whose names I eventually forgot; though their faces continued to keep me company during silent moments. We visited each other's homes, or met in the courtyard and made a lot of noise.

My cousin Lolek came often from Muranowska Street to play with Fredka and me, and tell us cliff-hanging stories about cops and robbers and exotic safaris in Tanganyika. The stories made little sense, but we listened anyway to hear how they ended. He drew for us the most fabulous cartoons of boxers, with muscles like balloons. When he tired of our company, he took his scooter and whizzed around the circumference of the courtyard, one foot dangling in the air, barely avoiding crashing through basement windows. When he had had enough of that, he went home. But in 1941 we could expect, with reasonable trust, that we would see him the next day. Lolek liked to visit with us. Unfortunately, that was not the only reason that he was a frequent guest at our house. Aunt Hannah and Mama encouraged him to spend time with us because we had more food than his family.

That year, I grew even more attached to my best friend, Janka, and her family who lived directly below our apartment. Mornings, I would jump out of bed, stretch out flat on the floor above Janka's room, press my mouth to a line on the parquet, and call down, "Janka! Are you awake?!" If she woke up before me, she would go to a corner in her room—not to disturb anyone still asleep—and would holler, "Estusia! Are you up?!" To communicate between floors we invented our own secret language.

Her older sister, Ala, and Ala's boyfriend attracted much of my interest. I loved to watch Ala as she sat in front of her tall vanity mirror to rouge her lips and comb her velvety-black hair into a pageboy. When she finished, she looked like a princess from *The Arabian Nights*. Her face was oval, her complexion tawny, her eyes large, dark, and almond shaped. I thought Ala was the epitome of adolescent beauty and chic.

Ala's boyfriend—tall with sand-colored hair, finely chiseled features, and as lovely to look at as Ala—called on her often. When they left the house holding hands, my heart skipped a beat. I cannot imagine where they could have gone. There were no parks to stroll in and the streets were unsafe. Perhaps they went to visit with friends?

When they returned, they would linger under the front archway near the gate, holding hands, gazing into each other's eyes, and talking until dusk and curfew drove the handsome young man away. Watching from the window, Janka would say, "They don't want to part." And I would add, "They are in love."

Miss Anka, Janka's nanny, still lived with them, but stayed mostly in the background. When I think of her heavily powdered round face, a thin line of lipstick on her lips, and sad, full-moon-round eyes, I am reminded of a mournful clown who cannot manage to feign laughter.

Nineteen forty-one was also the last year we could visit Aunt Hannah and Malka's houses, walk to the Ogródek, and run down neighboring streets to see friends. Of course, we knew we had to be very watchful and dash home if we heard a rumor of a German patrol seen anywhere in the ghetto. Girls Fredka's age went arm in arm to the "Deptak," a street where girls and boys strolled and flirted. Fredka rarely went there, not because she did not want to go, but because we were too proper.

That year, the streets remained packed with peddlers, beggars, young people rushing to keep a rendezvous with their dates, and pedestrians scurrying as if time were running out. In the ghetto, we lived life fast and in extremes. Everything was concentrated, crushed together, rendered more intense. The traffic flowed until a couple of Nazi soldiers would decide to make a sudden appearance. Then, an uproar would start and all the passersby and traders would flee. Those who did not run fast enough, or happened to stand in the wrong spot, often paid with their lives.

As soon as the sun touched the horizon, everyone in the ghetto was locked indoors. The streets stayed as hauntingly vacant, dark, and silent as a cemetery at midnight. Wails of hungry cats, clangs of toppling trash cans, and distant salvos of gunfire made the night air tremble. Yet life moved on in spite of horrendous adversities—until the end of that year when we began to hear rumors that we were to be deported from the ghetto.

4 Deportation

The rumors threw us into a state of panic. Various versions circulated: one claimed that only some would be expelled, namely, the refugees, old people, and children. Another version was that all the Jews were to be deported from Warsaw, with no exception. People reminded each other of the fate of Jews who had disappeared from other towns. Parents cautioned, "Don't talk so loud. The children will hear."

But in no way could they protect us from the fear we heard in their voices or the horror inscribed in their taut faces. "Are we going to die?" we asked without fully understanding death.

I saw stiff, lifeless bodies abandoned on residential stoops and sidewalks every day, and I took turns killing and being killed in make-believe play with friends. But I was too young to comprehend the finality that death really is. As a matter of fact, death did not terrify me as much as the possibility of being separated from my parents. I desperately wanted for us to live. But if we had to die, I wanted my parents to assure me that we would all meet death holding on to each other—like a joint transfer to the unimaginable.

Horrifying reports of massacres of Jews in Vilna, Biala Podlaska, and other communities stifled the air we breathed. Other hearsay opened a chink of hope. "Did you hear the latest news? Hitler is dead." There was talk of an armistice, of peace being declared, and for a short time we breathed easily. The worse things became, the greater the hopes that people placed on the war's ending.

I rehearsed in my head what I would do if Nazi soldiers came to get us. An impossible challenge. The soldiers, loud, rude, and fully armed, made me feel tiny, bare, and completely inadequate to interfere or speak my mind. I wanted to see the monsters bound, stabbed, cut, crumpled, slashed, and excoriated. But if they entered our house and I uttered a single word, they would surely shoot my neighbors to set an example, and worse— they would shoot my parents and me. So I fought them at night in my sleep. I clawed at their eyes and ripped at their faces when they went after my parents, sister, or friends. And I reasoned with them at the same time because I still believed that somewhere behind their unfeeling faces were hearts and a conscience. They were people, weren't they? I knew Tata did not jump at their throats for the same reason—to protect us and other Jews from punishment. And Mama would surely strike them with a heavy frying pan if she knew we would not be killed on the spot for her act.

"Should we pack our things?" Fredka and I volunteered to our parents. We had prepared a list of our favorite dresses and most essential items of clothing: sweaters, boots, coats, mittens, and outfits for every season.

Mama told us, "No, no. It's not necessary. Go and play instead."

Tata reassured us, "We will take care of everything. We will let you know of all that is important. Not to worry."

Fredka and I also recognized the uselessness of packing, only to be forced to hand everything over to the soldiers. To be practical, we dressed in multiple layers of underwear and dresses. We slept fully clothed in case the German soldiers descended upon us at night. Mama and Tata said, "It is not necessary, but if it makes you feel better, it's okay."

I made a small bundle of my cherished trinket collection that I kept in a drawer in Mama's beautiful vanity with the tall oval mirror. My collection consisted of birthday cards from friends; fountain pens and mechanical pencils I valued too much to use for every day; the shiniest, smoothest, reddest-tinged, most perfect chestnuts; and my very most treasured collection of small perfume boxes. I wrapped my treasures carefully in a neat parcel and kept it close at hand in case I had to grab for it and run.

Deportation began in the month of my thirteenth birthday, July 1942, when the Germans ordered Czerniakow, the head of the Judenrat, to deliver thousands of men, women, old people, and children to the *Umschlagplatz* (transfer station). The Judenrat followed the order by publishing a notice that a segment of the ghetto population would be resettled in the east. The deportation would begin in two days. Terror quivered in people's voices.

"Where will they send us, Tata? What will happen to us?" Fredka and I wanted to know. Our parents held us close and patted our heads lovingly.

At first, people tried to believe the promise that only a limited number of Jews would be affected by the decree. *Who knows, maybe I will be spared?* Everyone hoped. However, it did not take long to learn that the German authorities had lied to Czerniakow. As soon as it became apparent that no one would be spared, Czerniakow stepped into his office, locked the door, and remained there unresponsive to all who wished to enter. Eventually, his colleagues broke down the door. They found him sitting motionless, head resting on his desk next to an empty cyanide bottle.

The news of his death slipped out of his room, and out of the Judenrat, and was repeated by word of mouth through the miserable, crowded streets and courtyards, and was received as a communal death sentence. I felt the bitter taste of death brush my lips when the horrible news reached my ears.

During the first period of deportation, which lasted several weeks, only Jewish policemen rounded up people from the streets and homes and marched them to the Umschlagplatz. Ukrainian guards and German soldiers loaded the captured people onto freight trains and shipped them out of our lives. In return, the Germans promised to spare the policemen's lives and the lives of their families. The policemen naively believed that if they carried out this mission, the Germans would not enter the ghetto, bloodshed would be avoided, and only a small number of Jews would be deported from the city, as was promised. Instead, the Germans soon took over the process of deportation until no one in the ghetto remained. The Jewish police brought shame to themselves. People in the ghetto shunned and hated them for taking part in the deportation of fellow Jews.

At first, we did not know that deportation meant death. One thing was certain: if you were found hiding, you were shot on the spot. Furthermore, the German authorities had forced Jewish people to write to their families inviting them to join them in Bialystok and Minsk, where they worked and received food and clothing. Rumors of the letters circulated widely. As a result, some people marched voluntarily, and unknowingly, to the Umschlagplatz and to slaughter.

Miss Anka, Janka's nanny, lonely without kin and unwilling to be a burden to the Rotenbergs, filled a satchel with her most essential belongings. She put on her best blue suit and matching pumps, smoothed her woolly dark hair neatly back, put a dab of make-up on to look her best, raised her head high to give herself courage, said good-bye, and departed for the Umschlagplatz. Her departure left the Rotenbergs and neighbors with an enormous sense of loss and helplessness.

What better choice did Miss Anka have than relying on the promise to be treated more mercifully if she gave herself up? She was not a meek "sheep." Miss Anka was "somebody" with pride, hope, and courage.

Most people resolved to stay put at any price and not follow orders to march. The obvious escape was finding a hiding place in our homes during *Akcja* (deportation roundups). Some hid under mattresses of their beds, in cupboards, in drawers, in concealed rooms, and in other outlandish places and crevices that they could squeeze their bodies into to vanish out of sight. Parents with young children and infants took pillows with them to silence their cries. Our hideout was a carefully concealed room behind a wardrobe. All of us who lived in the same row of apartments, below and above us, agreed to shove a large piece of furniture against the door of the same room in their homes.

Some of our friends sought other ways of escaping deportation. They bought forged Aryan birth certificates and smuggled their way out of the ghetto. That too took great courage, even if their light complexions and Aryan-looking faces did not betray them. It scared the daylights out of me to hear stories of the dangers the people encountered on the other side of the wall. At any minute, in the street, they could be confronted by interrogating eyes staring them down. If Jews blinked, or in any way betrayed fear, they would be stopped and challenged to prove their Christianity. Often, the trapped Jews were delivered to the German authorities for a fee. The thought of concealing my identity among people who would hound me in the streets frightened me even more than remaining imprisoned in the ghetto with my people, even if it meant sure death. Besides, Mama would never pass, in spite of her Slavic features: high cheekbones, blue eyes, and peachy complexion. Polish was not her native language, and she spoke with a Yiddish accent. She had been chased out of her native shtetl in Belarus during pogroms when she was a young girl.

One day my parents sat down with Fredka and me for a serious talk. "The only way we can protect you is by sending you to a convent." We stared at them aghast. "Preposterous! You want to send us away? Never! We will not go," we both cried. Our fear of separating was so great that our parents gave up the idea.

Tata's Heroic Act

The Germans announced that only Jews with work permits—"productive workers" employed by the Germans or the Judenrat—would be exempt from the transfer. This provoked a desperate scramble for work cards. The men in our courtyard complex immedi-

Residents of the ghetto gather on a street corner to listen to a message on the loudspeaker.
Courtesy United States Holocaust Memorial Museum.

ately assembled at the house of Mr. Keinigsberg, the portly neighborhood leader, to find a way to avoid deportation. Afraid to let Tata out of our sight, Fredka and I went with him to our neighbor's house. We sat quietly in the next room with our friends—Keinigsberg's two daughters—and tried to listen to the critical discussion.

It did not take the men long to arrive at a unanimous conclusion: "One man has to go to the Judenrat to obtain work permits."

"Who will go?" someone asked. No one responded.

Suggestions followed: "The one who has fewest children. The youngest. The strongest. The nimblest."

No progress. They drew straws, but no one would dare risk the deadly street-deportation raids.

Then, Tata's steady voice rose above the arguing, "If we waste any more time, we'll all be dead. I'll go."

Tata. No! My heart shrank.

Tata went, not the youngest, nor the physically strongest. He was ill with tuberculosis; his spittle had crimson traces! He went and miraculously escaped a sudden raid by jumping into a ditch covered by wooden planks. The planks rattled under Nazi boots as Tata sat curled up in a corner. He waited for the pitiful cries of innocent people, and wild shouts of Nazis, and pops of gunshots to stop.

In that unforgettable moment when he returned home to us, white as a ghost, he embraced us and held us close. He chanted in disbelief, "Who are these automatons? How can they tear children from their parents, pile them onto wagons and cart them away like rubbish? I cannot understand. Don't they have children, wives, and mothers?"

He brought back the temporary permit for us to live.

The deportation proceded with twentieth-century efficiency and Stone Age values. Daily, German soldiers descended upon us with calculated abruptness and laid siege to blocks of streets. Suddenly, the air thundered with the beat of Gestapo boots rushing from the street toward our doors. Their bayoneted rifles clanged readiness for slaughter. First, they rounded up people from the sidewalk. Then they stormed into the courtyards and up the stairwells, moving ever closer and closer, shouting vulgar insults: *"Verfluchte Juden! Hunde! Raus! Raus! Schnell! Schnell!"* (Damned Jews! Dogs! Out! Out! Fast! Fast!)

We bolted into our secret room before they reached our apartment. We pulled the wardrobe to obscure the door to our hiding. While we cringed in our refuge, the soldiers searched every apartment, every corner, and dragged out everyone they could find. Hellish banging, slapping, kicking, crazed barking of dogs, pops of gunshots, cries, and whimpers rose from the stairwells and courtyard. But in our room, I heard only the violent pounding of our hearts.

Blood drained from me each time I heard the slapping boots entering our apartment and nearing our secret door. I died a little bit when they opened the wardrobe doors and drawers to look for plunder. I hated their voices, intoxicated with self-indulgent cruelty and bursting with joy when they found pleasing objects to steal.

We knew the blockade was over when the crescendo of wild shouts and stomping boots and soft taps of victims' feet began to fade from the courtyard. Eventually, all was quiet as a desert. We remained sitting, as though lifeless, till we could find courage to leave our hiding room to face what we would find. Still unsure that we could trust the silence, we shoved the wardrobe away from the secret door and looked out the windows to get a cursory glance. Then, as in a nightmare, we descended into the courtyard to look for neighbors and friends and mourn those who had been dragged off.

What we found after each raid was horrifying, the pain too great for words or tears to express. There was the body of our pregnant neighbor in a puddle of blood, her stomach slashed open. Red footprints led from doors of friends across the courtyard and clear out into the street. After one raid, eleven-year-old Jurek crawled out of his hiding under the mattress and appeared in the middle of the courtyard sobbing pitifully, "They found my mother." Then he took off, out into the street, running to find her. There was no stopping him. He was gone.

My beloved friends, Mata, Jurek, and Felusia, the splendid Frenkels, and other innocent neighbors were kidnapped while I sat silent like a stone in my hiding, praying to all the powers in the universe to spare them. I did not see them dead. None were buried. They simply vanished, severed from me, leaving me feeling limp inside, and terrified.

During one raid, my friend Lusia lay hidden in her bed under a neatly smoothed comforter and bedspread. She was as still as a corpse, I am sure of that. The German soldiers were done with searching our homes, storming down the stairs, and dragging neighbors away. Lusia's faithful little white dog ran after a German soldier, yelping desperately and snapping at his boots. The soldier turned around, followed the frantic dog to Lusia's bed, and dragged my beautiful friend to death. I had heard the frenzied barking, but remained frozen in my hiding. I learned of her tragic end later when we crawled out of our hiding to count the losses.

With each blockade my world shrank. The streets and courtyards became as vacant and still as canyons. When I stepped out of the courtyard to look down the sidewalk in the direction of the Ogródek, listening for a sound of life, only silence reached my ears. The silence was not silent at all; it crawled all the way from beyond the corners of intersecting, lifeless streets, and beyond that. I knew that the Ogródek was empty. But I could not be 100 percent sure that Mrs. Marisia and the other teachers did not live somewhere, somewhere.

I knew that my sweet Aunt Malka whose face never grew old, my beautiful Aunt Hannah with the smiling eyes and hair that flowed like waves when she danced, my two uncles with the same first name, Boris, and my fabulous cousins, Lolek and Moniek, were no longer in their homes. I never went there to check. But I knew their homes were as still as morgues when my parents began to talk about them in the past tense. I could not imagine them murdered and tried to make myself stop thinking about them. That was hardly possible.

People who die never leave you completely. My Aunt Hannah, my Uncle Boris, and my two cousins still show up in my recurring dream. In the maze of sleep, I see myself walking through familiar childhood streets and up a misty stairway to their door on Mura-nowska Street. I hear their chatter and clearly see them through the wall. But they will not open the door to me, nor will they have anything to do with me.

I remain standing behind the door, feeling baffled and deeply hurt by their rejection. When I wake up, I feel as if I had parted with them only yesterday. Their faces and rejections haunt me for days.

The unsettling dream returns less often as the years pass. That too is upsetting. If they vanish from my consciousness, then I let them transmute into nothingness.

5 No Place for Children

My fears became even more troubling once the German authorities declared all children under fourteen useless to the Nazi regime. Their order meant my immediate deportation. I was contraband, my life forbidden. Mama immediately cut off my long braids and fluffed my hair to make me look older. "Dressed in adult clothes you look much, much older. No one would guess you are not yet fourteen," she told me.

I asked, "Tata, what will happen if they find out I am only thirteen?" Tata squared his lean shoulders and said in an impassioned voice, "I'll burn their eyes out with acid. I'll never let them take you away from me!" I believed him. Rejected by the world, I clung to his assurances that I was safe—if only in his love.

Selekcja

A new order came like a bullet, sudden and shattering: "All Jews must report for a major *Selekcja*" (selection) at a designated street and an appointed time. The stated purpose of the compulsory assembly was to select only a segment of the ghetto inhabitants for "relocation." The rest would be allowed to return to their homes. It warned, "All those who ignore the order, or hide, will be slaughtered mercilessly by a select force of soldiers who will storm the buildings and search every corner and leave nothing unturned." That infamous Selekcja took place in 1942, in the fall, I think.

What to do? Hide behind the wardrobe that could easily be shoved aside, or follow orders and go, hoping not to be selected for deportation? My parents agonized. They talked around the clock and weighed the consequences knowing that, either way, death could be waiting. When they reached a point of exhaustion, Tata said, "Mania, what do you think we should do? We will follow your gut feeling and stay with the decision."

Mama hesitated, then said, "My intuition tells me we better not hide this time."

I do not know what swayed her. Perhaps the persistent threats got to her, and she reasoned that, being physically fit, we had a fair chance not to be chosen for deportation.

On the appointed day, we picked up a few bundles of food and other essentials, nothing much. We already knew where the deportation trains went. Together with our neighbors we joined the wave of trapped people, all proud and brave, but in no position to strike back. I tried to stay in the middle of the moving crowd, hoping the tall grown-ups would screen and protect me from the soldiers who stood guard on either side of the procession. In the distance, not far away, I spotted a line of German officers in important-looking uniforms. They glittered with emblems and stripes, and revolvers hung from their sturdy rumps. They stood tall and imposing like living statues—chests puffed out and arrogant eyes looking down on the marching bedraggled mass. Like self-appointed gods, the officers jabbed whips at people in the lineup and pointed: This one to the left, to the trains. This one to the right, to live a little longer. Sorting people like rubbish.

I moved forward with the line, my parents close behind me. My mind ordered, *Walk erect, look older than you are. Don't you dare cry. Don't let them see your fear. Looking bold is your victory. Stay alert, watch where they will point Mama, Tata, and Fredka; be ready to jump in line with them.* I felt an indescribable urge to flee. But where? Tear their eyes out! But how? Their rifles pointing at my heart stood in my way. The people and the entire world seemed a nightmare, spectral.

Slowly, we reached the line of the twentieth-century demigods busy doing their day's work. I felt a stinging tap of a whip on my shoulder and I moved forward. I turned my head back to see where Mama, Tata, and Fredka would be sent. The whip poked Fredka in the same direction I was sent. Mama followed behind us. Then Tata.

The heavy seconds it took for us to take these few steps are still as vivid in my mind as if it only happened yesterday. I remember the officers' pink jovial faces, their voices talking amiably to each other and laughing heartily. I wondered, *How could they chuckle while sending people to a crematorium?*

Mama whispered, "God in heaven. How can you permit this?"

We moved on, hearts shattered, outraged beyond imagination, and incredibly grateful that all four of us were spared and sent back home. Our gratitude seems as ridiculous as it was genuine.

Still trembling, I moved with the unescorted crowd toward home. My eyes refused to turn away from friends driven out of our lives like cattle and marched to slaughter. I ached for one more parting glance, one more touch . . . just one. Then I saw her in the parade of the condemned being prodded forward with rifle butts.

Janka! My heart screamed for my beloved best friend. Her beautiful dark face was yellow with jaundice, eyes aglitter with fever, arms clutching a pillow too close to her chest. I heard her pleading cry, "Mama! Mama! Mama!"

A short distance away, I saw Mrs. Rotenberg, Janka's mother, standing, wild-eyed, but not moving. I too froze in place, transfixed, cemented to the spot. When Janka was out of sight, Mrs. Rotenberg exploded with rage and anguish. She fell to her knees, her body contorting, her arms clawing and striking at the pavement. Liver-colored droplets of blood gathered near her until even the stones seemed to be crying tears of blood.

I remained silent. I was remembering Mama's words: "You must be brave to stay alive. Life is sacred." All I allowed myself was a soundless scream and emptiness—fathomless and frightening—while in the street around me people wailed in grief and misery for their loved ones who were dragged away that day.

Trains to Treblinka

We never heard from our relatives, friends, and neighbors who were dragged to the Umschlagplatz and loaded onto freight trains and sent to a mysterious place. But a few people managed to escape and come back. They crawled through the nights, took circuitous hidden routes, and were careful not to be seen—not even by peasants, who might give them away.

At every turn, I heard their stories of horrific train rides to a place called Treblinka, where our people were forced into gas chambers and choked to death.

The word "trains" now throbbed in whispers, laments, songs, and ballads that beggars sang at street corners. It evoked terrifying images of parting glances, fading gasps, final heartbeats, and unbearable longing for the lives that had been dashed away.

My Last Encounter with Janusz Korczak

Even in the worst times, individuals stood out in the ghetto like prophets and lit my way.

Janusz Korczak was such a beacon. Before the war, I had come to know and love him through his books. All Polish children loved him and the heroes of his stories as much I did. His protagonists were as real to us as the people we knew.

To the children at the *Dom Sierot* (orphans' home) on Krochmalna Street—founded by Dr. Korczak—he was a beloved father. Miss Jadwiga, a summer camp counselor who was raised there, assured me, "He loved every one of us as his own. The door to his room stayed open, always. We could come to him any time we needed. And we always insisted that he pull a bad tooth, because then it did not hurt."

His thin, heart-shaped face, strong and loving, remained etched on my mind when he came with his children to our courtyard performance before the ghetto liquidation. However, Dr. Korchak touched me most deeply in August 1942.

An order was issued: all the children in his orphanage must be delivered to the ovens of Treblinka, posthaste. Poles from the other side of the ghetto wall pleaded with him to agree to be smuggled out to safety. He was a national treasure. His talents must not be lost, they argued.

Dr. Korczak refused. Without a trace of hesitation he placed himself abreast the line with his children, told them they were going on an outing, gave each child a Jewish flag, and singing the "Hatikvah," marched with them through the streets of the ghetto, onto cattle train cars, and into the ovens of Treblinka. He knew the children could not be saved, and he did not want them to face extermination alone.

I, a young girl condemned to die at the whim of foreign soldiers, followed their progress through the ghetto streets as the news traveled from mouth to mouth. I listened in bewildered silence, and my parents mourned with us as they held Fredka and me in their arms. I was witness to this grave injustice, as was all humanity, especially those who had the freedom to speak out, but chose to remain silent.

By November 1942, the Nazi war machine had turned three-quarters of my people to ashes. Ninety-nine percent of the children were gone. Most of the people I knew were parents without children, widows, or widowers. I found it hard to understand how much pain and sorrow the human heart is capable of enduring without breaking. Nor could I fully understand the infinite force that lifts us above unbearable grief. The stomach demands to be fed, the mourning heart craves to be comforted; memories of loss turn to dreams. And so some miserable widows and widowers moved in together and held hands in public.

How can they do this? They are betraying love, cried my young mind, without understanding the complexities of love and life. The speed with which the present washed over the past simply shocked me. At night, when I could not fall asleep, I sorted out the situation. *People must remain irreplaceable, immortal in the hearts of the people they love. Parents must mourn their dead children every moment of their remaining days. So must husbands and wives mourn, interminably, the loss of the other.* I thought of fairy-tale princesses who sat in overgrown gardens mourning the death of their beloveds, never enjoying a single laugh until the day they died. I imagined ancient times when lovers jumped into the graves of heroes killed in fighting.

Fear of separation and death occupied my thoughts and dreams. *How could my parents and Fredka live without me, or I without them? If I were killed and they would cease to think of me, my existence would be erased.*

6 Subghettos

bruptly, the ghetto was sliced into three separate subghettoes at the start of 1943. Each subghetto contained a German factory and became a ghetto unto itself. Only people with work identification papers could live there. All others, "the unproductive," were to be deported.

I will never forget Mama imploring Fredka, "I don't like to ask you to do this, but our lives depend on you. You must to go to Justina's house and plead with Mr. Bursztin to give us work affidavits."

The awesome responsibility overwhelmed Fredka. She pleaded, "What if he refuses and we all die? It will be my fault. I am afraid I will fail."

Mama coaxed, "He won't refuse you. You have the best chance of all of us to prevail. You are Justina's (his daughter's) friend and Mr. Bursztin likes you."

Mr. Bursztin, a corpulent, charismatic man, was the only Jewish person I knew in the last days of the ghetto who brimmed with energy and self confidence; he looked as polished as a gold coin in Tata's secret collection. He ran the Schultz sewing factory for the Germans. That made him the king of the hill. The factory was located on our street, Nowolipki Street.

Justina Bursztin, with a mass of curly, ginger-colored hair, twinkling blue eyes, a sprinkle of freckles that called attention to her small upturned nose, and a bright laugh, had her father's exuberant nature and flirtatiousness. And she was Fredka's good friend. That was important, very important.

Of course, Fredka did not let us down and did as Mama asked. She rehearsed what she would say, then went to Justina's house, tears trickling down her pretty cheeks. She came back with work permits for Mama, Fredka, and me. My document was based on lying about my age, since children under the age of fourteen had to be surrendered and transported to the gas chambers. Tata remained without work and would have to live like the other "illegal elements" hiding among us.

And so, thanks to Fredka's courage, and thanks to Mr. Bursztin's power and goodwill, we found employment mending blood-stained uniforms for German soldiers whom we detested more than anything on earth. We remained in Warsaw a while longer, hoping for a miracle.

The Schultz subghetto formed a square bordering Leszno Street, Nowolipie, Nowolipki (where we lived), Karmelicka, and Smocza Streets. The buildings in the subghettos were virtually vacant. We were the sole occupants of a five-story apartment complex with tiers of furnished flats, still as death.

The streets bordering the three subghettos, called "wild areas," were out of bounds for Jews. No one lived there, officially. They were vast, deserted, silent, ghostly disaster areas. Only abandoned dogs, stray cats, and rats lived there freely. Although I never set a foot in the wild area, I often listened into the deep quiet for German soldiers on the rampage. While my ears kept guard, I heard the wind blow through broken windows of empty rooms and echoes of voices that I missed so much.

Soon after we obtained work papers, we moved to a ground-floor apartment in an adjacent building where we would later build a bunker underneath our flat. The prospect of living under the ground and not seeing the face of the earth had not yet entered my imagination. But my parents knew better. There was one other thing that Fredka and I did not yet know: Tata was a member of the resistance fighters that had begun to form after the news of Treblinka reached the ghetto.

My parents also picked the apartment for its location at the far end of the courtyard and for the window facing the front gate. That gave us time to spot Germans entering from the street and hide while they were crossing the yard. Work permits or not, we always hid from German soldiers.

We lived in the ground-floor apartment several months, from the beginning of 1943 until April when the ghetto was blotted out. I had no particular attachment to the isolated flat. I remember the tile kitchen stove because it kept us warm, and the living room window because I depended on it for mental escape and security, just as a sailor on a submarine depends on a periscope to welcome the looming freedom above and to look out for danger. And I remember the table where we entertained guests. For fear of being separated, all four of us slept on two single beds in an alcove located off the living room. The beds stood close together and I knew that I could be in my parents' embrace in one leap.

To fuel the kitchen stove, Tata collected wooden furniture from deserted apartments. Mostly, he removed doors from hinges, and carried them to our apartment. I was proud that Tata let me help him split the big wood doors and chop the strips into small pieces to fit the opening in our stove. He showed me how to hold the ax and how to swing it without lopping off my foot. He stood at my side to guide me: "First, we have to make room on the floor to place the door without bumping into things." I eagerly shoved objects aside while Tata held the door. He showed me how to prop up the doors on wood blocks to prevent damaging the kitchen floor, how to avoid knots, and how to split the wood with the grain. I swung the ax with vigor and pent-up energy, imagining that I was hacking down our killers, limb by limb. Best of all, when chopping wood, I was near Tata.

Fortunately for us, we had running water and we did not go hungry. We still had money to buy food that was smuggled in from the Christian side and sold on the black market.

Every dawn, Mama, Fredka, and I left Tata (the forbidden to live), to join the handful of the "useful and productive" at the Schultz shop. Of course, I left him with a heavy heart. *What if the devils with the scull-head emblems barge into our house and find him? I might never see him again!*

Still, some part of me looked forward to walking to and from the factory. It was the only time I got to see normal people: our surviving neighbors. Even the "wild" ones (the ones in hiding) would come out and mingle during that brief time. All other times the streets were desolate.

I loved the camaraderie among our people in the factory. Everyone offered assistance. "This is how you hold a needle. And this is how you use a thimble properly to make your work easier."

We even laughed sometimes at the bitter jokes we cracked about life. And Mama would say, "We must be going crazy. How can we laugh in this death box?"

But even in the darkest moments people go through the motions of life: they wash and set their tables, and even manage to utter a chuckle. That just is what people do.

At the factory, we mended uniforms stripped from wounded or dead soldiers. First we had to soak them in cold water to dissolve the blood stains. We all learned fast. Mama, a fastidious housekeeper who punched and aired the bedding daily and beat mattresses dutifully, had rarely held a needle before working at Schultz. "Phew, a button!" she would say squeamishly when we placed it in her hand to sew it on for us. At Schultz's, her disdain evaporated, and she did her part.

Mama took immense pride, as well as sorrow, in Fredka's and my mending proficiency. "*Moje dzieci* [my children] are so clever. Look how perfectly they hold a needle." She would boast and quickly add, "They really should be in school, or playing with other children. The Nazi devils will have to answer for this hell they created." The adults chuckled sadly and nodded. Fredka and I, the only living children in the group, were held dear. There was not a single old person among us.

We shared that deep caring with the illegals that hid among us. The most treasured in our midst was three-year-old Piotrek. He was the only toddler, living secretly with his mother in an apartment in one of the vacant buildings in our section. We all adored and protected him. We considered it a privilege to be near him, to run our fingers through his black curls, to kiss his round cheeks, to ooh and ah at his huge, moist, dark eyes and his extraordinary cleverness.

At dusk, we parted with our friends and reunited with Tata. The streets quickly grew silent as death, and darkness swallowed the subghetto. Not a razor-thin light could be seen in a window. Our security depended on being out of sight. The Nazis too felt safer keeping us in darkness.

Yet some of us dared the dark and forbidden distances that separated neighbors and friends. On occasion, one of my parents' friends would come out of the thin black air, appear at our door, and spend the night with us. At such rare times, I stayed up late into the night listening to adult conversations—soft and harmonious—just as it used to be. They gave me hope that there would be a tomorrow when they talked about the ingenious ways they were evading our persecutors. And when they reminisced about our blissful past and the people who had disappeared, I imagined being inside a dream. Bringing them back to my mind's eye and touching them in thought made death seem less final.

Our rare visitors were also our emissaries, connecting us to our people who were scattered only a few desolate streets away, but as out of reach as creatures on another planet. They were couriers of news and gossip, as well.

*   *   *

Once, we had a most unexpected guest from as far as one of the two other subghettos. It was Benio Posner, Fredka's and my dear old courtyard friend. He reached our house by walking through the secret labyrinth of dark basement alleyways created by the underground movement. We were overjoyed to see him alive, but so sad to hear him tell that his entire family had been marched off to the Umschlagplatz. He joined the resistance fighters and lived in a bunker on Mila Street. He had suffered a fracture and limped.

"It's a minor problem," he said. But we did not think so.

He left us when it was still dark. Frightened that we would never see him again, we blew out the light and stood at the window to watch his silhouette cross the courtyard. He moved with the agility of a cat, in spite of his limp. Besides having to navigate the secret passageways, he had to sneak across some streets that had no underground connections.

Bunkers

Late one evening, Mama, Tata, Fredka, and I sat at the kitchen table, a flickering carbide lamp in the center. In the pale circle of light, hidden from the rest of the world, time stopped for a short moment and the faces of my family gleamed in the spotlight, so vivid in the knowledge that they could be blown off into nothingness at any unexpected moment. Our room remained just so, unto itself, peaceable and unmolested. Tata turned to Fredka and me and said, "I have something important to share with you. You must listen carefully and keep it a secret. Soon, we and several friends will start building a bunker under our apartment. You understand that not a word can be uttered about it to anyone." I was not totally astonished to hear that. As soon as people learned about Treblinka, Jews began to build bunkers.

Tata immediately involved us in the project. "We have to come up with a secret trapdoor in the floor to lead us to the bunker, one that no German will spot. Can you think of a good place for it?"

Tense with fear and excitement, we came up with a number of possibilities, but Tata kept on encouraging us to think harder. Suddenly an idea beamed in my head. "Tata, the cabinet floor under the kitchen windowsill! It's wide enough to crawl through. The edges will hide the outlines of the trapdoor." Tata presented my suggestion to our bunker partners and they approved. I felt proud and useful.

My parents kept few secrets from Fredka and me. They involved us in many major decisions. That was wise. It proved to me that, though I was a child, I had the power to solve important problems. Furthermore, being informed gave dangerous situations a degree of transparency and made them seem potentially surmountable.

Later, Tata and his friends changed the location of the trapdoor to the powder room off the kitchen, where more room to crawl down was available. The entire floor, commode and all, lifted artfully from the foot moldings. Built-in stairs led down to the bunker. When the trapdoor was lowered, it left no clues to give us away.

To give us heart to accept the reality that we soon would be confined to a dark, dank bunker, Tata gave us running progress reports. He kept us informed about food, carbide, and other survival essentials acquired on the black market and stocked on shelves. He told us we would even have a dynamo generator. I could not quite imagine what it would do for us in this underworld, but I allowed myself to hope. Smuggling across the wall went on as long as Jews had money and non-Jews saw an opportunity to line their pockets.

The Informer

I saw him in the dark basement of our building, where I went to escape boredom. Playing in the open daylight was too dangerous. He was prowling in the area where our bunker was being built. A weak light beam crawled down from the open door on top of the stairwell and made him faintly visible. He was a skinny young boy, no taller than I. He moved as softly as a cat, peering into corners.

At first, he was not aware that I was observing him. I saw his face when he turned in my direction and looked up at me. In the semidarkness, his face looked pale, his eyes pitch black and arresting. I knew who he was. Everyone in the remaining fragment of the ghetto had heard of the boy who was seen roaming the dusky labyrinth of basements and reporting to the Germans the locations of bunkers. In return, they became his protectors and allowed him to live.

I glared at him angrily, accusingly, thinking, *What did they do to you to make you do such a thing?* He turned his face, raised his shoulders high, stuffed his hands into his pockets, looked straight ahead, and slunk away into darkness—with information I wished he had never acquired.

I immediately reported the incident to my parents. As always, they gave me credit for my alertness. "Why is he permitted to do this? Why is he not stopped?" I demanded.

"He is a child. We cannot harm him," Mama said.

"Besides, the Germans will be quick to replace him. He is less dangerous because we know to watch out for him," Tata added.

I think, underneath it all, we recognized the uselessness of our attempt to hide. But we were not ready to surrender.

The Gift of Moisze Miodowski

Imagine living in a world where nearly all ordinary pleasures are denied you. You are a child, but you seldom see the sky, or a butterfly, or daylight because it is not safe to be seen; you are working hard all day for an army of killers. Most of the sights and sounds around you are devastating. Then, suddenly, you hear a voice that is so sweet, and magical, and powerful that it carries your imagination beyond the barbs of your miserable reality. Such a voice belonged to Moisze Miodowski. Tata brought him into our lives. I remember what he told us about Moisze.

Before appearing in our subghetto, Moisze, a dark-complexioned young man, had lived in a small town some distance from Warsaw. One day, a gang of German soldiers stormed into his town, rounded up all the Jewish people, young and old, and lined them all up to be shot in the name of their Führer. Moved by an irrepressible impulse, Moisze began to sing the "Kol Nidre," the Jewish prayer sung on Yom Kippur, the Day of Atonement. His beautiful voice rose above the salvo of guns and caught the attention of one German officer. The officer let his finger slip off the trigger, walked up to Moisze, and pulled him aside. It turned out that the officer, a musician, was so enchanted by Moisze's voice that he told Moisze to hide under a heap of corpses, stay there until nightfall, and then steal away.

Moisze lay still under the cover of motionless limbs, excrement, congealed blood, and dead hearts until the burst of gunfire and marching boots faded and darkness fell. Then he dug himself out above the blanket of cadavers and made his way, walking only at night through forbidden streets and villages, until he reached our subghetto and joined the remnant of Jewish people and the resistance fighters. Tata first met him as a fellow resistance fighter.

Tata invited Moisze to live in a room next door to our apartment. I am sure that Tata's friendship soothed Moisze's loneliness. But Moisze's gift to us was no less valued. Sometimes at night, when the German soldiers were not likely to be near, Moisze invited us to his tiny, poorly furnished room to hear him sing for us. I liked to fold my hands on the table, rest my head in the crook of my arm, and listen to his angelic voice rise with such power that it lifted beyond the walls and ceiling, and above the night. I closed my eyes and let his voice float me into a world of warmth, softness, and dreaminess.

Moisze Miodowski was but a blink in my life. He stepped out of his room one day and never made it back. I could easily guess what happened to him. Though Moisze vanished from my life, his gift to me—showing me that beauty can transcend ugly reality—will live with me forever.

Executioners in Our House

One silent dawn, just as the sky began to slip out of darkness, all of us—Mama, Tata, Fredka, and I—felt eyes boring into us. As one, we lifted our heads from our pillows and saw a nightmare come to life. Two ruddy-faced German SS officers—shiny medals dangling from their puffed-out chests, glistening revolvers poking out from their hips—stood framed in the archway between our beds. The skull-and crossbones on their hats looked down at me menacingly.

The officers stood at ease, rocking slowly on their heels, hands folded behind their backs, and leather whips dangling between their legs. Their faces were as calm and hard as stone gods. Their interrogating eyes, cold as a lizard's, waited for an explanation of why we were still alive.

Certain that we were facing our executioners, we leaned to embrace each other but stopped in mid-motion for fear that we might trigger a catastrophic response.

Then, one brute shot a question like a bullet exploding the silence: "What are you doing here?!"

Tata's composed response followed. "We are working at the Schultz factory and have permission to live here."

The most frightening and decisive moments came when one of the officers addressed Fredka. She rose to her feet and moved toward him, a small, slender figure in a white nightgown, her beautiful, delicate face whiter than the white of her gown. She appeared like a vision of innocence. Her feet barely touched the floor and her eyes, though filled with fear, looked directly into the soldier's eyes.

Without taking his eyes off Fredka's face, the SS officer backed away until he reached the door. Then he motioned to the other SS man and both turned and left.

They did not leave empty handed. They took with them Mr. Sabatnik, Tata's friend who was spending the night in our apartment. As soon as they were out of sight, we ran down into our bunker and prayed to all the intervening powers in the universe to let Mr. Sabatnik return unharmed.

We sat, an hour long, cooped up in our hiding and fearing for Mr. Sabatnik's life and for our own fate. Suddenly, we heard footsteps nearing our trapdoor. We stopped breathing and listened. "It does not sound like boots," we concluded. Then, after several short taps on the trapdoor, we heard Mr. Sabatnik's mournful voice calling down to us.

"You can come out now. It is safe. It's me, Sabatnik."

We climbed out of our hiding, so happy that our friend had come back alive, and moved to tears to see his mangled face.

The SS officers had dragged Mr. Sabatnik from building to building, ordering him to knock on peoples' doors and give a friendly reason—in Yiddish—to let him in. The officers promised him all sorts of rewards if he followed their command. Mr. Sabatnik ignored the threats and the rewards. Instead, he told the people to keep silent, doors shut, and hide. The soldiers beat him to a pulp, but Mr. Sabatnik only repeated his warning each time he was forced to knock on another door.

Without raising a fist, Mr. Sabatnik had returned humanity to mankind.

Tata and Mama continued to share with Fredka and me topics unimaginable to any parent under normal circumstances; and equally unimaginable to children who never lived with the reality of Treblinka and the threat of a bloody uprising hanging over their heads. One day, my parents gathered us around the kitchen table, the coziest place to speak about the unspeakable, and informed us in a somber and rehearsed voice, "We have something very important to tell you. We know that you will handle it with the same stout hearts and smarts you have handled every other trying situation. What we want to tell you is: each one of us will have a tiny capsule of cyanide sewn into our coats to use only as a last resort."

We did not ask what the word meant. We had heard several people at the Schultz shop talk about taking cyanide rather than letting themselves be dragged off to Treblinka. We asked, "Can we see it?"

Tata went on to instruct us, "There is no need for you to see it, and you must not touch it. It is highly toxic. We will wear the coats only if we will be rounded up. The decision to use it will be strictly Mama's and mine. You must try to put it out of your minds for now, and leave it to us."

"I know, Tata, I am not afraid," I assured him. His presence and his directions were my shields. *As long as we are together, even in death—Tata, Mama, Fredka, and I, as one.*

7 The Uprising and the End of the Warsaw Ghetto

Armed resistance groups began to form after the news of Treblinka had reached the ghetto. My parents and neighbors had whispered about fighters preparing a network of underground bunkers for hiding and for entrenchment in case of bombardment a while before our bunker was constructed. In no time, they dug tunnels for movement from one position to the next and to get to the other side of the wall to obtain weapons from the Polish underground.

They made holes in basement and attic walls between attached apartment buildings so that they could walk unseen from the street. The dark basement alleys—virtual catacombs—and attic corridors traveled by the fighters quickly became familiar passageways for all ghetto inhabitants. Fredka and I stole moments of play in these secret passageways, hidden from the sky and German patrols.

Soon after our bunker had been constructed, small groups of fighters met there with Tata a few times. My parents never mentioned who the visitors were, but Fredka and I sensed it. We found it both frightening and hopeful. "At least we can strike back, defend ourselves," we said, trying to delude ourselves.

*   *   *

Early in 1943, we learned about isolated clashes between Jewish armed fighters and German security forces. We braced ourselves for retaliation. The punishment came with Himmler's order to abolish the ghetto in three days, in time to give the Führer a birthday present: a *Judenrein* (cleansed of Jews) Warsaw. At that point, most Jews had been deported from the ghetto and 99 percent of Jewish children had been killed. I counted in the 1 percent of surviving children.

Events erupted on April 19, 1943, with the entrance of German columns into the ghetto. Tanks, armored cars, and cars with powerful loudspeakers rolled down our streets calling for us to report willingly for "resettlement." An ultimatum blasted through the streets, courtyards, and windows, and into the remotest corners of our homes: "Unless all Jews follow orders, the Judenrat members will be shot and the ghetto leveled to the ground."

We defied the orders, grabbed a few bundles, lifted the secret trap door, and stepped down a thin ladder into the dank bunker. I felt banished. The low ceiling pressed down on me, damp walls closed me in. A dim, winking carbide lamp substituted for the sun. Small boxes, cans, and bags of food and carbide were neatly stacked on shelves. There was a corner bathroom, a sink, and a few scattered cots. We slept in shifts. We never took a bath or slept through the night. The monotonous ticking of the clock was our only link with the outside universe; it let us know when day was rising and night falling. How I longed for the sky, for open horizons, for the crisp blueness of day!

The strangers in the bunker became my family and my nation. Their slumping shoulders, their brave faces struggling to veil terror, and the kindness in their low voices sustained me. Piotrek, the sole toddler in our section of the ghetto, and his mother hid among us. "Shush, shush," we constantly hushed him for fear that his sweet chatter would give us away. Mama tried to lift our hearts with reassurances. "As soon as the civilized world learns about this savagery, they will come to our rescue." We were still unaware that the world already knew what was happening, but no one heard our cries and no one came to our aid.

Tata included a French tutor in this miserable underworld, and she made Fredka and me repeat French phrases after her. This was Tata's way of denying that his children had no future. Strangely, chanting the foreign phrases distracted me from the monstrous explosions above ground, and made me feel as if life would go on, in spite of knowing that death was a breath away. We stayed in the bunker several days and nights. But if you sit in a dark hole in the ground listening to the world crashing around you, you never stop sitting there. Some part of you sits there through all your life.

*   *   *

While we sat in our bunker, fighting raged in all three subghettos. Wehrmacht demolition teams rolled though streets, blowing up bunkers, rounding up their occupants, marching them to the Umschlagplatz, slaughtering people, and dynamiting building after building. Our bunker walls trembled. So did we.

Sometimes, an urgent tapping on our trapdoor, like Morse code, sent us into deathly silence. All eyes turned on the bunker leaders asking, *Who can this be?* A whisper, softer than a breeze, would seep through the trapdoor cracks, and the leader would declare, "It is safe. It is one of us." The carbide lights went out, a flashlight pointed to the ceiling, and a crack in the trapdoor opened wide enough to let several fighters slip through. The guests stayed just minutes, exchanged whispers with the bunker leader, picked up some things they needed, and slipped out into the exploding streets—like figures in a dream.

Against forces armed from head to toe, against tanks and war planes stood our poorly outfitted, inexperienced, starving bands of ghetto warriors. They took positions in street corners and lobbed grenades and Molotov cocktails at German columns. Equipped with flame throwers, mines, rifles, and guns, they climbed on rooftops, stepped in front of open windows, crawled through secret tunnels, and attacked German soldiers and their Latvian and Ukrainian collaborators.

There was no end to the young fighters' valor. They crept through confusing networks of sewers to get to the Aryan side to obtain weapons. Often the Polish underground betrayed them and did not deliver promised arms and instructions. Days passed and no word or help of any kind reached the fighters. Disillusioned, abandoned, ill equipped Jewish fighters continued their struggle. The Warsaw ghetto fighters battled longer than it took France or Poland to capitulate. Clashes flared up with fierce persistence even weeks after the ghetto had been burned to the ground and the Germans declared that the residential district in the Warsaw Ghetto no longer existed.

Boom! The trapdoor of our bunker burst open with a detonation so loud and close, I was sure the top of my head had blown off. The explosion sucked out all the air, and everything reeled under a cloud of dust and flying splinters. Stunned, we screamed as if our collective cry had the power to scare off our assailants. Perhaps we hoped that we would awaken God. In a terrifying instant, a horde of barbarians invaded our refuge. We no longer had a corner to hide in, nor even the liberty to drop to our knees, clench our fists, and smash the earth in fury and frustration.

How did they know the secret location of our trapdoor? Did the dark-eyed boy I had seen prowling in the basement lead them there?

"Raus! Raus! Vehrfluchte Juden! Hunde!" They stomped, kicked, jabbed rifles into our ribs, and forced us out into the street. We were shoved into a moving flood of ravaged people. We knew our destination: the Umschlagplatz and deportation to—Treblinka?

My parents whispered urgently as the pandemonium raged, "Hold on tight. We must not be separated."

I tried to reassure them, "I will never let go of your hands!" But my voice was gone. *If the crowd cuts me off, how will I call out to my parents?* Frantically, my mouth formed words, my abdomen heaved, but not a sound passed my lips. Tata noticed my panic and realized my dilemma. His fingers encircled my hand and drew me close to him as we stumbled forward. Mama cried out, "The child is in shock! I hope they burn in hell!"

Was I in shock? I remember being aware of my terror and of my resolve not to become a victim without the will to resist death. I was conscious of wanting to protect my parents and sister and not be separated from them. We locked hands and moved as a single organism to die as one, if die we must. The ground beneath us thundered and shook with detonations; homes crumbled around us; planes circled overhead dropping incendiary bombs. Enormous tongues of flames licked the sky and transformed it into unworldly spectrums of iridescence. Plumes of smoke, tall as towers, billowed. Ash and debris fell on our heads and coated our throats. The air stank of burning flesh, furniture, buildings, lampposts, and all that once supported life.

We passed heaps of corpses sprawled like discarded puppets with frozen expressions of horror: a stiff arm here, a charred leg there; torsos of parents flung across the bodies of dead children like protective shields. Their silent screams of love—like sirens of nobility—penetrated the pits of death. I yanked my face not to see, but their clay faces called to me to look, to acknowledge, and never forget.

I shivered and stared in horror. *Will I be like them? And Mama? Tata? Fredka? What will death feel like?* I hoped, I wished. *Not quite yet. We are not ready. I want one more embrace from Mama and Tata. No, one is not enough, more and more. More laughs with Fredka. More dashes to catch the rainbow. More suns to rise on peaceful days, as it used to be.*

I know these cannot be the exact words I chanted. But these are the words that still speak inside me when I think back to that time. In the wreckage of my memories, I still hear the suppressed scream in my throat: *Strike back!* with all the force of my indignation—a fury as formidable as the crimes committed against us. But I did not jump at the throats of the executioners. Nor did I march like a sheep. But, like any captive with a gun pointing at his or her skull, I knew that only a miracle would let me get back at the attackers. Even a child knows that the time to fight to defend yourself is before you are defeated.

I gathered my courage to endure and raised my head. I hid my tears from my parents because I loved them, and from my enemies because I did not want to give them the satisfaction of seeing my tears. I hoped that Mama's words would come true. "Time will shame them, their nation, and their progeny. Whoever delights in murder cannot inherit the earth."

Perhaps the reason that defeated warriors march silently, and condemned men walk mutely to the gallows, and people accept the fate of a terminal illness without making a scene is so that they can mobilize their strength for a dignified exit.

Trains to the End of Existence

We joined a sea of desperate people at the Umschlagplatz on Stawki Street, between the Aryan and Jewish parts of Warsaw. We were forced to sit on the ground, like bundles of waste to be loaded onto lines of freight trains waiting on a tangle of tracks. The tracks ran far into a misty distance, rounded a corner, and then vanished into the end of the world. The jangle of coupling cars, the clangs of bars bolting doors, and the barks of guards clashed dissonantly like a diabolic ensemble. Near me, mournful whispers of my people—like the laments in the Kaddish—rocked me gently. That was the only rational sound in this field of death.

We sat in this frightful place for hours, until dusk. We shivered and watched flames swallow the world in gargantuan gulps. The air crackled with burning buildings, with bodies trapped inside. It thundered with collapsing city blocks. It shuddered with the staccato of gunfire and the insults flung at us. Surreal mushrooms of smoke swirled in the wind and spread across the blazing sky.

Amidst this cataclysmic spectacle, Tata's gentle voice brushed my ears, "How can such breathtaking grandeur exist in this hellish upheaval?" Suddenly I had a sensation of standing outside the phantasmagoric reality, somewhat outside my own horror—as if I were careening down an abyss and what I saw on the way down became more real, more encompassing, and more immediate than my terror of dying.

I did not understand it then, but Tata was bestowing upon me another gift, one that would serve me forever.

Our turn came to be loaded onto the train. I was scarcely able to keep up with the flow of human cargo. The guards shoved and pushed us into the cattle cars, packing us tightly, body against body. Arms and legs tangled and wriggled for a modicum of space. Heads turned and twisted for a gasp of air. Beseeching, pain-filled eyes circled the car for a spot of floor to collapse on. Mama, Tata, Fredka, and I ended up pinned against a rattling wall. We struggled to hold on to each other, fiercely clutching a hand, a coattail, and silently praying not to be torn from each other. Our tongues felt leathery with thirst, lips crusty and cracked, throats dry from the smoke and ash we inhaled.

When the wagons were packed to the tormentors' satisfaction, the doors and bars slammed shut, and the train took off into the night. Our decimated city disappeared in the distance while the train plunged into the night. Random bullet shots pelted the speeding train for mere sport—ta-ta-ta-ta! I had been kidnapped and carried to a macabre end of the world.

That April night was the last time I saw Warsaw, my queenly city. Among the pyres and mountains of rubble floated my anguished longing for things to be as they were before the war. My mind flashed back to the Aprils when Fredka and I searched the lilac trees to find the first tiny buds; to greening parks with swans on silver ponds, to tranquil nights when Warsaw wore a crown of golden lights and my streets murmured peacefully. But most of all I longed for a sip of water from our kitchen faucet, a slice of bread at our table at home, not ever to be thirsty or hungry, and for human decency. And I wished to see the executioners impaled on their own bayonets.

After long, dreadful hours I recovered my voice, but I said little. There was no point in asking questions or complaining to my parents, whom I tried to protect. No one said much. Some groaned with pain. Some wondered, vainly, if there was a chance for escape. Some moaned, shook their fists at God, and whispered, "God, where are you? How can you let this happen?" Some asked, "Where is human conscience? Where is civilized man?"

Memory of a Good Train

With eyes closed, in the frightful darkness within, hallucinations of a prewar train ride to the countryside flashed into my consciousness with lightning speed; then I was right back in the desperate present, with the all-encompassing alertness of a hunted animal.

My memory flashed again on my last good train ride. I was speeding from Warsaw to a summer villa in Michalin. My face stayed glued to the window in complete awe. Trees and telephone poles took on a dreamy fluidity. Furry pines galloped backwards, their outstretched branches like wing tips, reaching out and then quickly withdrawing.

During that ride we stopped at small village stations under black, rectangular roofs. Peasants with wholesome faces and flowery scarves joined the crowd of vacationers. Then the conductor called, "All aboard!" The locomotive puffed gargantuan breaths of smoke;

the wheels beat out fresh rhythms and carried me past motionless ponds, solitary peasant huts, silky white birches, orchards, forests, and rectangular fields that stretched clear to the end of the world like patchwork quilts stitched by giants.

The train dropped us off near our villa. All summer long I chased butterflies and rainbows, played in pine forests, frolicked with my sister, cousins, and friends, and fell asleep to the rustle of trees and the prattle of gentle voices.

From Monday till Friday, mothers basked in the sun, munched bonbons, gossiped, and joked. They laughed nervously and made light of the fact that their husbands were left alone with the maids in the city.

Tata? Unthinkable! I was horrified at the women's calm.

On Fridays, mothers cooked up a storm and made the houses and themselves pretty. Freshly bathed children, I among them, galloped to the train station to greet weekend guests and experience a special romance with trains. We leaned into the tracks, stared into the horizon, and waited. First, we saw the locomotive with a lamp like a beacon. The passenger cars sauntered behind. The train seemed to come from nowhere; they dropped off our fathers and guests and disappeared, leaving a sense of mystery.

At the end of that summer, the train brought us back home and to a city nervous with preparations for possible war. Air-raid sirens shrieked over the cacophonous city noises to drill us into readiness. Still, people carried on as if it would never happen. Families shopped for the coming season, and went to movies, theaters, and restaurants as usual. Fear made hearts beat stronger and renewed zealous love for our land. We children sang patriotic songs and waved little flags that we made out of red and white paper. Exactly eight days before the war broke out, I sat with my beloved friend Janka on our favorite windowsill, from where we could see our friends playing in the courtyard. We leaned into each other and whispered, "I wonder what war would be like?" We concluded, "It would be very exciting and interesting." With childish innocence, we closed our eyes, crossed our fingers and made a wish, "God, let there be war." Tragically, God must have heard us. I was sure of that. Guilty!

The summer before the outbreak of war was the last summer of my childhood. War split my world into a time of happiness—pure as childhood bliss—and a time of darkness when the sight of corpses became a banality.

8 Tata's Last Word

At dawn, the train jerked to a clanging halt. Those close to the bullet holes and cracks in the walls reported what they saw: "Armed Germans and Ukrainian guards and people—our people, chased."

"*Oh! Boże drogi! Gotinew!*" (Dear God!), people sighed.

I pressed my arms into my chest to restrict my violent trembling. My mind was no longer entirely mine. It was doing things as if in a nightmare. I clutched my parents, forced myself to sit bolt upright, and tried hard to stay alert. After a short wait and solemn thoughts about our fate, we heard unbolting bars and rude shouts. "*Raus! Raus! Schnell.*" And they were upon us.

The train had brought us to the infamous concentration camp Majdanek, located among rolling wheat fields in Lublin. In no time our tormentors rushed us into a fenced-in field jammed with bedraggled people. We had had nothing to drink since they had chased us out of our bunkers. We pleaded for water. The soldiers playfully picked up garden hoses, aimed streams of water above our heads and let the water arch to the ground. Unable to withstand our thirst, we bent to the ground, dipped our hands into muddy puddles that formed around us, and scooped out droplets of water to moisten our lips.

I lifted my head to scan the field of annihilation for a sign of safety, an escape. A faintly familiar figure of a young woman clutching a motionless child caught my attention. I looked again and called out, "Mama, Look! Piotrek's mother!"

In her vomit-stained arms lay our beloved Piotrek, the last hidden toddler we had known in the final days of the ghetto. He lay as motionless as a clay doll with a tousle of black curls. Piotrek's mother turned her ravaged face to us, pale as death. She moaned like a wounded animal and stammered, "I killed him. I killed him. I swallowed the cyanide too, but I threw up. I wanted to die with him." She hugged and rocked the little corpse and wailed.

As far as I know, she was the only person from our bunker who actually swallowed the cyanide capsule.

"Achtung! Aufstehen!" (Attention! Stand up!) A band of wild guards began to shove us into groups, separating men, women, and children: *"Männer hier! Hunde! Frauen dort! Kinder da!"* (Men here! Dogs! Women there! Children yonder!) They ripped screaming toddlers out of the arms of hysterical parents. They bellowed, *"Los! Schnell!"* Wham! Kick! Shove! And Tata was torn away from us.

Unable to hold on to him, we called, "Tata! Tata!"

Mama screamed, "Samek! Samek!"

Tata called back our names, "Mania! Fredziuchna! Estusiuchna!"

We shouted encouragements: "Hold on! Endure! Stay alive! I love you! I love you!"

We craned our necks not to lose sight of Tata. With guns pointing at us—safety catches clicking—we were ordered to sit on the ground and wait for fate to roll over us. Gusts of biting wind lashed across the open terrain. Tata pushed himself to the front row and sat cross-legged on the muddy ground with the group of exhausted and grief-stricken men. We three sat with the group of women directly across from Tata, locking eyes with him. A short distance from us, children remained confined behind a wire fence in a muddy enclosure resembling a pigsty. The children clung to the fence pleading and yammering, "Mama! Tata! Where are you?" Their sepulchral cries horrified me. They milled around in their isolated space desperately, frantically. I could not bear to look in their direction. I feared that I too might be torn away from Mama and Fredka and thrown in with the children.

Tata was ill. He had a high fever and shivered with chill. He took off his jacket and wound it around his head to quell the cold. I could not stand the look of suffering I saw in his worn face. I was accustomed to looking into his eyes to find comfort—they always held kindness, steadiness, and reassurance. How filled with pain they were now!

I broke loose from the group of women and dashed across the field that separated us from Tata. He motioned me back, his face and eyes contorted with fear for my safety. I reached him and knelt down on the ground in front of him. "Please, Tata," I said, "You need not worry about me. They will not get me." I flipped the lapel of my coat and showed him the tiny, secret vial of cyanide sewn to the inside. "They will never get me, Tata. Remember, I have cyanide." I meant to reassure him.

He shuddered, his eyes burnt with anguish and love. He pleaded, "No, no! Don't do that! You must live!"

All life was coming to an end for me, crushed under the boots of barbarians. All lessons of nobility and the sanctity of life were piled on a pyre. From these ashes came Tata's message to me: "Live!"

Tata vanished like a dream, sheathed in the radiant light of virtue and unyielding values. He remained my archangel of humanism, calm and gentle as a whisper, dignified as the Masada site. He remained an immortal voice, a mantra as eternal as the current in a stream. "Yes, yes, there is a separating line between the worst and the noblest in men; neither purges the other." He vanished during a Walpurgis Night, leaving a pulse of goodness when the wrath of evil danced like Satan, sending my world up in flames.

9 *Majdanek*

Selection and Shower

Things continued happening outside our command or will. Soldiers shoved and shouted orders to move forward. Where to? The gas chambers? The reality of death, of not being, was incomprehensible and horrifying. An irrepressible inner force commanded me to shrink into myself, become invisible, watch for flying bullets and whips, duck in the right direction—every flinch, a wrong twist or turn, could be fatal. I remained alert as a hunted beast.

Suddenly, an armed, burly soldier stepped in front of me and blocked my way—green eyes, hard as flint, looking into me. He barked in German, "What are you hiding?" Maybe he is looking for money or jewelry, I thought. Frightened, but determined to hold on to my last treasure, I showed him a picture I had hidden under the lining of my shoe and pleaded, "Everything I had was taken away. That is all I have, a picture of my father. Could I keep it? Please. It has no value to others."

He leaned into me, placing the butt of his gun on my shoulder; the other arm darted out to take away the last thing I had left of Tata. He hollered a string of foul insults and motioned me forward. Mama and Fredka stared at me from the row of miserable marchers—their eyes wide with fear of losing sight of me. I too worried about their disappearance. Losing sight of each other could mean being separated forever. That would be beyond unbearable. I rushed to reach them.

The next stop brought us into a large room where the barbarians forced us to strip every stitch of our clothing. Nude, stunned, and humiliated beyond words, we had to form a line and walk in front of jolly SS officers in starched uniforms. With a snap of a whip held in white-gloved hands, they sorted us into groups. We knew precisely what the groups meant. The weaker-looking people were designated first for the gas chambers. The others were on reprieve until the next selection, when room was available in the gas chambers at this busy time. Our footsteps fell on the floor like drumbeats in a death march.

Mama in the lead stepped in front of an impeccably uniformed officer. I desperately wanted to drape my small fingers over her nakedness. The officer glanced at her, up and down, and pointed her to a group. She stopped at the head of the line to watch if the whip would separate Fredka and me from her. Its tip sent me in the same direction. But when Fredka stepped in front of one of the demons ruling over life and death, the whip pointed her to the group of skinny women headed straight for the gas chamber. In a flash, my stark naked mother lurched forward, taut and upright, and called out, "No! She is my daughter. Let her go with me!" All eyes turned to my large bosomed, small hipped, short, pathetic mother and to the pompous, booted, insignia-and-medal-decorated SS officer. He shrugged and the whip tipped Fredka to our group.

We felt immense gratitude. "We are so fortunate! So unbelievably fortunate! That SS man had a drop of a conscience," we said to each other as we embraced.

It is unthinkable that we felt thankful to the brute for granting us a few more days to live. Still, I am pleased that things went that way. I was proud of Mama's swiftness and courage that day. It took half a heartbeat for her to recognize that she wanted Fredka to join our group and to act with such extraordinary daring. Our survival depended 99 percent on random luck and 1 percent on instinct and grit. Without the 1 percent pluck, you were 100 percent dead.

They handed us bars of soap and rushed us into shower stalls. The soap did not fool us. We knew it served as a ruse to lure Jews obediently into the gas chambers. Trapped and chased, we stepped under the showerheads and inhaled the choking vapor of disinfectant in the water: witnesses to our own deaths. I did not scream; no one screamed. What was the point? No one would hear. I pressed my arms into my chest to restrict my violent trembling. I felt as if it were the world shaking with a ravaging force.

"Schnell! Hunde!" They chased us out of the stalls. We absolutely could not believe we were alive. We scampered like frightened rabbits to dodge the bursts of vulgar shouting, the gun barrels, the whips landing on our backs, and to not lose sight of each other. They thundered orders for us to pick up wooden clogs and caftans—stinking of fumigation—from benches and get dressed. *"Schnell! Schnell!"* All we now owned was one scratchy, loose caftan and a pair of oversized wooden clogs. No underwear, no stockings, no coat. But we three had each other and drew succor from that. Everyone else was alone in this brutal world.

In spite of all the horrors, I was glad to be among the living. I hoped and wished that our suffering would pass like a terrible nightmare. In mute fury, I thought of ways I might find revenge, including pushing the killers into the ovens that they had waiting for us.

A ring of electrified barbed-wire fences with guard towers isolated Majdanek from the rest of the world. Behind the fence we, all women, lived in rows of drab, one-level barracks. A tall, brick chimney lurked above the fence. The chimney spewed black clouds of smoke and the souls of my people. I always avoided looking in that direction. Few blades of grass grew on the worn-down soil, and the spidery smoke erased the sun's glow. A distant patch of blue sky, like an opaque window to a dream, hung above me as I marched to and from forced labor. Cold winds whipped across the flat and empty terrain, tearing at my skin. The guards' omnipresence clawed at me like death.

Our barrack bore no resemblance to a home. It looked like warehouses for discards. You entered and faced a three-tiered stack of bare wooden shelves supported by vertical posts. The planks, our bunks, ran the length of the wall. When we came back from work, we immediately crawled into our bunk slips to allow others to pass. The narrow strip of floor in front of the bunks left little room to walk. These coops were our "homes." This is where we spent the few hours allowed us between work shifts and *Appells* (roll-calls). This is where Mama, Fredka, I, and several hundred women slept, packed side by side like cigars in a box. We had no nightshirts, no pillows, no linen—just what we wore, and a scratchy, lice-infested blanket. We three cuddled into one another as we dropped off to sleep. Tragically, all the others in our barrack were alone.

Searchlight beams crashed in through the bare windows opposite the bunks and looked into all corners of our barrack. The exposed windows invited the eyes of armed guards cruising outside. But the windows also brought in the sky, pure and as unreachable as freedom.

We had a communal washroom with long rows of pipes with spigots above narrow troughs. I cannot recall if we had hot water, how we dried ourselves, or how we washed the single caftan and blanket we owned. I clearly remember being tormented by lice.

We rose at predawn, squinted into the murky darkness to find our clogs and *puszkas* (tin cans) stored at our feet, slipped into our clogs, and landed on the floor with a loud clatter. We tugged at the dresses we wore—the same ones we slept in—to straighten creases and look presentable. Cold, exhausted, and bleary-eyed, we clutched our puszka and shuffled to the latrines, open ditches behind the barracks; to the communal washroom; and then to outdoor queues for a slice of coarse bread and chamomile tea ladled into the puszka. We never parted with our puszka for fear of losing it. Our lives literally depended on the miserable tin can.

We barely gulped down the few precious morsels, and we were rushed to the Appell in the center of the field, in front of the gallows. We stood as silent as death itself. Guards smacked whips against their polished boots and screamed orders for us to form perfectly straight rows, stand at attention, and not flinch—not an easy task when your head is light with hunger and you tremble with cold. No one dared to miss the Appell. People who failed to report on time hung from the gibbet in the center of the field. For days, they drooped from the rope like broken puppets to remind us of what might happen to us if we strayed. The corpses swinging in the breeze, the sadistic screams of the guards, the panting of their dogs, and the pops of guns sealed the morbidity of our semiexistence and made the silence of my people scream.

The guards counted our heads, hollered more warnings, divided us into groups, and led us outside the camp to work in secluded, green fields, flat as tabletops. Above our heads hung a strip of sky and, etched behind it, barbed wire fences. The field stretched far into a desolate distance and came to a dead stop in front of a black forest, marking the end of my horrifying world. I often pressed my ears to the impenetrable wall of isolation to hear if a world still existed. I heard only the chilling silence of indifference. It was painful to imagine that, in truth, a short distance away, people sailed on silver lakes; they entertained family and friends in warm homes, and children played and laughed.

Rain or shine, predawn until dusk, we worked in the fields, thrusting shovels into the hard soil to dig up squares of turf, heaving them into wheelbarrows, pushing the heavy loads to spots dug bare by other Jews, and placing them there. Some days, the early spring winds lashed at us mercilessly. When the pain of cold became unendurable, we waited for the guards to turn their heads, and then quickly stepped close to the person in front, placed our lips on their backs and exhaled a puff of warm air. I received the sparse blast of comfort with immense gratitude.

At dusk, the guards ordered us to get in line, marched us back behind the barbed wire fence, and locked the heavy gate. I tried hard not to shuffle, or appear weak and fit to be gassed. To accomplish a passable stride, I pressed my aching toes into the wooden clogs to stop them from slipping off my feet.

Cold, famished, and exhausted, I lined up in front of the gallows for another Appell, to be counted and to endure whatever other insults the soldiers decided to inflict. When that agony ended, I followed the reek of cooked turnips and joined another line behind a steaming vat. In one outstretched hand I held out my puszka to receive a ladle of turnip slop. With the other hand I grabbed a slice of bread and shuffled off with Mama and Fredka to our barrack. The bread was dark, dense, and had the consistency of mud mixed with straw. I savored every crumb of bread and every drop of the slop.

We never had enough food to sooth the pain of hunger. Mama would sometimes say, "I feel tempted to steal a piece of bread for us. But how can you steal from people who have so little?"

I do not remember anyone in our barrack stealing. Perhaps I have forgotten. Or it may be that we devoured our rations too quickly for anyone to snatch them from us.

In Majdanek, where diarrhea ran rampant, we had no real bathrooms. Instead, we had to trot to open trenches located behind the barracks and in front of the barbed wire fence, where armed guards watched us from their towers. Going to the trenches was terrifying, humiliating, and, of course, unavoidable. Afraid and embarrassed about squatting in front of the guards, I picked the farthest spot from the towers, turned my back, crouched as low as I could without falling in, and fought my fear of being shot and drowning in the muck. Many did die that way. I never succeeded in finding a spot far away enough to shut out the loud voices of the guards in the towers, nor could I understand why the soldiers did not turn their heads in shame. In anger, I muttered to myself, "They are savages! Savages! I hope the stench chokes them to death, every one of them!"

After every trip to the trench, Fredka pleaded bravely, "Mama, please, Mama, let's go to the gas chambers right now. What's the use? They will kill us anyway. Making them kill us is the only power we have over them and over our destiny. Please, please, Mama. I don't want to endure this humiliation any longer."

Mama scolded her lovingly, "You must not say that. We are still alive and we have each other. There is infinite dignity and honor in fighting for life. Life is sacred. We cannot give up. You are innocent and good. They bring shame to humanity and they will pay for it."

Only those who struggled with us can know how hard we fought to keep our faith in goodness from dying. At night, after long hours of hard labor, we lay on bare bunks—

rows of starved and bereft women—illuminating the darkness of our existence with po-etry. Our barrack's poet laureate, sixteen-year-old Gutka, was always the first to start. Words and melodies poured out of her like musical lamentations. Slowly we all joined in to memorialize the sanctity of simple moments when life was good and right. Our verses screamed against the atrocities and the executioners who ruled our universe. We eulogized the good people who dangled from gibbets outside our door, and the innocent souls that floated on plumes of smoke. We had no pencils or paper to record our words for history to remember. Our verses were written on the wind.

When our songs and whispers stopped, the black night hovered like death. Sporadic shrieks and moans rose amidst the rhythmic breathing sounds of sleep. Bodies tossed and writhed with fright. Yellow searchlight beams burst in through the windowpanes and slipped back into the dark. Gunshots and barks of German shepherd dogs made the night air shiver. I squeezed into Mama's embrace, silently cursing the shameless savages as I dropped off to sleep.

News about Tata

No matter how closely we clung together, we did not always manage to land on the same work team. One morning, Fredka was marched off with a separate work team. On the way, she passed a line of hollow-cheeked Jewish men approaching from the opposite direction. She recognized the face of one man and called out, "Where is my father? Do you know?"

He replied, "Look at the truck," and motioned to the truck that followed closely behind the men. She looked up and saw a heap of corpses shaking as the truck rolled over the uneven ground and past her. A choking stink of gas fumes hung around the truck.

Horror-struck and alone, Fredka continued on her forced march. She worked that day in silence. She did not utter a sound until she lined up next to Mama and me for the evening Appell on the open field in front of the guards and gallows. Then she whispered a lament, "I saw Tata. He is dead."

We stood mute and rooted to the spot, unable to talk, unable to cry in front of the goons with guns, and whips, and faces like steel, who watched every move we made.

When we joined another column of living dead to collect a single ladle full of the evening turnip swill, Fredka muttered the rest, "I saw Tata's corpse. I smelled the gas fumes." She wailed, "Let's go right now to be gassed."

She pleaded, "Let's put an end to our humiliations and torture. They will kill us anyway. Mama, I don't want to live this way."

At that moment, my sister was dearer to me than ever. I had to help her bear her despair, or else I might lose her as well. I swallowed hard to force boulders of tears down my throat. I remained as mute as scorched earth. How I wanted to stab the life out of them! Tear their hearts out!

Mama too fought back her tears. Silently, she rocked to steel herself. Then she raised her wan skeletal face and said, "Now, we cannot be sure what the man meant. We do not know for certain if he did not make a general remark, 'Look at the truck.' He might have meant that is where Tata might be. We do not know for sure. Tata might still be alive."

We knew. We remembered how sick Tata was when they wrenched him from us. But denial is a scab that covers raw wounds.

That night, in spite of our clawing hunger, we could not swallow our rations. We hid them out of sight like animals in the wild that cannot be sure of their next meal. The wind blew colder through the thin walls that night, and the darkness of our existence felt more strangling. When we curled up on our bunk plank, we clasped each other tightly and held on, as one holds on to his last breath. Life without the others was unimaginable.

I lay in Mama's embrace on that brittle night not letting go of Tata's image. He remained my absolute hero. If he had ever upset me, it was all erased by the love and examples of goodness he left within me. That perfection remained my anchor.

Brigitte

One morning at the field, a guard sent Fredka, a few other women, and me to a ditch piled full with personal items—photographs, wedding bands and other small jewelry, gold dental crowns, and more—and ordered us to sort them. Suddenly, Brigitte, a pretty young German overseer known to us for her cruelty, appeared at the edge of the ditch shouting and ranting, thrashing the ground with a whip in a fury. She pointed a finger at Fredka and yelled, "I saw you look at that picture!"

Fredka attempted to explain, "I had to look to know in which pile to place it." Before she could finish, Brigitte pounced on my sister—a delicate, skinny fifteen-year-old—flung her to the ground and whipped, kicked, and mauled her curled-up body with a ferocity I will never forget.

Everyone in the ditch felt Fredka's pain, although the whip never touched us. When Brigitte tired of hurling her insults and her whip, she walked on with an air of utter contempt.

Careful not to be noticed by guards, I moved close to Fredka, who remained limp and coiled up with pain. I propped up her wounded body and shushed her as she whimpered like a small puppy. Deep welts on her back showed through her ripped caftan. Gashes, like angry scribbles, covered her back, arms, and legs. On the march back to the camp, a kind woman and I propped our shoulders under Fredka's arms to help her walk straight and pass unnoticed by the guards while others marchers formed a protective screen around us.

The following day, Fredka still could barely stand upright, and we had to risk hiding her under the long collective bunks when we left for the Appell and work. When Mama and I came back, Fredka met us with news. "Mama, finally all our suffering and humiliations will be over! While you were gone, German soldiers rounded up everyone they could find, asked our names, and wrote them on a list."

Of course, no doubt existed in anyone's mind that being on the list meant being next for the ovens. What remained for Mama and me to do was as clear as drawing in the next breath. We immediately traded places with two women on the list so we could die together. At the following morning Appell, when a guard called out the two women's names, Mama and I joined Fredka's group. This posed no problem because none of us had any identification. The guards escorted us to an awaiting freight train, and we dashed toward an unknown, frightening destination.

10 *Longing*

Sometimes I plunged back into introspection about all that had been dearest in my life. I imagined that if I were free to walk past the barbed wire fences, I would find my best friend, Janka, just as she was before the time of madness—a beautiful, olive-skinned girl with twinkling dark eyes. I imagined that if I would reach out to touch her, she would not vanish into air as she did in my dreams.

Reveries flashed and vanished in my head—as rapidly as only thoughts can—when I stood at attention at Appells, when I looked away from heaps of corpses, when I marched to and from work, and when I collapsed on a trembling train floor. Some part of my mind tried to remember that sanity existed—must still exist somewhere. As in a dream, I found myself looking into Nowolipki Street, where we moved from Mila Street the summer of my ninth birthday, one year before the apocalypse. Our street had tall buildings with iron-work balconies and was abuzz with happy noises. Mama was deliriously happy with the move to a "better" neighborhood, a roomier, brighter flat on a second floor, with a balcony and tall windows.

The windows in our new apartment gave us a wide view of the entire courtyard and looked directly into the front archway with an iron gate to the street. In the morning, sun streamed in to spotlight cozy corners and rare oleander and eucalyptus plants that Mama proudly placed on the floor. I liked to fling a window open to call out to friends playing in the courtyard, observe neighbors in new outfits, or watch the clouds mutate into giants and dragons. Later, in the ghetto, I stood watch at the windows for German soldiers entering our yard.

At home Mama set a tone of song, laughter, and wonderment. "Look at the clouds crowning the sun! Look at the yellow in this yellow flower!"

Noticing miracles hidden in the mundane is a gift Mama passed on to us.

"Mama, I want a doll just like the one I saw in Bracia Jabkowski's big store window," I would beg.

"It is very expansive. You will have to save money for it," Mama responded. I immediately began to save my *groszy* (pennies) in a tiny porcelain piggy bank. Every so often, I shook the coins out on the table to count them. When the heap grew big, Tata showed me how to stack the coins into towers of ten, to conveniently add up the total.

While I waited for my dream doll, Mama said, "No problem. I will make you a doll right away. It will be just as beautiful as you can imagine."

She took out a towel, spread it out on the table and rolled it lengthwise, folded the roll in half, then twisted one folded end into a ball to form a head. She tied a string under the head and placed the doll into my cradled arms. She made the same doll for Fredka. We had as many instant dolls as we wanted.

We swaddled our babies in shawls, just as real mothers do. We dressed them in imaginary gowns and jewels, and turned chairs upside down to make cradles. In no time at all, the furniture in the room changed into towers, castles, parks—anything we could dream of.

Sometimes, Tata crossed over to our imaginary universe. We built trains with a row of chairs and raced to made-up worlds. Tata sat in the front chair, the locomotive, puckered his lips and blew two short whistle blasts: "Toot! Toot!" He imitated metallic rasps and chugs, and we were off.

Tata's love became my treasured endowment. When he was no more, and I was far from Nowolipki Street and innocent childhood, I brought him back in my mind to remind me that goodness exists—even if only in my memory.

Tata's jewelry workroom was the liveliest and most interesting room in our apartment. It bustled with the voices and activities of four employees who sat bent over a long table creating wondrous bracelets out of gold ingots. With a thin pipette held in the mouth, and a tiny torch in front, they melted pieces of gold. The molten gold quivered in hand-held asbestos bowls and shimmered like tiny liquid suns—a beautiful sight! They poured the gleaming liquid into forms to cool. Then they hammered, filed, and shaped small gold loops with pliers, soldered them, and produced glamorous gold bracelets.

I popped into Tata's workroom whenever I felt bored, or wanted his advice or his attention. If he was not too busy, he cheerfully talked with me while he worked away.

"Tata, I have got to tell you something. I will never speak to Zosia again. She called me a name."

"Did you ever call anyone a name?"

"Never!"

"Think about it. When you remember at least once doing the same, come back and tell me."

It did not take long to jar my memory. "Tata, I remember one time . . ."

"Did you forgive yourself for it?" I stared at him. "If you did, you might consider forgiving Zosia."

Tata was my hero, his kindness and cool logic, my inspiration.

On Fridays before sundown, Tata's workshop was silent, workbenches cleared, and tools placed out of the way. The house looked scrubbed. The fresh scent of soap and tangy aromas of favorite dishes wafted in the air. A white damask cloth and silver candelabra adorned the table. When dusk crawled up to our windows, Mama lit the Sabbath candles. She lowered her head and rounded her arms above the flickering candles as if embracing the spirit of Sabbath, and said a brief prayer. We ate gefilte fish, chicken soup, and *babkah* (coffeecake).

On the Sabbath our street was quiet. The shops were closed with iron bars and padlocks, families strolled unhurriedly, and the pungent aromas of *tshulent* (a Sabbath meal) flowed in the breeze.

The Sabbath tshulent was as customary in our neighborhood as matzo was at Passover. Preparations for that holiday meal began on Friday and set our kitchen into a frenzy of activities. Mama was busy peeling, chopping, stirring, tasting, and smacking her lips. She put the ingredients—potatoes, meat, stuffed derma, and seasoning—into a large pot. She wedged a smaller clay dish with *kugle* (noodle pudding) in the center and placed a heavy lid on top of the pot. She wrapped the top with layers of newspaper and secured it with a string, then carried it to the baker.

Before sundown, our street was humming with harried women, small children in tow, carrying the tshulent pots, wrapped like presents, to the bakery. The baker shoved the pots into a large oven filled with glowing embers. The pots remained in the ovens overnight, simmering very slowly. *Voila*, a holiday meal was cooking without breaking Sabbath rules against striking a match or interrupting the holiday rest. The ingredients mingled, the potatoes turned brown and flavorful, and the noodle pudding formed a delicious crust on top. Mid-day on Saturday, neighbors and maids carried the steaming tshulent pots home to be shared with family and friends.

At night, as I lay on hard barrack planks ensconced in Mama's emaciated arms in Majdanek, my stomach knotted with hunger, I often sipped the memories of tshulent and home, like an elixir.

Holidays were extra special at home, even though my parents were more concerned about how people behaved toward one another than about God. I only remember going to the temple with my parents on Simchat Torah, a joyous holiday celebrating the one-year cycle of the reading of the Torah. However, Mama and Tata clearly loved Jewish traditions and cultural values, and the historical links the holidays symbolized.

Passover in our house evolved as a grand production of cooking, silver polishing, and happy chatter; it culminated on the night when everyone I loved most sat around one glistening table and celebrated the Seder at my Aunt Malka's house.

On Saturdays and high holidays, Tata took Fredka and me on walks to feed the swans at Krasinski Park, or to Saski Ogród (Saxony Garden), where young lovers kissed under bows of acacia trees. We promenaded on the regal, tree-lined Marszałkowska and Królewska Streets. Distracted by clanging trolleys, elegant store windows, and fancy bonnets on ladies' heads, I often fell behind Tata. With my head still in the clouds, I ran to catch up and clasped the nearest hand. An unfamiliar face would look down at me, or Tata would call out, "Estusia, pay attention!" I turned and ran to my father, shrinking with embarrassment.

Absolutely no pâtisserie ever equaled the renowned Ciastka Hirszwelda, where fashionable people sat at small tables sipping tea from extra-thin glasses. Stopping there for *ciastka tortowe* (cream pastry) was the crowning treat of our outings. I have never tasted its match.

Warsaw was the grandest city in the world. A more beautiful city did not exist, except in fairy tales. And where else were children lucky enough to speak Polish? No strange-sounding language could possibly have as many words to express exactly what you mean as does Polish. I was certain of that.

This is how Warsaw and my childhood before the war remained inscribed on my memory, its loveliness more real than reality, and exponentially grander in relief against the tragedy of loss. In my selective memory, Warsaw glows in a golden radiance of lilac trees against open blue skies, air filled with fragrance, joyous play, rich sounds of good neighbors, kindness, and faith in love. Magic train rides to the country in the summer and the coziness of home were emblazoned in my memory and became shelters in my mind from a world crumbling around me. I believe that paradise was conceived by those who experienced hell on earth.

11 Skarżysko

Before the train reached its destination, it halted for a pit stop on an embankment. Mama and I insisted on staying in the car to avoid the guards outside. Fredka cried and pleaded that she had to go. Not to be separated, we all got off the train. We feared separation more than death. By the time Fredka finished, the guards blew their whistles, let out a volley of rifle shots in the air, cursed, and swore. We ran frantically to the train, stumbling into the nearest car, not the same one we left. That coincidental switching of cars saved our lives.

The train continued on its doomed way, until it came to a prolonged halt. Unable to see outside the windowless freight cars, we listened to loud exchanges of commands and the recoupling of our car. After more shouts, clangs, and jolts, we were off for a short and final ride. The doors flew open and we were chased out.

Our train arrived in Skarżysko, a slave labor camp. Tragically, the two women with whom Mama and I had traded places in Majdanek met their end there.

How many months did we stay in Majdanek? I do not remember, though the time felt endless. I do not remember the air growing warm—I was always cold. Nor do I recall any sound or sight of birds. Perhaps they flew where the picking was better. However, I remember the green fields beyond the barbed wire fences and trees growing heavy with leaves. No flowers. Maybe the wildflowers died when we dug up the turf and moved it senselessly from place to place? Or perhaps I was too sad to see them? I calculate that we stayed in that forsaken camp from April until summer—about two months.

Skarżysko had no crematoria. Jews worked there until they dropped dead, or a German soldier chose to kill them at a whim. The camp had three separate *Werks* (branches): Werk A, Werk B, and Werk C. HASAG, the long established German ammunition firm, operated all branches. Thanks to Fredka's need to hop off the train for a pit stop, we boarded the wagon that went to Werk A, where bullet shells were manufactured. Had we remained sitting in the same wagon, we would have landed at Werk C, where people worked with gunpowder. This would have been worse than immediate death. The workers on Werk C turned a ghoulish yellow-green from the gunpowder, called pitrina, and looked frightening even to us. The powder destroyed their lungs, and they died after a few months of work. Fredka had saved our lives again!

Our transfer from Majdanek to Skarżysko saved us from immediate death. Skarżysko had other advantages: men and women lived in the same camp, in separate barracks located on opposite ends of the camp, and people did not disappear as rapidly because their labor was useful to the war. However, Skarżysko had its own horrors. Here too electrified barbed-wire fences imprisoned us, and armed guards stood in towers reminding us that we were open targets. When the light of day grew dim, searchlights beamed down from the towers and followed us everywhere.

We lived in smaller barracks, sleeping on bare planks in double bunks. I slept with Mama on the upper berth because I was still afraid of the dark. Fredka slept alone below us. We still lined up with puszkas to collect a ladle of soup and a slab of coarse bread, and for Appells. Our wardrobe remained the same: a loose caftan over a bare body and wooden clogs on bare feet. And, as in Majdanek, we could not leave the barracks after dark.

Daily, like clockwork, armed guards marched us out of the camp and down a deserted road to the factory, where we worked from sunrise to sunset—or sunset till sunrise when we worked night shifts.

The floor where we worked was as large and hollow as a coliseum. It had rows of troughs filled high with bullet shells. Hundreds of pathetic people, including Mama, Fredka, and me, sat bent over the troughs, our hands whirling in perpetual motion, sorting bullet shells. A short distance from the tables stood lines of giant, thundering machines with turning turbines tended by sallow, emaciated people.

A few skilled Polish people, who lived outside the camp, served in limited supervisory positions. But the main overseers were Germans. Two of them I cannot banish from my memory. One was tall, blond, wiry, nervous looking, and vicious. His sharp-featured face, his intense eyes that peered into everyone he passed, inspired instant fear. We nicknamed him *Totenkopf* (Deathhead). When I spotted him walking the floor—always with a whip dangling at his side, I looked away, hoping to become invisible.

The other unforgettable overseer sauntered down the isles looking handsome and relaxed. Actually, he had the appearance of an amiable burgher from whom you would not feel compelled to turn your face away. He did not seem to care much if we worked frantically. He had other interests in mind; and at such moments I felt grateful for my pathetic looks.

From time to time he stopped at one row, glanced warmly at one scrawny Jewish girl who still was beautiful, then walked away. A few minutes later, the girl rose from her seat—her shoulders rounded as if trying to hide her body, head down and eyes staring at the floor—and walked down the center isle to the overseer's office at one end of the floor. She walked up a few steps, opened a door with sparkling windows, and disappeared. Every one of us pretended not to notice her rising from her seat and walking the long stretch of floor, but we did not miss a detail, nor did we ignore her sorrow. When she walked back to her seat, she seemed even smaller, and everyone tried even harder not to be seen looking her way or letting our faces betray our thoughts.

Outside the barbed-wire fence in Skarżysko stood a dark forest. I stared into it whenever I marched to and from the ammunition factory, or when I ran from our barrack to the latrine, or when I lined up for headcount at Appells. The forest and the patch of sky above me became windows to my dreams and hopes. Before I fell asleep, I imagined allied bomber planes veiling the sky and dropping bombs. I conjured up waves of flames chewing up the barracks and fences and the ruddy-faced guards, and I saw myself floating between the breath of freedom and death.

Sometimes I dreamed of leaping into the forest, running between shafts of moonlight, and escaping into freedom. As soon as I tried to figure out where I, an unwanted Jew, would find this freedom, I ran into trouble. I imagined hiding in the forest till the end of the war. But that presented a problem. I was afraid of the dark. I also knew that armed soldiers, with bright searchlights and drooling German shepherd dogs, combed the woods for runaways. I knew that beyond the forest too I would be hunted. So I shut my eyes, quivered with hopelessness, cuddled into Mama's arms for protection, and appreciated the momentary comfort. While the forest lured me ceaselessly, I remained as frightened of it as I was of waking up to each new day.

The Miracle of Finding Two Cousins

Sometimes, on our way to the latrines or to the communal washrooms located in the center of the camp, we passed men and exchanged a few words—just a customary sharing of surnames, home towns, and brief inquiries about family members who might have been seen in another place. One day, Mama struck up a brief conversation with a man who crossed her way.

"Did you say your name is Wakszlak?" the man asked. "There are two Wakszlak brothers right here, in this very camp. They are from Działoszyce."

"They must be my nephews! My husband had a brother in Działoszyce," Mama stammered in utter disbelief and rushed off as fast as her wooden clogs would allow her—although careful not to attract the attention of the guards in the towers—to share the incredible news with Fredka and me.

The discovery filled us with excitement as well as caution. "Maybe we are not related at all, in spite of our common surnames? How will we meet them? What will they think when they see us looking like this?" Fredka and I fretted.

Mama remained hopeful. "Maybe they will be able to help us with food?"

She took the first opportunity to walk to their barrack and returned triumphant. "See, I told you they must be Tata's nephews, Max and David. I saw them! They were so glad to see me."

"Are they as consumptive-looking as we?" Fredka and I wanted to know.

"Not at all; they appear well fed and well dressed," Mama said.

Later, the three of us walked to their barrack and Mama called them out to meet us. We waited only seconds for them to step out, but the seconds were heavy with fear of being seen by the guards and apprehension about how this miracle would turn out. Although I was deeply grateful to have found two living cousins, I felt nervous to meet them for the first time under such circumstances.

Two perplexed young men stepped out of the barrack and moved slowly toward us. No doubt they tried to make sense of the unusual meeting with their newly found family—three frightened, starved women in tatters. Fredka and I stood back, shyly searching their faces for a clue how to show our emotions. I immediately took note of their robust appearances. I stared at David, an angular, darkly handsome lad with soft brown eyes. I noticed Max's serious face, regular features, and round friendly eyes looking at us quizzically. Beyond that, I thought, *Do they have bread to share with us?*

But I did not ask. Later, when Fredka and I were out of an earshot, Mama asked them if they could help us with food. "We are starving," she said. They promised to help with bread and asked if she would mind washing their shirts in return. Mama jumped at the opportunity.

We saw our cousins from time to time, when Mama brought their washed shirts to them in exchange for bread. No safe place or time existed for visits.

Max and David came to Skarżysko under barbarous circumstances, but not as handicapping as ours. They had their own warm clothes to protect them from harsh Polish winters, and they managed to conceal small gold items in their clothes to trade for food. Furthermore, the two young men worked in a small engraving shop supervised by a decent German overseer. He helped them with food, talked with them, and did not ignore their humanity—a rare occurrence during the time when those who were in power became beasts.

Trading and possession of currency and valuables were strictly forbidden in Skarżysko and all concentration camps. All material things had to be surrendered to German authorities. Even a slice of bread obtained illegally was punishable by death. Still, some secret commerce existed and some prisoners lived on more than the starvation rations. Polish plant supervisors who lived in town provided the link for trading gold for bread.

Mama Confronts a Kapo

Every day after the Appell we were marched to work and back past a gate guarded by armed Germans and Ukrainians—and Jewish *kapos* (policemen) with clubs—and onto a road surrounded by desolate fields. As in Majdanek, the distant, dark forest marked the end of my world. Flanked by armed Ukrainian guards, we silently walked in line, keeping our eyes to the ground to avoid hateful faces of guards and the sight of a gun barrel. We moved slowly and laboriously, in spite of being prodded. Our features remained as motionless as clay. The wooden clogs felt heavy on our feet as we dragged them over the dust- or ice-covered road. Our shuffles resounded like funereal drumbeats.

On our march back from work one day, a kapo at the gate pounced on an emaciated man and proceeded to kick and pummel him. Without a thought of the consequences, Mama, who looked like a walking skeleton herself, jumped out of the line and yelled out sharply, "Stop! Shame! This is your fellow victim! You will be haunted even in your grave for this brutality!"

I thought, *This is the end of her, and us.* But the kapo immediately stopped. The German guards remained silent while their dogs tore at their leashes. The march continued without a further incident.

Hiding from Shears

To wash our lice-ridden hair, we had to risk our lives by sneaking away from our factory worktable; we would steal suds from mammoth bullet-washing machines, run into the factory lavatory, quickly take turns washing our hair over the toilet, and return to our workplace before being noticed. This was a dangerous undertaking, but Fredka and I had it all worked out with precision.

First Fredka would leave her seat and go directly to the lavatory. I followed with my puszka, sneaking close to the huge, booming bullet-washing machines with vats of steaming suds. When no one appeared to be looking, I quickly dipped my puszka into a vat, filled it with boiling suds, and continued to walk, on trembling legs, to meet Fredka and take turns to wash our hair. I was first. Fredka, in a panic about being caught with the contraband, forgot to add cold water, and dumped the scorching liquid on my scalp.

Within days my scalded scalp became infected and covered with lice-infested mange. I could barely endure the itch and pain, but that was not the worst of it. The Jewish camp head-nurse found out about my condition and marched down to our barrack to look for me—to shave my hair, I assumed. With my hair gone, I would look younger and uglier, and my life would be in greater danger. I was not ready to die. So when I saw her coming, I hid behind the barrack.

After a talk with Mama, the nurse left. I did not doubt that Mama touched a sympathetic chord in the nurse's heart. However, I took no chances. For days, after long night-shift hours, I hid behind our barrack to keep watch for the nurse. When I spotted her moving toward our door, I bolted, hid behind the farthest barrack, and waited for her to leave.

Eventually, word of the hunt spread through the camp. Moved by my struggle, a few women appealed to the nurse and extracted from her a promise not to shave my hair, but to cure my scalp. Too frightened to trust, I ignored her reassurances and desperately kept up my vigil to dodge her. When I finally gave in, she kept her promise. My poor sister endured my plight with the pleading eyes of a penitent praying for forgiveness, though the accident was as much my fault as hers. Eventually my scalp healed, but the lice stayed.

The Rabbi's Daughter

The rabbi's daughter, a skinny young woman with dusky-blond curls and sad eyes, occupied the bunk next to us. She rose quietly before each dawn, hunched her slender shoulders above her thin torso as if to hide a secret inside her body, and went on her way. Mama tried to engage her in a conversation, but the rabbi's daughter looked away—like a forlorn, trapped little creature with a thousand-mile-stare into the distance.

People in our barrack, all as totally alone as the rabbi's daughter, could not understand the cause of her extreme timidity, but everyone felt that she was a little more special because she was the daughter of a well-respected rabbi. I rarely took notice of her; I was too busy trying to stay alive. Until one day I heard people say, "The rabbi's daughter was with child. She delivered her own baby squatting above a hole in the latrine. The baby drowned in the muck."

The image of the new life drowning in the fathomless pool of excrement left another crack in the innermost part of me.

The rabbi's daughter grew even more pensive and evasive. The rest of us receded a little further into our own sorrows and struggles to survive the next moment.

Typhus

Only two latrines located at a considerable distance from the barracks existed in the entire camp, one for women and one for men. They were platform-like constructions with rows of holes over which one had to squat. Below was a trench. I dreaded running to the latrine at night. In addition to the fearsome guards, rats, thousands of them, came out in the dark to scour the ground. Clusters of squeaking little pink newborn rats squirmed in corners. The darting rodents, the armed guards, the yellow searchlights, the barbed-wire fences, and the pitch-black forest looming behind them were nightmares come true.

To avoid the frightful trips to and from the latrine, we all peed into puszkas, then we opened the door gingerly, looked around the corners, and tossed out the urine with lightning speed to avoid being caught. Once, Mr. Aronowicz, a block kapo, suddenly stepped out of the dark and caught me at the crime. He screamed, raised his whip, and ran toward me. Mortified, I slammed the door behind me and dashed back to our bunk. He followed and stood over me, lashing me furiously with his whip.

In a flash, Mama, flinging herself between his whip and me, screamed, "Stop! I will never forgive you this! My blood will spurt from my grave and haunt you forever for what you are doing to my child!" Mama was very dramatic.

He stopped, bowed his head, and defended himself. "When you pour this filth out on the ground, I have to pay for it. I get whipped mercilessly."

That was true. *Battenschlager* (a Polish/Yiddish nickname meaning whip striker), the German camp commander, punished the kapos for the filth the Nazis made us live in.

That monster assigned the block kapos to catch nightly quotas of rats. If the kapos fell short of the commander's expectations, he increased their quotas, as well as their punishments. Ironically, that beating and, above all, Mama's outcry saved my sister's life.

One day Fredka could not rise from the bunk to report for the morning Appell and for work. We tried to prop her up and to coax her, but to no avail. She looked frightful. Red blotches covered her emaciated body, her eyes shone with fever. There was nothing Mama and I could do but leave without her. We pleaded with her to remember to pull a blanket over her head to avoid being seen, and to stay still till we came back.

That evening, when Mama and I came back from the factory, our hearts sank. We could not find Fredka. Mama tore through the barrack like a fury. I followed. We ran to the camp infirmary, stopped in front of each window and called endearingly, "Fredziuchna! Fredziuchna!"

We moved from window to window, calling her name until Fredka's terror-stricken face appeared behind a grimy windowpane. Her lips formed the words, "Mama, Mama. Help me!"

Mama called to her that she must have heart and fight to stay alive. "We will come back to you every day. You know that. I love you! We cannot go on without you." I rushed off not to miss our bread and soup rations. I left Mama hiding in the shadows, pushing herself up on her tiptoes and stretching her scrawny neck to get closer to Fredka, and pleading lovingly. "You must be strong. Don't forget to come to the window to look for us tomorrow. I will be here every evening. You must not give up."

Soon, the dark, the curfew, and the threat of death to both Fredka and herself drove Mama away, and Fredka was left feeling abandoned.

Commander Battenschlager often stalked the camp in slow, deliberate strides—his neck turning to all sides like a searchlight, a whip swinging in one hand, the other hand thrust behind his hunched back, a shiny revolver dangling from his hip, and a German shepherd at his side. When we saw him, we saw death. For sport, he would collect the sick from the infirmary, take them to the forest behind the barbed-wire fence, and shoot them.

The thought that Fredka might be killed while we were separated from her terrified Mama and me. Mama could not rest. Fredka's name never left her lips.

As soon as we returned from work, Mama dashed off to rap on the infirmary door and to plead with the kapo nurse to give Fredka the coarse slab of bread she brought—Mama's ration. I do not know if Fredka was able to eat it. I am not sure whether the kapo ever gave it to her, or just ate it himself. After Mama left her ration of bread with the kapo, she moved on to search the windows for Fredka's ghostly face and to call to her love and encouragement. Mama grew more gaunt. Her face turned into a mask of hunger, pain, and suffering.

Just when things looked darkest, Mr. Aronowicz came to our rescue. To expiate his guilt for flogging me, he told Fredka to hide in the latrines whenever Battenschlager showed up at the camp. Burning with fever and fright, she followed his instructions. When Battenshlager left, Mr. Aronowicz let Fredka know that it was safe for her to return to the infirmary.

Thus, my sister's life was saved.

Small marvels sometimes happened even in concentration camps. One late evening after work, on the way to the infirmary, Mama noticed a bright sparkle on the dusty ground. She bent down and picked up a tiny crystal. She examined it in disbelief. It was a small diamond with beautiful facets. Filled with gratitude and hope, she rushed to Max and David to ask them to trade it for something nutritious for Fredka. "She needs nourishment to give her strength, and maybe something delicious, if possible. A treat to make her feel good," she said wistfully. My cousins managed to trade the diamond for a little bit of butter, a piece of white bread, and a tomato—something that we had never seen in the camps. Mama carried it to Fredka like manna from heaven.

Miraculously, Fredka survived her illness, the infirmary, and Battenschlager's raids. She came back to us looking less like a human being and more like a pitiful, starved, hairless bird with pinched cheeks, bony forehead, two sharp bumps under mournful eyes, and spindly long legs. When I saw people cringe looking at my sister, I felt like crying out, "This is not Fredka. This is a mirage. Fredka has a beautiful heart-shaped face, a flawless, translucent complexion like alabaster, lustrous sand-colored hair, and eyes clear and blue as the sky. This is only a mask of suffering you see."

But I said nothing. I let Mama boast, "*Moje dzieci* [my children] were so beautiful to look at. Fredka was doll-like. What have they done to us?!"

Worried about Fredka's deep sadness, Mama gently coaxed her to talk about her tortures. "*Shvelbelle*" (little lamb), she murmured into Fredka's ear. "It was so terrible for you. Shush. Shush," as she caressed Fredka's shaved scalp.

"You will never know, Mama. No one will. No one can imagine," Fredka moaned. "The sick looked like mad ghosts with festering wounds, scabies, and mange. They wandered around, hallucinating, landing on top of me. I was so petrified of them. They talked gibberish, flailed and tore at me. I could not get them off me. I had no strength left. I wanted to die, Mama. I want to be dead."

Fredka bewailed the sick that rolled off their bunks landing on top of each other, the stench of corpses rotting on the floor, the foul odors of excrement in barrels standing in corners.

Mama listened and whispered, "Shvelbelle, how awful it was for you and how awful for me that I was not able to be at your side." But Mama never failed to remind Fredka how lucky she was that she survived the unbearable suffering and how lucky we three were that we had each other.

We clung together more than ever. The suffering of the other seemed harder to endure than our own. We lied to spare each other. "Oh, I'm not so cold, not so hungry; I can take it." In the few quiet moments before we stretched out on our bunks for a brief night's rest, we tucked our heads into each other's lap to find comfort. Lovingly, we caressed Fredka's prickly skull, and combed our fingers through the other's hair to pick lice and nits—to relieve the tormenting itch. Our barrack comrades affectionately nicknamed us, "the three monkeys." No wonder: hunger and suffering transformed us into three barely human-looking creatures holding on to one another for love and security—like monkeys. Love sustained us.

12 Częstochowa

The seasons rolled from summer to winter, but I never noticed the leaves changing colors. At predawn and at night, when we marched to and from work, the distant trees loomed dark, like phantoms. I never felt the warm touch of the sun.

Winter was most unbearable. Our feet felt like icicles, our wooden clogs skidded on the slick ice and it was hard to march. Wind knifed through our thin caftans and chapped our bare arms and legs raw. The cracks in our skin got infected by filth and lice. I had large patches of oozing, festering scabs on my limbs and cheeks. My frost-bitten toes turned into swollen, red little pillows and itched unbearably when they thawed. I was hungry and cold beyond description.

Late in the summer of 1944, the guards marched a group of us from the camp to a train depot and ordered us to climb onto waiting freight trains. They shouted, shoved, and bolted the doors with iron bars. We sank down to the floor, and we were off.

Where to? No one dared to guess. The train chugged, the floors banged against our sore rumps as it rattled over the uneven ground, until we arrived at another concentration camp in Częstochowa.

The camp in Częstochowa was virtually indistinguishable from Skarżysko in every respect. It was run by the same German ammunition company, HASAG.

As before, electrified barbed wire fences cut us off from the rest of the world, and we lived in stark communal barracks. We continued to freeze and be pestered by lice, and I continued to be so hungry that I ate my breath.

Max and David continued to work in a small engraving shop. They still gave us much appreciated slabs of bread, and Mama washed their shirts secretly under the cold water faucet in our communal washroom.

Every day at the crack of dawn, we were marched like lines of insects past a heavily guarded gate and across a desolate field to enter a windowless ammunition factory to sort bullet shells. Even in this netherworld of walking corpses, Fredka and I contrived games right behind the backs of German guards. While our hands darted into barrels to scoop up fistfuls of copper, finger-length bullet shells to discard the ones with imperfect points, Fredka and I whispered to each other a rhythmic refrain: "*Para, nie para, nic*" (A pair, not a pair, nothing). The object was to guess the matching bullet-shell-point combinations in each other's fist. Mama kept an extra eye out to warn us when a guard looked our way.

Miraculously, we remained children and persisted in our world of imagination even when death breathed down our shoulders. Sometimes Mama's rare ripple of laughter erupted and stunned her. "I must be going mad. How can I find humor in the grave we are in?" she reproached herself. I guess the sound of one's own laughter is nearly as essential for survival as a sip of water.

After sunset, we shuffled back to assemble at the Appell to be counted and insulted. Then we queued up to collect a ladle of thin porridge and a too-small slice of coarse bread. When this ordeal ended, we returned to our barracks and clambered onto our bare banks to sink into frightful darkness and fitful sleep.

Mama's indomitable faith that the Allies would triumph in the end and right all wrong kept us going. Eventually, she even found a glimmer of conscience in a most unlikely source—a German section guard at the factory. The first time the guard stopped at our station to rush us with our work, Mama looked up at her and said, "They are only children, and they are very tired and hungry." Surprisingly, the guard remained standing, asking questions and listening with civility—all the while gathering clusters of bullet shells into her hands and helping Mama get her work done.

The overseer returned daily for short visits with Mama. My mother told her about our sunny life before the war and the degradations imposed upon us, and upon the entire world. The woman listened politely and revealed to Mama a hint of contrition. "I am a soldier doing my duty for my fatherland. German soldiers are following orders. We have no choice."

"You must be out of your mind to speak so boldly to a German guard! You are crazy," Fredka and I pleaded with Mama.

But Mama turned a calm face to us—eyes wide open and brimming with confidence—"Don't be so scared, I can tell that she is not out to hurt us. Besides, I think that I pick up a hint of fear in her conversation. Mark my words; she is afraid of defeat and revenge. She is afraid that victors will treat them with the same savagery they inflict on their neighbors." Of course, Fredka and I did not put much stock in Mama's "wild" postulations, but her daring gave us courage to dream of the impossible.

Then another unbearable winter came, 1945. Memories of normal life slipped further into the distance. Still Mama kept up her propaganda. "You are good and as innocent as angels. They are shaming mankind. Wait until the world finds out about the camps."

But time brought only dead silence. No one heard our calls for help. No one came to our aid. Not a blip or a single word of hope penetrated our seclusion. Were the Allies slaying the Germans, or the other way around? We had no idea. We starved and shivered with cold, hopelessness, and despair. We remained condemned to relive eternal darkness every passing second. The pain and humiliations multiplied by each setting sun and recurring season. But Mama continued to promise, "If we survive, we will be soothed for our innocence and our suffering. The world has a conscience," my romantic—or perhaps mad—mother insisted.

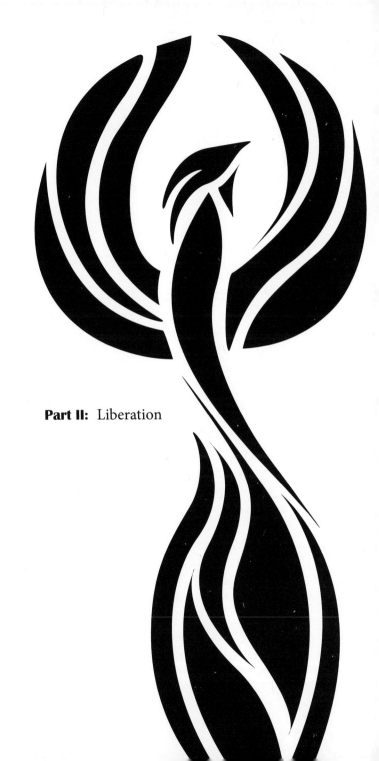

Part II: Liberation

13 *A Miracle*

On a mid-January night in 1945, an earsplitting rumble of bomber planes broke the long silence and made the darkness tremble. We lifted our heads from our bunk planks and whispered, "Could it be?" In a few seconds, flares, brighter than a summer's day, lit up the sky. Violent explosions shook the earth relentlessly. Mesmerized and in total disbelief we murmured, "Allies? After all these years?"

When the bombardment would momentarily pause, the silence—morbid as death—filled us with dread. "Don't leave. Please, please don't leave. I will not mind dying," we prayed in chorus. It may sound strange, but in the death camps, the prospect of being blown up by Allied bombs was the only happiness we could hope for. Such a death would be merciful. Such a death would be our victory over Nazi gas chambers.

The detonations continued for hours and we began to imagine the unimaginable. As if in a dream, we peered around the doors. No guards were in sight. We shuffled out of the barracks, one at a time. We crouched forward and muttered, "Be careful. The Germans might be hiding in corners. Who knows where the demons are?"

Mama, Fredka, and I stole across the camp to Max and David's barrack to seek protection and guidance. We located seats in a corner and hoped that if we sat quietly and proved not to be any trouble to them, my cousins would let us leave with them if the improbable happened and we were liberated. We knew they would see us as burdens on the snow-covered roads with people unfriendly to Jews. Unlike the three of us, my cousins remained in fair physical shape and had warm clothes, leather shoes, and some money. Mama, Fredka, and I were walking skeletons without proper footwear. We had no place to return to, no home. Warsaw was no more.

We sat silent and spellbound, teetering between fear of annihilation and euphoric hope of liberation, and listened as aerial bombardments gave way to ground artillery thudding from a distance, then ever closer toward the camp. We wondered, "Is it possible the Russian troops are near our gate?" The young men discussed at what point they should risk sending scouts to check the gate and possibly beyond.

"Who should go?" they asked. Everyone volunteered.

Careful not to act in haste, they questioned, "What if the Germans come back and punish us for going past the gate? Could this be a ruse, a trap the Germans are setting up for us?" It was impossible to grasp what was happening.

As the air raids let up, and the barrage of artillery drew closer, the men grew bolder. They sent scouts as far as the gate. They returned swiftly and reported, "The gate is open. There are no guards at the gate!"

The scouts continued to explore past the gate into the no-man's-land encircling the camp. All proved positive. The German guards were gone.

When the first tinges of gray dawn began to lift, the scouts reported that people were leaving the camp. With lightning speed, the men in my cousins' barrack organized themselves into groups based on their areas of origin. Max and David told us they were leaving without us. They were heading for Działoszyce, their hometown, to see if they could recover anything of their past lives. "Follow us there," they said. "We will wait for you." They bid us good-bye, and suddenly, in a flash, they were gone.

We were stunned. What to do? Where to go?

We left the barracks and joined the milling crowd of starved, agitated people who were as confused and scared as we. We had nothing to take with us. We had only to summon our strength, push one foot in front of the other into an unfamiliar landscape outside the gate, and hope to find salvation down the road. "We must run! The Germans may return," we urged each other forward. Our legs and breath disobeyed.

Like three apparitions, we followed the fleeing crowd of people who looked like their own marching shadows. We passed through the gate. Outside we saw no signs of habitation. My breath was shallow with suspense. My mind cautiously scanned, absorbed, and hoped. Not a bud of life sang out. Before us was only a desolate snow-covered field.

Mama, a small skeletal figure, shuffled forward, pushing against the icy wind. Her shoulders hunched over, bracing against the cold. Passion for life burned in her intense blue eyes. She searched the horizon for food, cover, and a road to safety.

Adding to Mama's otherworldly appearance was her outlandish hair color. It was tinted navy blue. During our last days in the concentration camp, we felt a panic because Mama's hair had began to turn gray, and older people counted among the first for extermination. We found someone willing to barter a small envelope of fabric dye in exchange for our ration of bread. In the only dish allowed us, the puszka, we collected small puffs of steam from a narrow valve that protruded from the kitchen barrack. We managed to collect enough steam to dissolve the dye, and frantically rubbed it into Mama's hair. The result threw us into a slight terror. In desperation, we looked at each other wondering, what have we done? We tried hard to convince ourselves that navy blue hair was probably safer than gray.

Fredka, my beautiful sister, looked the most frightful of us. Her once softly rounded face was now hollowed by angles and craters; her bright blue eyes were dimmed with pain and fright. Her thick hair that once bounced with waves and hay-colored tendrils had been shaved. To hide her humiliation, she found a rag and wrapped it into a turban to cover the stubble growing out of her scalp. The turban ballooned over her skeleton frame and made her look like a strange bird. Her long caftan swayed from her body like a sack on a stick and trapped the icy wind against her bare skin.

Fredka had always been the most despairing of the three of us. In the concentration camps, she had pleaded repeatedly for us to surrender to the gas chamber and be spared the humiliations. Her anguish inspired Mama and me to struggle and persist even harder.

I am less able to describe what I looked like at fifteen on the dawn of liberation, since we had no mirrors, but I could not have been different from the others. I imagine that my eyes, encircled by moon-shaped shadows, stared out of my emaciated face with the same pain and despair as the eyes of the other survivors. I recall wrapping my arms round my body to sooth the gnawing pain of hunger, cold, fear, longing, and confusion. My bare feet burned with cold inside oversized shoes. Unlike Mama and Fredka, I had real shoes, not wooden clogs. I got them with the help of my two cousins just before liberation.

After walking for what seemed like hours, we heard military vehicles, rowdy voices of soldiers, and hoots of laughter in the woods beyond a hill. It was hard to imagine people with such light hearts. We hesitated a moment, listening. "Russian soldiers!" we cried out with relief. We caught our breath and rushed toward our liberators—our eyes misty with gratitude. They were our sole hope of rescue from the cold and hunger, and a promise of safety. Startled, the soldiers looked at us and backed away.

Confounded and in total disbelief, we explained who we were, how long we had been praying for their arrival, and how desperately we needed food and shelter. They turned their heads and waved us away. "We have a war to fight. We cannot help you." They warned, "It is against the law to be in the street after dark. You must move on and find shelter before curfew." To send us off quickly, they gave us a few slabs of bread.

We felt as if God himself had withdrawn his hand and slammed shut the gate to paradise! Swallowing our humiliation, grief, and fear, along with the bread, we walked on searching for relief from our misery. Lured by memories of life as it was before the war, we walked along the road hoping to find food, shelter, and contact with an accepting community in the center of Częstochowa.

The city overwhelmed us with unfamiliar streets and whirling traffic. Strangers passed us avoiding our glances. From our appearance they knew, *Jews from the concentration camp*. I would like to think some felt compassion. But nobody met our eyes or stopped to offer help.

I envied the sure and purposeful stride of the warmly dressed pedestrians. "They are on their way home as we once were," I thought. I wanted to follow their steps. But I had nowhere to go. I was lost. All I knew for sure: I was alive, hungry beyond words, numb with cold, and I had my mother and sister to hold on to. I wanted to live, and I believed that we were deserving. Mostly, I only thought of surviving the night.

We were frantic to find food and shelter before curfew. At times, the three of us joined small clusters of other survivors; at times we roamed alone. The only assistance we received was from fellow survivors who told us where to find an abandoned pickle factory. We climbed through a shattered window and ate dill pickles on the first full day of freedom.

As night drew close, a couple of our people gave us directions to an abandoned school. We walked through half-deserted streets, picking our way across slick patches of ice and mounds of snow until we found the school. Gingerly, we opened the door and stepped into an empty lobby. Frightened faces of survivors looked down at us from a wide staircase in the center of the floor. We sighed with relief—our people.

They welcomed us immediately and soothed us with kindness. "You can stay here. You'll be safe. Find a place on the floor in one of the classrooms upstairs."

There was no heat, no lights. Most people had bedded down on bare floors for the night. Mama spotted a vacant paper closet and immediately rushed to it. "Who knows how long we might have to stay here? This closet is perfect," she declared.

And she was right. At night, she slept curled up on the bottom of the closet. Fredka and I slept next to her on a shelf we removed from the closet and propped up on two chairs we managed to find. We lay folded into each other in the most compact way, not to fall off, with heads resting on opposite ends and cupped in our hands. Evenings, we sat on the bottom shelf and found comfort talking with our new friends. The sides of the closet held us like the walls of a home, almost. This was the coziest we had been in a long time.

On our first night of liberation, we and our new friends whispered our stories of the day we thought would never come. We asked with concern, "Where are you from? Where are you going? How will you get there? Do you think that the Germans might come back? Did you find food?" Then, when everyone was quiet, we were left with our own thoughts.

We stayed in the abandoned school for six days for fear of not finding another shelter. During the day we looked for food and help. Sometimes Russian soldiers took pity on us and gave us bread. On one occasion, we dug potatoes out of an ice-crusted field. We ate them raw; we had no way to cook them. One day, some acquaintances in our shelter shared a herring with us, although now I'm not sure if it was a wishful dream or if it truly happened.

Evenings, we returned to the school and our new friends. Everyone felt pressed to run from the German troops at the front line, to return to their hometowns to look for surviving family and old friends. We had no clue where to turn.

One night, roars of a drunken Russian soldier woke us up. A frozen water pipe had burst outside the school and the water gushing into the street attracted the soldier, who happened to be strolling by. With a raised machine gun, he rounded up a few helpless men on the first floor and ordered them to close the hole in the pipe, "Or I will shoot you!" The men asked, "How can we do it? We are concentration camp survivors spending the night here. There is nothing here in this abandoned school to repair the broken pipe."

The intoxicated soldier insisted, "Find straw, and stuff the hole! Follow me!" And we heard the pounding of the soldier's boots mounting the stairs. Before long, the soldier was upon us. He lit a match, stared into our closet, and asked, "*Zenshtshyna tshy mushtshyna?*" (Man or woman?).

Mama signaled us, with a touch of her fingers, to stay down and not stir. She responded in Russian, "*Starushka i malutshkeh rabiati*" (An old woman and little children). He left us alone and moved on to round up more men.

When the soldier pulled the trigger of his machine gun and shot into the air, everyone let out a loud, pent-up scream, simultaneously thinking he or she was hit by the bullet.

The collective sound of our cry shook the walls and so startled the soldier that it sent him running into the street and away forever.

The next morning Mama declared with absolute resolve, "We must leave Częstochowa and move on."

Fredka and I asked, "Where, Mama? Where can we go?"

Mama had a plan. "We will go to Kielce and look for Tata's distant cousin who lived there before the war. A man in the Skarżysko camp told me he saw him in another camp. There is a chance he is alive and returned to his hometown. You never know."

"Do you know him?" Fredka and I asked.

"No, but he is family."

"He is probably dead. It's useless," we insisted.

Mama patiently reasoned, "Kielce is only one hundred kilometers from here, and it is on the way to Działoszyce where Max and David went. If we do not find Tata's cousin in Kielce, at least we will be closer to look for Max and David." Of course, we could not be sure if the two ever made it to Działoszyce, or if they would be glad to see us.

"This is the only chance left," Mama insisted. "We must try." The next morning we were on our way to Kielce.

14 The Old Woman in Kielce

We set out into a cold unknown, marched to the train station, and climbed onto a freight train. It took us a whole day to reach Kielce, one hundred kilometers away.

We arrived at the Kielce train station, a huge, dimly lit hollow packed with passengers streaming in and out of the building. The three of us remained standing, isolated, not recognizing anything or anyone, and not being recognized. Welcomes and happy greetings rang out like echoes from the past. I remembered when trains took us to green country villas where smiling aunts and uncles waited for us. There were no greetings for us now. People glanced at us and quickly looked away. Columns of gray dusk seeped through tall windows. An alarm went off in my head. "Curfew is almost here. We must find shelter. But where?" A hum droned in my ears as if I were drowning. Only a miracle could save us now.

Suddenly, we heard a barely audible chant-like call, a whisper as if rising from way down, almost where our feet touched the ground. "*Uhmhoo? Uhmhoo?*"

The word *Uhmhoo* stems from a Hebrew word meaning "of the clan, or of the people." It was adopted in Yiddish and used as a greeting, as well as a code word to find another Jew among hostile people.

"*Uhmhoo*," we murmured with relief, careful not to call hostile attention to ourselves. We banded together with four other survivors and slowly walked out of the train station. We moved forward without a destination, guided only by the drive to live. We meandered through narrow cobblestone streets with humble little stucco houses, with small doors and roofs leaning close to the sidewalks. I remember peering enviously through lacy curtains on windows lined evenly at my eye level, and noticing shadows of figures flitting back and forth in the glow of home. I was gripped by a yearning so fierce that I almost forgot that I stood on the outside on this descending winter night, feeling pressed to outpace the nearing curfew.

As darkness gathered, lights glowed in windows, luring us on and filling us with longing and fear. I am not sure what terrified us more, the freezing night or breaking the curfew. We dreaded authorities—their guns, their indifference, and their power. To be caught breaking the curfew was unthinkable.

A group of young hooligans noticed us and began following us with their dogs. They taunted us, chanted anti-Semitic slurs, hurled stones at us, and laughed uproariously. They set their dogs on us, thrilled by the sight of our flinching and retreating in fear. The gang tormented us with the total approval of adults who either looked on indifferently or were amused by the spectacle. Trapped and defenseless, we stared into the dark streets for a place to hide. Nothing. I looked up at the darkening heaven in utter bewilderment and wondered how the stars and moon could still hang in the immense sky when our people were so desperately abandoned.

Then, a few houses down the street, a door opened. A stooped old woman stepped out, a silhouette in darker black than the black of night. She looked in our direction, saw our situation, and rushed to position herself between us and the volley of stones. Shaking her fists at our tormentors, she screamed, "Stop! What are you doing? Stop this cruelty right now!" She advanced at them with the bold courage of uncompromising values. Scornfully lecturing them, she cast such shame on them that the hoodlums disbanded, while threatening they would return to teach her a lesson.

I looked with disbelief at this apparition who took on the band of bullies, while others younger and far more able stood by. She turned her face to us—pale in the white moonlight, a toothless crescent smile and friendly upturned wrinkles. Her eyes held me with kindness, held us all in a spell of gratitude and relief. She ushered us into her home and spoke in the voice of a loving aunt, "How cold you must be! Come in, quick. You must warm up." She shut the door behind us and continued talking to us, "Oh, Jesus Kristus!

Look at your clothes! I must find wood to add to the fire. I must give you something warm to eat."

Her home was one dimly lit room furnished with the most basic essentials: a table with a couple of chairs in the center, a bed leaning against a side wall, and a large clay stove at the far end.

The old woman pointed us toward the stove. We reached out for the faintly radiating warmth. A sizzling kettle stood on top. In the corner, a black cat that was curled up in a ball lifted an arched back and hissed at us. I felt strangely secure for the moment under the wings of this old woman. She scrambled for wood kindling, apologizing for her poverty and inability to feed us properly. All she had to share was a thin gruel.

When the fire was out, she made beds for all seven of us by placing blankets on top of the stove and on the floor near it, to let us feel the warmth trapped in the clay. There was something familiar about this old woman. She was the goodness and kindness that I had known once and still hoped to find.

She talked with us into the night, wanting to know us. She chatted about her daughter, who would come home soon. She cautioned us to pay no attention if her daughter grumbled about our presence. "She is a good person, but worries too much. She'll complain a bit, but will get over it fast."

The daughter came, a handsome young woman. We overheard her whispered admonishments, "You cannot afford this. You are putting yourself at great risk with our neighbors."

Then she settled down to listen and join the conversation. Gradually, I slept safely in the house whose door shut out the hostile night.

When the first lights of day returned, we went back to the wintry street to continue our wandering. But Mama's persistent reassurances, "The world has a conscience," were validated. I left feeling grateful and desperately puzzled. If the old woman could do it, then why didn't others?

My question recalled a Jewish legend that Tata had told me: the fate of the world rests, at any given time, in the hands of thirty-six righteous people, the Lamed Vav Zaddikim. They perform Tikkun Olam, the healing of the world. They do not know they are among the thirty-six, and neither does anyone else. They just go about their everyday lives, doing what is right and good. They go unnoticed because of their humble nature and commonplace vocations. When I was a child, Tata told me that they will always be among us. I believed him. I am a grandmother now and still believe.

I am sure that the humble old woman in Kielce was one of the Zaddikim. Mirrored in her humanity, I now see the beacons of my other heroes who kept my soul from dying. I see my father whose kindness and courage remain immortal. I see Dr. Janush Korczak who joined the starving orphans to be delivered to the ovens of Treblinka. I see Raul Wallenberg, Oscar Schindler, individual resistance fighters, and all of the ordinary people who paid the supreme price to live by their values.

The Lamed Vav Zaddikim may be only legend, but what if they are not? What if our fate depends on there being enough righteous people?

15 The Two Russian Soldiers

We stepped off the threshold of the old woman's house, inched forward, looked into unfamiliar streets. "Which way do we go?" The sun hung high in a clear sky and a sparkling coat of snow covered the streets. Mama stood between Fredka and me. She reached out to clasp our hands and squeezed them tightly to her body. Looking straight ahead, she declared, "We've come out alive, what a miracle! This wandering too will end. If we find Tata's cousin today, we will no longer be so alone. If not, we will have to look elsewhere for help. We cannot give up now. We have survived."

We walked toward the center of the city, the most likely place to find help. To give us hope, Mama chattered, "We have family in America, you know. I am sure they are worried about us. All we have to do is find them."

She listed aunts, uncles, and grown-up cousins as she shuffled through the snow and shivered with cold. "My brother Abe and my sisters Riva and Sonia went there after World War I. That is what we should have done, gone to America. But who knew? Who could have imagined that a whole nation would go mad and murder innocent people and children?"

Fredka and I reminded Mama that she had been separated from her siblings ages ago.

Who knew if they were alive still? But she continued, unperturbed, "You know, I was the youngest of seven children, all much older than I. They adored and babied me. My sisters tied beautiful ribbons in my hair. They will be happy to know we are alive."

She talked into the void. Fredka and I paid only peripheral attention. We were too concerned about survival and what we might have to face the next moment. Still, in spite of not putting much faith in Mama's prattle about family in America who were completely out of reach, I felt emboldened. America! The word rang with promise. I imagined a sunny country where everyone ate. Of course, we had no addresses of our relatives. "I know their names. We'll find them," Mama reassured us.

The old city of Kielce, located in southeastern Poland in the Holy Cross Mountains, was a rail junction and market center for agricultural and mineral resources from the surrounding area. Before the war, Kielce had a vibrant Jewish community with streets abuzz with commerce, theaters, libraries, schools, and, I imagine, happy voices. But in the winter of 1945, Kielce was grim and gray even when the sun shone. The Jewish community had been erased.

Unable to find help, we wandered the streets without direction. We looked enviously at people who had money to stand in long queues in front of stores. We inhaled aromas of fresh bread wafting in the air and swallowed droplets of saliva at the thought of eating. We gaped at chimneys puffing smoke and hallucinated about being in cozy rooms with crackling fires and pots of food bubbling on stovetops. Lights in windows filled my head with dreams of home—a reality as remote at that moment as a fairy tale. Horse-drawn carts, a few automobiles, lines of army trucks, and tanks with Russian soldiers rolled down the streets. All headed toward a destination.

We roamed the streets for endless hours, never getting close to finding our cousin. When twilight began to creep up, we gave up our search and turned full attention to securing a shelter for the night—a task that filled us with despair. Just before night was upon us and we had reached the limit of hope, we stumbled upon a survivor who directed us to a room occupied by a kind Russian soldier.

The Russian soldier's room was located in an imposing building occupied by the Red Army's support corps, in the center of Kielce. The soldier, a tailor, did not live in the room. He came in every morning, sat down at his sewing machine to do his work, and left at the end of the day. He was a quiet, kind man, and shared the room with homeless survivors who wandered in from the street, including us.

The tailor's sewing room was grand and virtually empty of furniture. It had a high ceiling framed by elaborate moldings, an elegant parquet floor, and three French windows that beamed light in. The single sewing machine in front of the center window and a couple of chairs in the middle of the floor looked lost in the majestic space. Most of the parquet floor was occupied by squatting survivors, who drifted in, rested a few days, then moved on in hope of finding a home. No one stayed there as long as the three of us did. During the day, if we did not step out to look for food and a way out of our isolation, we rested on the floor and talked about our experiences with the people who shared our fate. We chatted to forget our loneliness, to be reminded that life can be beautiful and decent because it once was.

The burly Russian tailor sat at the sewing machine near the window, mending uniforms and listening intently to our conversations. He looked up from time to time, but rarely said anything. Dark unruly curls dangled to his forehead as he bent over his work and guided a piece of uniform under the needle. As he listened, his machine picked up speed, and he leaned closer into his work as if he expected to sew up his feelings or stitch himself an answer.

At night, we divided the floor into a checkerboard of rectangular sleeping spaces, spread out rags (for those lucky to have found any), and slept pillowing our heads on our hands. We scrupulously respected the invisible lines that separated neighbor from neighbor.

People who die don't just disappear. They turn up at odd moments and fill empty corners. The Russian tailor's room brought back memories of my favorite aunt, Aunt Hannah, Mama's older sister and Lolek's mother. Her apartment in Warsaw was just as airy and bright. Sunlight streamed in through tall windows, turning tawny shades of parquet floors into gold. My aunt often returned in my daydreams, humming her favorite waltz from the *Tales of Hoffmann*. She danced in her light-footed way with outstretched arms to embrace me; her tall and slim figure swaying, silky auburn hair bobbing, eyes smiling softly. Just as I imagined reaching out to her, the picture changed. I saw her face, no longer smiling, framed in a window of a dashing freight train, and she was gone. I remained sitting on the bare floor, feeling deep longing and gratitude that I was once touched by my Aunt Hannah's grace.

The Officer

A Russian officer often came to visit with our host. We discovered that both soldiers were Jewish and had teamed together to make it possible for survivors to stay in the room. The officer too was middle-aged, as judged by my young eyes, but much different from the tailor, both in demeanor and appearance. He was tall and slender, and looked distinguished in his Russian fur hat and officer's coat tightly fitted at the waist and fastened with a wide leather belt. His softly furrowed, lean face looked serene and reflective. His pale blue eyes met ours directly and touched us with kindness. He often pulled up a chair to join the circle of survivors, asked questions, listened with interest, and cheerfully responded to our inquiries about life in Russia.

He spent more and more time in our corner, getting to know the three of us and holding long philosophical discussions with Mama. Mother, a sharp, opinionated observer, enjoyed the conversations. We looked forward to his visits. We did not know it then, but an idea had begun to form in his mind.

It is hard to remember how long we stayed in the room of the two kind soldiers. We had no clock and no calendar. Our hopes rose with the sun, and dimmed as it touched the earth. We looked out the French windows and said hopefully, "I think the days are getting longer. When spring comes, it will be easier to find food and get around." And Mama promised, "Oh, yes! We will get away from this murderous Europe, from hate, cold, and hunger, to a sunny country where no one starves." But the thought, "What if it doesn't get better?" never left any of us. Of course, Mama would never allow it to be said.

Gradually, we began to look more human. Fredka's hair grew in soft waves. The scabs on her face healed, and her beautiful, translucent complexion returned to her still gaunt face. A glint of life returned to her sad blue eyes.

Mama held her back straight again, her gaze was confident and direct, and no one stared her down anymore. The navy blue tint in her hair wore off. She fussed over Fredka and me and tended to our six-by-eight-foot plot on the floor as if it were home. As soon as we woke up, she made sure that the rag we slept on was neatly rolled up and tucked against the wall and behind our backs. She combed her hair back neatly and reminded Fredka and me to do the same. "Don't wrinkle your forehead. Sit up straight," she began to nag again just as she did before the concentration camps. Of course, this annoyed us, but Mama was also very quick to catch us at our best and be generous with praise, "You are so beautiful! You walk with grace. You are so clever!" Her declarations of pride made us self-conscious and concerned not to let her down, but also prodded us to strive and set high goals for ourselves.

I too stopped looking at the world with the hopelessness of a concentration camp person. I am convinced that my face and posture showed it. We somehow found rags to wrap around our shoulders to keep us warm. As bad as things were, the intoxicating taste of freedom gave us courage. Even if we lacked means and had no obvious place to turn, electrified barbed wire fences no longer confined us. We were free of armed guards stationed every few feet, ready to storm down on us. No soldiers with whips and German shepherd dogs hounded us. While our suffering continued, there was a meaningful distinction. And we had hope now. I had the heart to try again: for my own sake, for Mama's and Fredka's sake, and for the sake of those I loved who had not made it out of the camps. Their lives and love gave me purpose and direction.

The First Trip to the Market

A miracle! We found a few groszy on the street, the first currency we had touched since the day we were deported from Warsaw. We passed the treasure around, from hand to hand, and discussed what to do with it. We decided to go to the market. And we did! I am sure that it must have been Mama's idea. If it were up to Fredka and me, we would have saved the money for fear that we might never see another grosz.

I still remember the dizzying joy and fear I felt on that walk through winding streets and reminding Mama, "Hold it tight. Don't lose it! Be careful!" The last time we had gone shopping, long, long ago, we were different people and did not stand out in a crowd. Now we looked at each other as we arranged our rags for best effect, and asked, "How do I look? Do I look very terrible?"

"Oh no! You look much better than when we left the camp," we reassured each other.

As we drew closer to the market, the crowd grew denser, the noise grew louder, and we grew more nervous. We avoided asking for directions and let the rising din of voices and clucking hens guide us. Most people carried bulging bushels and baskets. Sensing Fredka's and my discomfort about feeling poor and out of place, Mama said, "Soon we'll do the same. We'll buy whatever we want." I liked hearing her say that, although I could not imagine what that would be like. The prospect took away my breath.

The sight of heaps of food piled on tables at the market overwhelmed us. In reality, it was a small market, but we saw a royal banquet. We gaped at the bright arrays of carrots and beets as would a blind person who suddenly gained sight.

I yearned to reach out to the heavenly mounds of potatoes and bread, and gorge myself. To this day, bread and potatoes taste like pastry meant for kings. We stared greedily at butter, meat, and milk. We had not seen such luxuries for so long. Our stomachs ached with hunger. We nudged each other and cried out, "Look! Look! Live chickens!" Chicken soup steamed in our imaginations. "Geese!" What feasts appeared in our minds! "Eggs! Eggs!"

We ogled everything, and the merchants ogled us with suspicion. We did not look like promising customers. What do we buy with our few groszy? Our eyes groaned. Mama stopped at an array of candies and declared, "We are going to buy one candy and share it."

"Mama, you've lost your mind!" Fredka and I cried out. It seemed preposterous that Mama would decide on such a luxury. We pleaded with her to come to her senses. But Mama persisted, "Poverty needs sprucing up from time to time to blunt its bitterness. My parents were very poor in Ciasnik. When there was little food in our house, your grandmother spread a white cloth on the table to cover up our poverty and lend dignity to our existence. This one candy will remind us of how good life can be and how much we are to enjoy life."

Mama bought one candy in a crinkly bright tissue wrapper. We took turns to suck on it as we walked back to our room, and reminded each other, "Suck slowly and don't swallow the taste quickly. It will last longer this way."

That day at the market and the sweet taste of the candy are still with me today.

The Officer's Proposal

The Russian officer continued his visits to our room and took special interest in us. He often pulled up a chair to our corner and talked with us about his life in Russia, and listened eagerly as Mama shared stories about our life before the war. We learned that he was a chemist, happily married, led a comfortable life, and had no children.

Fredka's beauty and quiet ways always won other people's attention, as well as my love and admiration. She was a skinny, serious, and delicate seventeen-year-old who evoked a protective impulse in others. The Russian officer was captivated by her.

He had a private talk with Mama when Fredka and I were not paying attention. He told her that he and his wife wished to adopt Fredka. "I thought about it for a long while, but I had no heart to approach you," he said. "I thought how difficult it would be for you and for her to separate. I finally concluded that it might be her only chance for a better life."

"Think it over. Think about it. My offer has my wife's heartfelt support. We want to help. It will be a wonderful chance for Fredka. She will have a good home, education, a bright future, and love from my wife and me. I know that it will be unimaginably painful for you, but think what it will mean for your child," he urged.

Mama was stunned. Let Fredka go to Russia and never see her again? Now, after she had seen Fredka near death countless times, through death selections in the ghetto and then in the camps, when Fredka had typhus and was piled up with a heap of dying people in the infirmary. How can he ask that of her? No, she could not do that.

But was she selfish to deny Fredka this opportunity of a life she could not give her?

For two days Mama argued with herself, walking around with a preoccupied stare. Finally, Mother resolved to let Fredka decide.

When Fredka heard the offer, she cried out, "Never! Never!"

They might as well tear off my limb, I thought, but I said nothing. Living without Fredka was unimaginable.

"Consider it carefully," Mama urged. "I don't want to give you up. You know that you are dearer to me than my own breath. I have been agonizing about it for days. I cannot give you up and I cannot deprive you of such an outstanding opportunity. The officer is very kind. His wife too wants to adopt you. Think what it may mean to you. You'll be loved; you'll be comfortably looked after—school, home, food, all the things I cannot provide. Our future is so uncertain."

Fredka clenched her fists and protested, "Never! You cannot make me do that. I would rather die!"

Mama wrapped Fredka in her arms and cried with relief. We all cried. All three of us knew that it was impossible.

We remained together as one, to struggle and to overcome.

16 *Parting with Mama*

We remained in the Russian tailor's room in Kielce for about eight weeks, waiting for winter to pass and hoping for a miracle to get us out of our isolation. It was too cold to go to Działoszyce to look for my cousins, Max and David. Furthermore, we lacked the means to undertake the trip, even if the weather were warm.

The people who passed through our shelter were our eyes and ears to the world. They brought news from different parts of Poland and about people who were as lost as we. We listened raptly to their stories, hoping to borrow an idea, a plan of action. And we did come up with a plan. Sadly, we had no inkling what we were getting ourselves into.

Our plan was an indirect consequence of political maneuvering among the Allied victors. In 1945 new boundaries were being established. In compensation for the Polish territories annexed by the Soviet Union, Poland gained, and renamed, a number of German cities: Breslau, now Wroclaw; Boyton, now Bytom; and Königshütte, now Chorzów. Many Germans left their homes in these new Polish cities and fled to Germany. They left in a hurry for fear that they would be treated as badly as the Poles had been under the German occupation. The majority of the German fugitives left most of their belongings behind.

Concentration camp survivors who had passed through these newly acquired Polish cities told us, "The doors of the abandoned homes are open wide. Strangers help themselves to everything they find. The property belongs to no one. Everyone is free to take it. You should see the riches people carry away!"

This could be our salvation, we thought. We did not want much, just enough to trade for some food, shoes, writing paper and a stamp to send a letter to America, and means to get out of our entrapment. After discussing and weighing all possible risks, Mama made a difficult decision: Fredka and I would go alone to Bytom—the closest newly-Polish city to Kielce—to find a few abandoned trinkets to get us started, and Mama would remain in Kielce. She reasoned, "Someone must stay here to make sure we do not lose our floor spot. Without it we may remain without a roof over our heads. You two go and I will stay."

This was the first time, and by no means the last, that Mama made an important decision for us, but put the responsibility of carrying it out on Fredka's and my shoulders. The heaviest responsibilities she mostly assigned to Fredka.

The thought of separating was unbearable. On the other hand, the fear that if we did not seize the opportunity we might remain lost in this inhospitable land forever was equally unthinkable.

One cold morning, Fredka and I walked out of the room. Before we left, Mama hugged and hugged us. She warned us over and over to be careful. "Stay safe and come back without delay. And keep out of the way of Russian soldiers!" They had a reputation of raping the women they had liberated. Actually, our best protection was our sad appearance—two frightened, emaciated girls in tatters. We told Mama not to worry, and we left.

Mama stood at the door and watched us climb down the stairs. When she could no longer see us, she walked over to the window, opened it, and leaned into the icy air to watch as we disappeared from her. Mama later told us that she was seized by fierce remorse and panic and prayed for us to turn around and come back.

She never once left the room until we returned, and grieved to the people, "How could I have let my children out of my sight? I am insane!" She imagined the horrors that Fredka and I might encounter on the way. Endless scenarios flipped through her mind and grew ever more terrible with every day we were gone. "How will I ever find my children? What have I done?" I heard these gruesome details so many times that I remember them as if I had actually been there myself.

Fredka and I walked down to the train station. We had a couple of slices of bread with us, but we had no idea how we were going to accomplish our mission. Where would we find shelter and food? How would we get on the train without tickets? How would we find the treasures that were waiting for us? We improvised as we went along. "We must stay alert and careful," we reminded each another. Having Fredka near me was the only security I felt.

Our first mission was to find the train to Bytom. We consulted the train schedule on the wall, located the right platform, and waited for the train to arrive—still not sure how we would get on board without tickets.

The train pulled in. We reasoned, "Let's watch other passengers to figure out what car to board."

We noticed that the well-dressed people climbed into the passenger cars. "They have tickets," we concluded. All the others poured into the freight cars at the back of the train. We knew where we must go.

A shoving crowd carried us onto a freight car. No one wanted to be left out to wait for a later train. It was February and the war was not yet over. The next train could not be counted on. Uprooted people on the move carried their household possessions on their backs like crabs. We carried nothing. The seats on the floor were quickly filling up. We slipped through the crowd swiftly, like eels in a stream, and angled for seats against the wall where we could rest our backs. Regrettably, we had had a war-time of experience in making ourselves barely visible, a war-time of training in identifying the safest spot and aiming for it with lightning speed. These habits had saved my life. Ridiculously, I still find myself swimming through a crowd and landing in the best seat in the house, even if it doesn't serve a reasonable purpose any longer. I am sure I embarrass my children at times.

Another survivor characteristic that I am not able to shed is being mindful of good hiding places in my house and the houses I visit. I can rattle them off in a split second. I am still programmed to be alert to danger even though true peace and sweetness of life have long been real to me. I might add that finding the best hiding places gives me an advantage when I play hide-and-seek with my grandchildren.

We sat quietly, reading the faces of people in the crowd. We waited anxiously for the door to close before someone in authority would step in to throw us out for having no tickets. A mournful whistle blew, couplers clanged, the train jerked, the steam engine puffed, and we were off, hearts nearly shattered with fear.

People settled down, sighing with relief. Fredka and I leaned back against the rattling planks. Cuddling up to each other for warmth and security, we listened mindfully to the conversations among strangers tossed together from different corners of Poland. We hoped to pick up useful information, but dared not join in the conversations or ask questions. The train gained speed, drafts of icy air blew in through open windows, and darts of sunlight flickered on passengers' tense faces—faces I was not entirely sure I could trust.

The distance between Kielce and Bytom is 160 kilometers, but I remember the trip lasting hours, endless hours. At the train station in Bytom, Fredka and I slipped away from the crowd and walked through unknown streets, lost and numb, asking each other, "How will we ever find the deserted houses filled with things?" We felt empty of friends and people we knew, and empty of ideas about where to find food and a place to sleep or hide from danger. We walked, prodded by hope and fear.

After a long while, we encountered two young Jewish women as lost and desperate as we were. We clustered together to roam the foreign streets in search of a door to salvation. We stuck our heads into silent buildings and withdrew as quickly as we heard a murmur. Before long, dusk caught up with us, the streets grew quiet and empty, and alarm rang in our heads. "We will freeze to death or, worse, they will arrest us for breaking the curfew!" Just as we saw ourselves falling off the edge of existence, our luck held out again. One of our new friends pointed a finger at a dark building, silent as a tomb, and said firmly, "This one looks empty. We're going in."

We opened the main door, entered gingerly into a lobby, and tiptoed up the stairs. We stopped on each landing, held our ears to doors, and then cautiously stuck our heads into unlocked and abandoned flats. We shuddered at the echoes of our own footsteps. When we felt satisfied that we were alone in the building, we decided to spend the night in an apartment on the second floor. We reasoned that it would place us close to the street if we had to flee, and far enough away from it to give us time to hide if we heard soldiers at the main gate. Each of us picked a place to hide, just in case. Then we stretched out on the floor for the night.

Fredka and I were grateful for the companionship of our new friends. We talked into the night, sharing our stories of the past and our hopes for the future. We asked each other, "Where did you live before the war? How did you survive? Do you have family in America or somewhere else?" We gave each other hope, "We are alive. And free. Maybe we can go to Palestine, or America; maybe other places will let us in?"

We talked in whispers till we fell asleep from exhaustion, though never completely dropping our guard. We went cold with fear when distant sounds of slamming doors and footsteps on the sidewalk woke us. We shuddered at the creaks and groans of thermal expansions and we murmured in alarm, "Did you hear that? What could that be?" Then we fell asleep again, but not for long.

At some point, boots slapping on the pavement and boisterous voices of soldiers startled us. We cried out in unison, "Russian soldiers!" We jumped to our feet and listened to the clamor drawing closer and closer.

We still had hope. "Maybe they will stomp past our building and leave us in peace." But the soldiers halted at the front gate to carry on a loud discussion. "Are they deciding our fate—whether or not to enter the building?" we wondered.

Then the front door slammed open, a rumble of soldiers' feet reached the stairs, and raucous voices echoed throughout the empty building.

In a flash, we scampered into cupboards, cabinets, and drawers, and disappeared from sight without a trace. I slipped into a tiny cabinet, shut the door, curled up tight as a fist, and pressed into a dark corner, head turned away from the door—as if this would help erase my existence to any villain who looked inside my hiding place. Stiff with fear, I lay rolled up in this tiny safe that could be broken into at any moment, conscious that my fate was floating on the fickle whim of luck. The violent thrashing of my heart pounded in my ears. I felt as trapped as a bird in a cage, knowing I could be set free by the whim of one righteous beat of one human heart, or not. This time, it was not the power and force of a government that threatened us. We were at the mercy of a few soldiers out for a good time or for spoils of war to send home to their sweethearts.

The silence in our room was as palpable as the clamor of the Russian soldiers stomping through the building, slamming doors, laughing loudly, bumping into furniture, climbing ever closer, till I could hear them on our landing.

Suddenly, their voices lost force. A door flung open, but the boots remained outside the room. A verbal exchange followed, and a final verdict. *"Nitshivo!"* (Nothing here!) Spared again!

The drumroll of boots beat down the stairs. The front door slammed shut. The rattle of rifles and the ugly voices—intoxicated with unchecked power—slowly faded in the distance. But we did not fully trust the quiet and remained motionless in our hiding places until the familiar creaking sounds of the night droned on without interruptions. Then we crept out from our hidings, feeling giddy with our good fortune. I felt like God's chosen, forgetting to ask why He put me in harm's way in the first place. We all huddled close together and talked about our fright as if we were casting stones off our chests. Eventually, all strength seeped out of us, and we dozed between restless starts.

When dawn and the sounds of waking traffic reached our windows, we lifted our heads from the floor and began to plan our next move. "It's getting light," we warned each other, "We might get caught and punished for trespassing."

Gingerly, we looked out the window to figure out how to steal out of the building without being noticed. "Let's wait for the streets to fill, then we'll blend in with the crowd," we decided.

We pondered, "Where do we go from here?" The experience of the past twenty-four hours had taught us that we came too late. The flats had been picked clean. But the tall tales we had heard from others, the promises we had made to ourselves, and our desperate cravings would not let us give up, not just yet.

As the traffic increased, we slipped out of the abandoned building and joined the early morning crowd. We meandered through strange streets and never came close to finding success. At midday, our new friends departed, leaving Fredka and me alone.

We gave up hunting for plunder and concentrated on finding shelter for the night and food. We walked and walked. Crowds streamed past us without seeing us. We searched for a sympathetic face to approach and ask for assistance, only to be rebuffed by evasive glances.

By day's end, our energies and spirits spent, we felt light-headed with fatigue, hunger, and fear. Then we heard, "*Uhmhoo?*" Kind eyes looked up at us and the voice of a young man gasped, "*Uhmhoo?*"

"*Uhmhoo*," we whispered back.

"You must get off the street before night falls or you will freeze to death. You need food right away." He led us to a building, pointed out an apartment, and said confidently, "Go there right away. Jewish people live there. They will feed you and house you for the night. Not to worry, just go."

We walked up a couple of flights of stairs to a door and knocked timidly. A voice asked, "Who is it?" Unsure of the safest thing to say, we responded with a quivering mumble, "Please open the door. *Uhmhoo*."

The door opened slowly, and the two of us stood agog, staring into a room that looked like a dream. The room, oh so heartbreakingly inviting, so homey! Delicious aromas of food wafted in the air. Lilting sounds of voices spoke Yiddish. And a circle of people sat eating at a table covered with a tablecloth. A chandelier radiated coziness to every corner. I was astonished that we did not faint on the spot. Such civility we had not seen since we lost our home, but we dreamed of it incessantly.

The people looked at us with smiling, sympathetic faces. Fredka and I introduced ourselves and begged to spend the night. They reached out to us with open arms and soothing voices. "Of course, of course, come in." They motioned us to the table. "Sit down. We will get you something to eat." There was no need to explain about cold, hunger, and curfew. They asked no questions; they knew. They made room for us at the table and reassured us, "You are welcome to spend the night with us. We will borrow pillows and blankets for you from our neighbors downstairs."

I felt enveloped in dreamlike warmth that made my knees buckle. Food was set in front of us. We ate with gratitude and forced restraint so as not to spoil the civilized mood. Oh, how the food melted every fiber in my body! Comfort permeated my skin, my bones. I consciously rolled every morsel in my mouth, trying to hold on to every crumb, suck every drop of taste before it disappeared. Our hosts talked with us slowly to give us time to eat. We had to use all our willpower to stop gulping our food.

The caring manners of our hosts brought back memories of visits with aunts and uncles, in rooms sparkling with candlelight, lively conversation, and love. I yearned for the secure arms of family, who, long ago, caught Fredka and me when we stumbled, fed us when we were hungry, and fetched us to our homes and beds when we were tired. I felt my determination rise to face the next challenge to find a meal and shelter, to stay alive and reclaim the goodness that once was ours.

Grateful, but dazed with fatigue and worry, we sat around the table with our kind hosts, trying hard to listen, not to nod off or ask for more food. Finally our hosts announced that it was time to go to sleep and asked, "Would you mind running down to our friends, in the apartment below, to fetch your bedding while we make room for your bed?" This simple task led us to a complicated entanglement.

The neighbors, another small group of young Jewish survivors, were just as friendly as our hosts, and asked us if our hosts had fed us. We were still very hungry. Fredka's eyes registered both hope and resignation, but before she could say, "Yes, we were fed," as I knew she would, I quickly responded with vagueness, "Yes, we were fed a little bit, earlier in the evening." My voice must have betrayed hope. Food was set for us at the table. It still tasted as wonderful as the first morsel we swallowed earlier that evening. But Fredka flashed furtive accusatory glances at me whenever she could, and I knew why. While we ate, someone carried up the mattress and bedding for us.

"As you were at six, you'll be at sixty, only more so," my mother used to say. That was certainly true of my sister and me. Through thick and through thin, we responded predictably in ways true to ourselves. Fredka was, and remained, pedantically scrupulous, very sensitive, and meticulously conscientious, and she excelled in whatever she undertook. When she was a child, she never missed doing her homework, rarely let our parents down, did what was expected of her, and did everything well. She drew beautifully, she organized play performances with friends that delighted everyone, and she never lied. I, on the other hand, was easier going. I got in trouble in spite of myself. I got lost while chasing shadows in the forest, got caught in rain storms, and watched flashes of lightning split the summer sky while sitting on tree branches. I often got sidetracked by the sheer joy of the experience, and I had faith that good would follow. I simply was less aware of danger and failure. I always found a patch of sky even in the darkest pits and held onto it.

In the concentration camps, Fredka always did her full quota of work in the ammunition factory. I often fell short, even though I was physically stronger than Fredka, especially after she had had typhus. Fredka was always the first to focus on the disgrace we were subjected to in the camps and the first to want to surrender, to end it all. Mama and I had more heart to fight and persist.

As soon as we left the neighbor's apartment to rejoin our hosts where we would sleep on a real mattress, Fredka stopped on the stairway landing in front of a window and said, "I am not going up! I am not going into the apartment! I am embarrassed! You did not tell them the truth that we were fed a full meal. How could you?!"

I pleaded, "I did not really lie; I lied a little. What difference does it make to anyone, except to us? Besides, how will the people ever know what we did or said to their neighbors?"

Fredka did not budge. "I am not going back. What if they found out from the neighbor who carried up the bedding?" The embarrassment of being caught at a lie was intolerable to her.

"So what if they find out? It's not important," I said.

No matter how hard I pleaded with her, Fredka was not going in. "What else can we do? We cannot walk out into the night," I reasoned.

Fredka climbed up on the windowsill and said, "I am not going into the apartment. I will jump out of the window if you insist." At that moment she had had enough of it all, including me.

I was beside myself. Fredka's threat seemed ridiculous, but her despair and exasperation were real. I looked at her; I looked down into the black courtyard. The hard cement pavement glistened in the moonlight. Although I knew my sister's penchant for drama, her outlandish threat petrified me. I pleaded with her. I promised that I would go in first and make sure that they did not know that we ate again at the neighbors. She did not budge. "I will do anything you want. Anything you will ever ask me to do, just get off this sill," I said. She finally gave in and stepped down. Despondent, and ashamed, she followed me into the apartment.

We spent that night sleeping on a real mattress, something we had not done in two years. Our heads rested on pillows. A warm blanket covered our bodies. We fell safely asleep listening to the soft breathing sounds of friends. But the image of my sister standing on the windowsill threatening to jump into the night stayed with me.

*   *   *

The next sunrise we left. Despite the failure of our undertaking, Fredka and I felt lucky that we had not been raped by the Russian soldiers and that we had not frozen or starved to death. We longed to be back with Mama, and we missed our rectangle on the floor, in a room where we knew no one, except the two friendly Russian soldiers. We could easily imagine how relieved Mama would be to see us, how out of her mind she was with worry.

Shivering with cold, we walked to the train station feeling as alone as when we had arrived in Bytom. The streets remained foreign and the faces of the crowds distant. We repeated the process of finding the right train and a spot to rest our backs in a freight car full of poor strangers who stared at us from time to time. Furious gusts of icy wind blew at us again through open windows as the train picked up speed.

After hours of sitting on the rattling floor, Fredka and I decided to walk up to the window, stretch our cramped limbs, and watch country scenes scroll past us. A tall young Polish man joined us and struck up a conversation with us. He took note that we were more bedraggled than the rest of the passengers and asked us who we were and how we happened to be on the train. His voice and face conveyed sincerity and politeness, and his conversation was intelligent and kind. He was saddened by our brief responses to his questions, and expressed shock at the inhuman behavior of people toward one another. One of his remarks still rings in my mind.

He asked, "Why did Jewish people, throughout the centuries, cling to their identity with such tenacity, even at the cost of incredible suffering and loss of lives? Why didn't they give up their identity as many other ethnic and religious groups had done?"

The answer seemed obvious to Fredka and me, but I am not sure that we made it clear to the man. We knew that conversion to Christianity had not protected Jews from persecutions. Jews who had obtained Aryan identity documents and Christians who had distant Jewish ancestors were hounded down and killed. Often, their own Aryan coreligionists betrayed them. The same was true during the Spanish Inquisition and other waves of persecutions against us. Under such circumstances, why would you want to leave family and sever links with history to enter a world that so despises you that, if your heritage is discovered, you may be killed anyway?

We said, "If a change of faith is dictated by true conviction, conversion might be worth the price. But if your existence among a people depends on lying and keeping your true identity hidden, that is quite another matter."

The conversation lingered for a while and a few other passengers joined in and listened politely. Fredka and I felt self-conscious and on guard, but the conversation was exceptional and restoring, perhaps because it was the first conversation we had had with strangers in public since we were liberated. We felt good to have held our ground and affirmed our identity.

Fredka and I had been gone from Kielce only three days. But in this situation, time cannot be measured by normal units. Mama's life was restored only when the door to the room opened and we stepped in. She rose from her corner, stood rooted to the spot for a few seconds, and stared at us as if seeing a miracle. Then she rushed to hold us, and wailed, "How could I have let you out of my sight? How could I ever forgive myself? I did not know how to find you, where to look."

Fredka and I were grateful to be back with Mama and out of the cold. Mama asked what happened to us, and rang her hands in alarm as she listened to our travails. I complained that Fredka had threatened to jump out of a window into the black night. Fredka complained that it was my fault because I had lied. We forgot to worry about the failure of our undertaking, or about what to do next with our lives. We held on to each other and felt enormously fortunate to be reunited. We were grateful that we were spared the worst that could have happened. We vowed, "We will never separate again, no matter what happens." We slept peacefully that night, the three of us together on our plot on the floor. I lay cradled in Mama's arms. Her cushiony body draped close to mine, as if to shield me.

That is how I fell asleep every terrible night during the war: in Warsaw during brief pauses between bombardments, on bunk planks in concentration camps, and in strange shelters during our wandering after liberation. Mama knew I had a lot of heart to cope with adversities in bright daylight, but I was petrified of the dark. Fredka, on the other hand, was much braver at night than I, but she found the indignities we suffered by day impossible to endure. That is when Mama focused her full attention on giving her courage to fight. During daylight, Mama never let Fredka out of her sight and fought savagely to protect her from danger.

17 The Night

Signs of approaching spring brought hope as well as terror to our hearts. "Look, the snow is melting and days are getting longer! We must leave Kielce soon. If we delay, another winter might overtake us. We might remain trapped, forgotten, lost forever in this bloody Europe," we warned each other.

Finding her brother and two sisters in America was Mama's ultimate goal. But we did not have their addresses, we were penniless, and the Iron Curtain cut us off from the West. Mama said, "Our only hope is to go to Działoszyce to look for Max and David."

"What if they are not there?" Fredka and I cautioned.

Mama did not let up. "That is where they said they were going when they left the camp. They also told us to follow them to Działoszyce and that they would wait for us. We must try to find them."

That undertaking had many risks. Działoszyce is many kilometers from Kielce. We did not know just how far. It was still cold, and snow covered much of the land. We had no money for tickets or provisions for the trip. Furthermore, we had no idea if Max and David had reached Działoszyce, or if they were still there, or whether they really wanted to see us. Taking all these uncertainties into account, we could not take the chance of losing our floor space in the room—the only bit of security we could count on. But even that was tenuous. The two Russian soldiers could be transferred at any time.

One of us must remain in this room to secure our space, we all agreed. "Fredka will stay. She is too frail." That is what Mama said. But I think that Mama counted on the Russian officer and his wife taking care of Fredka if we did not make it back.

Having reached a decision, the three of us walked to the train station and learned that none of the trains stopped in Działoszyce. We would have to get off some distance from our destination. We had no notion how far Działoszyce was from the nearest station, how we would get there from the train stop, what terrain we would encounter, or how friendly the peasants in the area were to returning Jews.

Leaving Fredka was hardest. The terror in her eyes mirrored Mama's and my fears. So much was up to us and so much was out of our control. We tried to imagine a happy reunion with Max and David, but we knew that we could not count on it.

Mama and I boarded the train without tickets—a humiliating experience all by itself. We remained on guard and ready to respond to the unexpected. We were cold and hungry. It still amazes me how long people can survive without food, how much severe cold we can endure and still stay alive.

We got off the train on an open platform at the designated station, unknown miles from Działoszyce, and stepped into snow-covered countryside. A few narrow streets with rows of small, drab houses converged at the station. A cluster of peasants, bundled in warm clothes and clutching an assortment of baggage, milled on the platform for a while, then vanished with the speeding train down the track. Others walked into the distance with sure steps. Isolated huts and barns were scattered in the white distance. Beyond the farmhouses was nothing but open country and stillness.

We strained to look into the horizon in hope of seeing Działoszyce in the distance. It was useless. An immense, slippery-gray sky merged with a sea of snow stretching as far into the distance as we could see. Questions darted into my mind. *Start walking? In which direction? How far? Will we reach Działoszyce before night? If not, where will we find shelter for the night?* I looked at Mama, hoping that she knew what to do next.

Mama looked back at me. She did not have any answers yet, but her face told me that her mind was working. Her eyes searched the area with the intensity of an animal in danger. She took note of horse-drawn carts loaded mostly with hay. "One of these wagons may be going to Działoszyce. We will ask for a lift," Mama said.

We approached several peasants on carts. Mama promised to pay for their kindness as soon as we reached Działoszyce and reunited with our cousins who would give us the money. They grumbled back, unfriendly. After several rejections, one man told us to sit on the edge of his loaded cart. He informed us that he was not going as far as Działoszyce, but in the same direction. He was nice. He cautioned us that it was getting late and that we might not be able to reach our destination before nightfall. He was wondering how we were going to make it dressed as lightly as we were. He asked why we were going there. We responded with caution, divulging as little as possible.

The cart rolled, cutting tracks in the fresh snow. Our bodies shook with the rattling cart. The wind whistled. The man shouted occasional commands to the horse. His whip cracked the air and landed with sharp slaps on the horse's back. The horse wheezed. The man reminded us not to fall asleep. Mama pointed out to me how lucky we were to have found such a decent man. "You see you cannot give up. We will get there. You'll see." But I heard fear behind her optimism.

The cart and the horse plodded slowly through snowdrifts. Groves of bare trees with branches like twisted talons floated in the distance. Every now and then, isolated farmhouses, with pillows of snow on pitched roofs, rolled toward us as we neared them, then floated away into the crisp white endlessness.

Each appearance of a snow-incrusted farmhouse set me thinking, *Would they let us sleep in one of them?* I took note of the watchdogs that ran toward us like furies. Their dark leaping bodies looked starkly ominous against the pure blanket of snow that stretched to every corner of that world. *How will we ever walk past them to ask for shelter?* I wondered.

We rolled with the wagon in a semistupor until the wagon stopped abruptly. The nice man told us that this was the end of our ride. We thanked him. We did not hold it against him that he did not offer shelter against the freezing nightfall. We knew better than to set our expectations high. His willingness to give us a lift was more than others were prepared to offer. He pointed in the direction of Działoszyce and took off in another. Stiff with cold, exhaustion, hunger, and fear, we let our feet sink into the snow that reached well above our bare ankles. A sharp pain cut through my flesh. We turned our heads to watch the man draw away with his cart. We felt very alone. Our last crutch vanished with the wagon that left us at the end of the world. "What now?" we asked each other. "How far to Działoszyce? How much progress can we make plowing through this desert of snow on foot?"

We started to walk, pushing through snowdrifts, sliding past clusters of ice. We walked and watched the sky grow dim. We walked and squinted into the distance, hoping to see a hint of Działoszyce. Nothing! The biting cold made us forget our hunger. At some point my Mama said, "We will have to walk up to the next farmhouse and ask for shelter before it gets dark." We rehearsed what we would say.

Nearing a farmhouse horrified me. The watchdogs growled and barked ferociously as they dashed at us with bared fangs. I was petrified and tried to back away pleading, "Mama, I am afraid, let's go away. The dogs will bite us, they will tear us apart."

Mama, from whom I had learned to be afraid of all dogs, big and small, courageously repeated what others had said to her: "There is nothing to be afraid of. The dogs are more afraid of you than you are of them." I continued to back away. Mama, who was as frightened as I, said, "You can't turn back. The dogs will not bite. You cannot show them that you are afraid. Act bold. We will walk to the farmhouse. We must find shelter." With Mama in the lead, I did just as she directed, but we were turned away repeatedly.

We stumbled from farmhouse to farmhouse, each of them separated by endless snow. A red sun began to sink on the rim of the horizon and deep twilight was already behind us. Still no one let us in.

We trudged forward until night engulfed us. With each step the universe grew more empty, eerie, and silent. The desolation was endless and the sky unforgettable in its calm blinking splendor. We were abandoned by God and man.

I know that I whimpered with pain, though I was trying to hide my despair from Mama. I know that she too moaned, even though she tried to give me heart. We both trembled with cold and moved forward, weak and light-headed. Silence filled the white emptiness.

We came to a frozen stream and had to cross an ice-covered trestle. I looked at the slick ties sparkling in the moonlight and thought, *God, if I slip and fall between the ties, a sheet of ice will carry me down. I will drown!*

"I cannot do it," I told Mama, who took the first step, shook and trembled, and stumbled across, sometimes on all fours.

Mama, now on the opposite bank, called for me to cross. I searched in vain for a way around the trestle. I raised my eyes to the sky in hope of finding an inspiration, a way out. The sky hung there in the indescribable glory of a myriad stars, just blinking the fact that "the universe just is."

Mama called again, "You must cross. You see, I did. Don't be afraid. We must go on and find shelter in one of the farms ahead. Come now."

I put one foot on an icy tie. I slid, but did not fall. I lifted my second foot and put it in front. I teetered. I bent down and crept on all fours. When I was close to the opposite bank, I lost footing and slipped. I grabbed hold of the tie in front of me, and held on with my arms. The lower part of my body dangled between the ties above the frozen stream. My fingers burnt with cold and my arms trembled with strain. The weight of my body was pulling me down. "I cannot get up, Mama. My hands cannot take it! I am going to fall!"

Mama called, "No, you are not falling! Your hands will not give way! They will hold! Kick your legs toward the bank in front of you! Pull yourself up! You are almost there," she pleaded. "I will pull you in! Just reach for my hand! Here! You will make it! You must!"

I struggled to swing my body toward the shore. It seemed impossible to hold on for another second. My mother's voice called, unrelentingly, "Here, here, here is my hand." My legs reached for the bank. I found a foothold. Mama's hand reached out and grabbed hold of me. Kneeling on the snow, she pulled, all the while giving encouragement. I heaved, and pushed with all the strength left in me until I reached the icy bank and fell into Mama's arms. Everything in me quivered. I was so cold and miserable, but so grateful to have escaped death in that frozen stream.

I never forgot the goodness of being alive that I felt at that moment, in spite of cold, starvation, and abandonment. I understood on that night—as I did many times when I was in the profoundest depth of suffering—that the primary meaning of life is life itself, and it must be revered. On a level beyond words, I understood the glory of looking forward to a new sunrise and seeing the magnificence of another night. Life was so vivid because it had nearly slipped away. I was not too young to understand life's tribulations and its majesty.

Mama's thoughts, when she stood at the edge of the stream calling desperately to me, are easy to imagine. She brought us out of the conflagration of the Warsaw Ghetto uprising, out of countless "selections" for crematoria, and out of concentration camps. We were free now, but Fredka was far away and alone, I had almost drowned in a frozen stream, and there was no one she could call to for help. It is equally easy to guess her relief when she held me in her arms again. She too looked up at the sky, grateful that life had not punished her one more time.

We held on to each other and continued to plow forward, squinting into the sparkling darkness, hoping to see a silhouette of Działoszyce in the distance. We ignored frantic watchdogs, knocked on several more farm doors. No one let us in.

When the cold seemed beyond endurance, and I lost all hope for mercy, Mama insisted on knocking on "one more door." A gaunt farm woman wrapped in a faded babushka stood at the half-open door, leaning on it as if she were about to close it, at the same time studying our faces intently and listening. A man's gruff voice called from the back of the house, "Close the door! Who are you talking to?" Mama hooked her nose around the open door and begged to let us stay for the night, or else we would surely freeze to death. She promised to pay her as soon as we found our cousins in Działoszyce.

"Wait," the woman said, "I have to ask my husband." We waited and listened to her soft, pleading whispers, and her husband's scoffs. She returned with a sad face. "My husband said that we cannot let you stay. We cannot afford it. We are very poor."

Slowly, she began to push the door shut, but her eyes stayed with us. Mama remained standing on the threshold, pleading, "My daughter and I will freeze to death if you turn us away. We are not asking for food, just a corner out of the way. We will leave at the crack of dawn."

"Wait, I will talk to him again," she said resolutely and walked away. We waited inside at the door, listening to the woman pleading on our behalf. That fact alone gave me comfort. The man rebuked her, but the good woman persisted until his tone began to soften, and finally the husband sounded resigned. The woman returned. "You can stay in the barn. We cannot give you any food, and you will have to leave before sunrise. Follow me." Our gratitude knew no bounds.

The kind woman led us to the barn. She told us to sleep on the loft and cover ourselves with the hay, and she reminded us one more time that we must be out at daybreak. We thanked her profusely and promised not to be any trouble. We climbed up the ladder and collapsed on the hay, exhausted and relieved. We cuddled and piled hay over our bodies trying hard to stay warm.

Mama and I talked briefly about the next day. We assured one another that Działoszyce could not be much farther. I asked Mama, "Do you think we will find Max and David?" We both realized that if we did not locate them, we would have to turn around and trudge right back to Kielce where Fredka was waiting. Our return journey might be as difficult as the one we had just completed. For the moment, we thought ourselves lucky to be inside the barn, chilled only by slim puffs of icy wind blowing through gaps in the walls.

We slept till the last glow of the moon vanished and we heard a voice coming from the hut. The woman appeared at the barn door and said, "You have to leave now. You can come into the house for a warm drink. But we cannot feed you. And you must leave right away."

We followed her into their little house. It was barely more than a hut. The place was as poor as the homes of most Polish peasants whose burdensome lives had not changed perceptibly in centuries. A few simple, essential pieces of furniture and utensils stood neatly arranged in the one-room house. Light streamed in from a small window and lifted the gloom cast by the low ceiling. Something was cooking on top of a clay stove, but no food aromas wafted in the air. The woman shared with us a hot, diluted beetroot drink. She chatted briefly with us, but she was anxious for us to leave. The man hardly looked up at us. Both seemed uneasy about our presence in their house, especially the man. We understood that they feared what their neighbors would say about letting Jews stay in their house. The woman pointed us in the direction of Działoszyce, and told us we did not have far to go. We thanked them for giving us shelter and a warm drink, and we left.

We were again in a lonely, white planet. No distinct outlines separated the ghostly shapes of trees and desolate white-clad huts in the immense shadowless emptiness. A fan of golden sunlight rose from the horizon, promising time to find our cousins before it sank back into darkness.

Still feeling lost, I looked up to the sky and gasped at the truth of our insignificance to heaven and man. In utter loneliness, I held onto Mama and, summoning visions of hope to obscure the starkness of our reality, I pushed toward life.

18 *Działoszyce*

Działoszyce sits at the confluence of two tributaries of the Nidzia River in the middle of a vast forest in Poland. It developed from a gamekeeper's village established by Polish nobles almost a thousand years ago. Favorably situated for trade on the high road to Kraków, it was well populated by the twelfth century. Jews were first permitted to settle in Działoszyce during the reign of Kasimir the Great in the mid-fourteenth century. Before long, they constituted the majority of the population. For hundreds of years, Działoszyce thrived, with a bustling Jewish community contributing to the growth of the town until the Nazis killed more than 10,000 Jews, leaving fewer than 2,000 impoverished Christian inhabitants.

Tata's brother Jacob, Max and David's father, left Pinczów, his hometown, when he was a young man and settled in Działoszyce. He married Aunt Cerka, started his own jewelry business, and in time had three sons, Max, David, and Itzhok, and a little, darkly beautiful daughter, Hanna, the absolute sweetheart of the family. Eventually, the family moved to their own house near the town square.

Shivering with cold, hunger, longing, and exhaustion, Mama and I wandered into the outskirts of Działoszyce the same morning we had left the farmhouse. This was only about twenty-four hours after we had left Fredka alone in the room in Kielce, but hardly ever had one day and a night lasted as long, or tested our endurance as thoroughly. We paused to gather courage, get oriented, and figure out the safest way to start our approach. Before us stood a small town, encircled by wintry pastoral views. A smattering of pedestrians walked down narrow streets; they were bundled in dark clothes, boots, babushkas, and peasant caps. The streets stretched into a traceable distance and stopped at a large open area that looked like a *rynek* (market square). A few horse-drawn carts rolled by. Longingly, I listened to the clip-clop of the hooves and the sounds of farm animals dissolve into the big sky above me. Everything seemed heartbreakingly serene and harmonious; everything belonged—except us.

Unsure of ourselves, we started to walk toward the market square. The town felt as foreign and threatening to us as all the other places that had kept us out. We trudged, half sparked by the hope of finding my cousins, and half frozen with fear that they were no-where to be found. We peered into windows, wishing for the miracle of spotting them inside a room.

It did not take us long to reach the cobblestone marketplace surrounded by somber houses with uneven roofs and mostly empty store windows. Timorously, we approached a few strangers and asked if they knew of our family, Wakszlak (Tata's family surname), who once lived in this town. Did they know Max and David? Someone pointed to a house at the bend of the town square and said politely, "This was the Wakszlak's house. The Germans took them all away. They are probably all dead."

My heart lurched. My uncle's house stood like a tombstone commemorating the lives stolen from us. Mama and I whispered, "Uncle's home. Should we go there?" We had no idea who lived there, nor did we trust it to be safe to knock on the door.

Torpid with dread, we remained standing in the square until a young Jewish man noticed us and recognized our panic. He rushed over to offer help. We asked pleadingly, "Max and David Wakszlak, do you know them? Are they here? Do you know?"

"Yes, Max and David are here," he said, and gently advised, "Don't go to their house. It's not safe to do that. Wait here. I will find them and fetch them to you right away. You will be okay; you are among Jews now."

The relief we felt when we saw Max and David is hard to describe. They looked at us kindly and were glad to see us. We tried to share with them our wandering from town to town in hope of finding family and help. The words fell from our shivering lips like heavy stones. Mama talked fast, as if our heads were under a guillotine and our lives depended on her message. She made sure that she did not leave out her concern about Fredka. She repeated over and over, "We left Fredka alone. Fredka is alone in Kielce. We don't know what might be happening to her." Mama continued to plead until we heard Max and David say, "Don't worry. We will take care of everything. We will get Fredka here and you will all stay with us. But first we must get permission from the people who live in our house."

"Permission? What will happen to us if they refuse?" Mama asked.

As we walked toward their house, Max and David shared the bitter insecurity of their own situation: "The Jewish survivors who come back are not welcome in this town. Strangers live in our house and enjoy all our family possessions. We had to plead with them to let us stay in a tiny attic room on the top floor of our own house. Their concession was not an act of kindness. They had an ulterior motive and we know what it was."

"At the moment, we have no legal recourse. Authorities grandly ignore the rights of Jews. Jews who show the least inclination to claim their properties are threatened by a vigilante group that is dedicated to ethnic purity. The father and the two sons who live in our house are leading members."

The precariousness of my cousins' existence frightened me. In addition, I remembered Max and David leaving the concentration camp after liberation without us. Would they leave us again if we had to run from danger?

Fortunately, my cousins managed to get permission to share their miserable room in the attic with us. David volunteered to go to Kielce to bring Fredka to us. He accomplished it with incredible ease and speed. Within a couple of days we were reunited. But still not safe.

After Max and David ran for their lives from the liberated camp in Częstochowa, they hopped on passing trains, hitched rides on horse-drawn carts, and walked on snow-covered roads until they reached their hometown.

When they finally knocked on the door of their own house, a soft-mannered woman answered. Her pale blue eyes scrutinized them cautiously. Immediately, she guessed who these two young men might be. Before my cousins had a chance to finish their introduction, she stepped back and said in a rehearsed voice, "I don't know anything. Not a thing. Come back when my husband and my sons will be home."

Max and David returned. The woman with the quiet face and averted eyes opened the door. "Wait. I will tell the men you are here."

"Everything in the foyer was much as it was when we lived there: the same knick-knacks my mother chose, all as familiar as her face," Max recalled.

"We waited a few seconds. A door opened and three men stepped into the foyer and quickly pulled the door shut behind them. All three were lean and well groomed, cool eyes piercing and waiting for us to speak. We drew ourselves up and looked back, unflinchingly, into the three sets of chilly eyes. Calmly, we introduced ourselves and said: 'We hope that room could be made for us to stay in the house till we find a place to live.'"

"Yes," the elder son replied crisply.

"Could we take a few minutes to walk through the house to retrieve memories?"

"No," was the answer. "You will stay in the attic room partitioned off from the storage area on the third floor. You will keep out of any other part of the house, and don't ask to see or touch anything outside your room."

Max and David assumed that the father and two sons had ransacked the house and had found some of the valuables that Max had helped his father hide. My cousins conjectured, "If they are as evil and greedy as we have cause to think, they will let us stay in the house long enough to lead them to the treasures they had missed. Then, they will try to cut our heads off. We must outsmart them: retrieve what we can find, hide it well, and then slip out of town before they kill us. We decided to take that chance," Max reported.

Of course, Mama, Fredka, and I became instant accomplices. Luckily, we managed not to lose our heads. Therefore, I can tell the tale of our colorful experiences in Działoszyce and our narrow escape.

The Room

After Max and David obtained permission for us to stay with them, we watched Max unlock the front door to their house and we stepped into a cozy foyer. All doors surrounding the foyer were shut tight. My cousins left the lights turned off and motioned us to the staircase. The care my cousins took not to disturb the people who occupied their house served as a warning.

Gingerly, we tiptoed up the dim stairwell to the top landing, opened a creaking door, and stepped into a ramshackle room. I am not sure you could call that crudely finished storage area with a low, slanting ceiling a room. A cot leaned on two opposite side walls, leaving no more than a yard of floor space between them. A small window wedged between the two cots admitted a shaft of sunlight.

A coal-burning stove stood in a corner near the door. The stove, like the window, played an important part in our lives. The stove became Mama's joy. It brought her a tiny step closer to recovering the power of giving. Nothing made her happier than standing in front of the stove and cooking for us—nothing, except watching us eat what she had prepared. It was as if she were ladling life into us. The stove also kept us warm.

There was hardly any space left for the four of us to stand up or walk. Two had to remain seated when we were all in the room. We had no chairs. A wooden makeshift table hung from the wall under the window. We ate sitting on our beds. At night, Max and David shared one cot. Mama, Fredka, and I slept in the other, squeezed together so as not to fall off.

My cousins always measured up to new challenges. They knew people with whom they could trade; they rounded up a few dishes, cooking utensils, and, most importantly, food. We stored our few belongings on top of the stove, on the makeshift table, and under our cots.

There was another barely discernable door on the wall next to Max and David's cot. It was roughly two feet by three feet, and its perimeter was outlined by a hair-thin rectangular crack. That door led to a musty attic with insulation hanging between beams. What lay hidden under the beams made up in great measure for the pathetic squalor our cousins chose to endure.

The room was our refuge. Its thin door and walls kept us insulated from the bigotry outside. It was the place where we shared thoughts over meals and talked over plans for the future. The tenuous serenity in the room sheltered our dreams.

The window was my escape. The bucolic views stretching beyond the crooked roofs of the town lured me. The trilling birds were my messengers. I heard them only early in the morning before the courtyard filled with rowdy children who shattered our peace.

Sometimes Fredka and I had to step to the back of the room or sit on a cot in order not to be seen by a gang of kids gathered in the yard to catch a glimpse of us through the curtainless window. They jumped from side to side and craned their necks every which way to catch sight of us. The minute we stood up or stepped toward the front of the room, they hollered, "I see her! I see her!" and burst into a chant, "*Żydóweczka Hajusia / Miała Żydka Beniusia*" (A Jewess Haya / Had a Jew-boy Benjamin). They laughed uproariously. Their barking dogs joined in the merriment. At those moments, Mama turned to us and reassured us, "That too shall pass. Those ignorant kids are not important." She gave me courage to continue believing that what I saw beneath our window was an insanity that we would soon leave behind.

Passover

The first Passover after liberation arrived with the melting snow. The approaching holiday and hints of spring stirred us with excitement and nostalgia. One afternoon, Max and David burst in the room and declared, "We and our friends decided to bake matzo for

Passover. Of course, we will have to do it discretely not to provoke the anti-Semites." Then, they turned to Mama and said, "Aunt, do you know how to bake matzo? Everyone is counting on you." Mama was the only surviving Jewish mother in town and was revered for what she represented.

Mama mumbled, "Bake matzo? I don't know. I think I saw matzo being baked once. I think we can figure it out."

Only if one considered how isolated our tiny Jewish community was could one imagine the complexity of this undertaking. Ingredients had to be secretly gathered, and a cooperative baker had to be found. But resources were pooled, ingredients collected, and people shared what they knew about baking matzo. A cooperative baker was found.

The baking took place deep in the night. Mama, Max, and David left the room on tiptoes, like conspirators of a dark plot. To keep the traffic at a minimum, Fredka and I remained alone in the morose room with the moon shining in through the windowpanes. My heart ached with jealousy of the people allowed in the bakery and with fear of letting my protectors out of my sight.

"Go to sleep," we were instructed. But who could sleep on a night when matzo was being baked? On that night, every Jew in Działoszyce stayed wide awake, quivering with the satisfaction that comes with standing up for something you value, even at the risk of severe punishment.

The baking of matzo continued until bands of orange lights rose on the eastern rim of the sky, then the handful of matzo bakers tiptoed to their rooms.

The following day at sundown, we had our Seder in the room. We sat across from each other on our cots and took delight in the matzo. But so much was missing! It was like sitting in the front row in the theater and the curtain never rose.

Passover in our household before the war evolved like a grand theatrical production, starting with Fredka looking out the window, pointing to the trees in the courtyard garden, and crying out, "Look, look! Passover is almost here! I have proof. I see buds on the lilac tree. I can wear *skarpetki* (knee-highs) and my new dress!" Every year, at the faintest hint of Passover, Fredka began to argue with Mama to let her wear knee-highs and frilly spring dresses, even if the city shivered with cold.

Our streets bustled with holiday preparations, and a brightly smiling sun looked down upon us approvingly. Men came into courtyards carrying huge, steaming vats of water and calling out in Yiddish, *"Alles wird gekosherd!"* (Everything is made kosher!) Women rushed down to the courtyard with arms full of dishes. Prattling voices, clinking dishes, and clouds of steam rose above the sizzling vats.

The houses in our neighborhood were just as alive with activities. Mothers busily replaced everyday dishes with holiday porcelain, and polished everything for the occasion. Spicy aromas of *goose-griven* (similar to bacon) mingled with delicate, lemony fragrances of matzo-meal cakes and macaroons cooling on baking racks. Children could hardly contain themselves. We squirmed with anticipation of the first Seder evening.

On the day of the first Seder, mothers swept houses clean of the last crumbs of bread, set the tables, and completed the final touches. As the day progressed, you could feel a serenity descending on the neighborhood.

Just before dusk, Fredka, our parents, and I dressed in our holiday finest, left our house, and stepped into a reverently quiet street. We boarded a shiny, black *doroszka* (an upholstered horse-drawn carriage) and were carried through the twilight to Aunt Malka's house to celebrate.

Aunt Malka lived on Pavia Street with the Pawiak Prison at the far end of the street. I was frightened and curious about the people hidden away behind the tall prison wall like ghosts in a cemetery, but I liked visiting my aunt's house a short distance away.

Aunt Malka was married to Uncle Boris, a tall, dark, good-looking, and likeable man, noticeably younger than my aunt. It was an open family secret that Aunt Malka had a difficult time keeping my uncle to herself and had to deal with outside competition. When my two cousins, Dudek and Josek (much older than Fredka and I), were home, their house rang with clever conversation, laughter, and Dudek's beautiful singing. When they were out, the house was melancholy and quiet.

During Passover, their house glowed with joy. Smiling Aunt Malka and Uncle Boris moved in tandem to welcome the whole family and to keep everyone happy. Beautiful, vivacious Aunt Hannah arrived with my stiff and pedantic other Uncle Boris, and wonderful cousins Lolek and Moniek. Fredka and I curtsied and kissed their hands.

At sundown, everyone sat at the festive table. Uncle Boris took the traditional seat, propped up with a pillow at the head of the table. A silver goblet stood in front of him and a ring of wineglasses glistened in candlelight. When all were seated and the conversation quieted down, a shortened version of the traditional reading of the Haggadah proceeded.

Fredka and I, the youngest children at the table, eagerly read the customary four questions asking why this night is different from all other nights. The retelling of the Passover story followed. The adults often joked about the lengthy wait for the holiday dishes, but I looked forward to hearing the story of sadness and hope, of slavery and freedom, of cruelty and mercy, and of miracles.

A feast of holiday dishes followed amidst lively talk and laughter. We celebrated late into the night. Fredka and I beamed with pride to stay up late with the adults while most of the children in Poland were fast asleep.

The ride back home was most special. I leaned back on the cushioned doroszka and admired the fairy-tale images and sounds of the sleeping city. The tall buildings resembled paper cutouts under the starry sky, and the sharp clip-clop of hooves punctuated the silence. The darkness seemed enormous under flickering streetlights, but I felt safe sitting close to Mama and Tata.

As soon as the coachman reined the horse to a stop in front of our building, I jumped out of my seat and dashed for the gate to be first to claim a turn to ring the bell. Then I waited to hear the custodian's hacking cough and string of curses for being ordered out of bed to unlock the entrance at such an un-Godly hour.

As we stepped into the courtyard, I held my breath to hear the slam of the iron gate, and to hear the shower of echoes bounce off the sleeping courtyard walls. We walked softly to our house and laid ourselves to bed, resting in the glow of the Passover celebration. On the night of the first Seder, everything was different and exceptional. It remained a memory that I often recalled during dark times when my soul thrived only on dreams.

19 *Awakening*

Despite many harsh experiences, our stay in Działoszyce restored us. Our cousins and a small community of Jewish survivors took us in. Fredka and I were free to walk in the fields and meadows that rolled beyond the outskirts of the town. Our hearts found room to grow again. New people stepped into our lives, and life was returning in tiny sips!

Our appearance improved. Looking in the mirror, I saw a lean girl with a serious face, dressed in a plain skirt and blouse, and shoes. My once-hollow cheeks and skeletal body were rounding out. But every gain creates new needs. I was absolutely miserable because I did not have the money to buy a bra. Today, young women step out proudly without wearing one, but when I was a young girl in Działoszyce, young ladies were embarrassed about their bodies. My shame about not wearing a bra was so great that I often walked stiffly with minced steps in order to minimize the bounce of my breasts. To make matters more unbearable, David would tease me—as big brothers often do—"Oh, look at it bob like balloons!"

Fredka was beautiful again. Mama too lost her ghostly appearance, but sadness and unease still showed in the pinch of her brow. We had used clothes given to us by our cousins and friends. Mama, Fredka, and I never had money in Działoszyce and never entered a store.

I even had a best friend again, Estusia Turkof. She had lost her family and had survived alone on false Aryan papers. Her uncle, the only other surviving member of her family, managed to find her after the liberation. They came to live in Działoszyce, her uncle's hometown. Estusia was my age, petite, and graceful. A sprinkle of coppery freckles on her short nose almost matched the color of her honey-blond hair, and her wide blue eyes evoked trust. Estusia was capable of such lightness of heart and lifts of joy, in spite of the incredibly sad memories she carried locked inside her.

I often walked across the market square to visit with my best friend. We shut the door to her room, and hours passed unnoticed while we shared our stories and hopes. I still remember the bright yellow sun at her window and two big, black, round shadows of our heads on the wall behind us. "How will we ever find each other after we leave Działoszyce?" we worried. We knew we would soon have to leave, but we had no inkling where we would eventually live.

We tried to imagine ourselves in the future, but that baffled us. We had no role models. We did not know what the world was like beyond our recent experiences. Our war images were useless now.

Yet pictures spawned in our young minds; princes would find us on our unknown path; small, simple homes would rise on hilltops in friendly towns, doors would open to us, we would have lots of good food, and everyone would smile.

Sometimes we tossed away all serious thoughts, and we practiced popular dancing steps as we sang for accompaniment. Having a friend who shared the pain of loss, the magic of hope, and the power of imagination helped me find steps into the world of the living.

The Fields

Fredka and I had three other friends, all a little older and all boys. They had lived in Działoszyce before being sent to the concentration camps and knew the area well. Fredka, my best friend Estusia, and I depended on the three olive-skinned boys with smiling eyes to take us to solitary green fields at the outskirts of town, away from prejudice and hostility.

We never left the room to see our friends without first sticking our heads out the door to check that no one else was on the steps. Then, we tiptoed down the stairs past the doors that always remained closed tight. Sometimes a door would crack open and quickly slam shut till we were out of sight.

Occasionally, we encountered the woman with the immobile face and discrete blue eyes on the steps. She always looked away and drew close to the wall as she slipped past us. Even though she tried to ignore us and pinched her mouth into a tight line, I was not afraid to raise my eyes to search her face for a hint of kindness. When I ran into the sons with the ramrod backs and icy stares, I wanted to disappear.

To meet our friends, we had to cross the lively market square framed by a ring of houses with jagged roofs, wrought-iron balconies, and half-empty stores; and a sidewalk paved with large uneven rectangles.

All traffic in Działoszyce traversed the square. Even the shepherds led their flocks across the square on their way to pasture. Fredka and I enjoyed crossing the bustling place, despite our fears of being spotted by the neighborhood kids who liked to taunt us. We walked arm in arm for extra security, and relished the thrill of being in the midst of humanity. We tingled with the sheer adventure of moving with the stream of normal life.

One day Fredka and I suddenly ran into a flock of goats at the market. Frightened, we turned our backs and walked briskly away, hoping they would leave us alone. Instead, the goats pranced close behind us.

"Stop! Stand still!" People called out to us. But we were too frightened to listen and too embarrassed to make a spectacle of ourselves. So we whispered encouragements to each other, raised our heads in a nonchalant way, and speed walked across the square with the line of bleating goats hopping behind us, all eyes staring at us.

When we reached the edge of the square, we made a dash for an iron gate facing us and pushed it open. We slipped inside an empty courtyard and slammed the gate shut in front of the goats. We caught our breaths, collected our dignity and wit, glanced at one another and burst out laughing with immense relief. This was our first adventure since liberation—a small thrill, a little laughter, a little fear, but no true danger.

We learned later that goats will follow anyone in the lead. If we had been calm enough to pay attention to the people calling to us to stop, this ridiculous situation would have come to an immediate end.

The narrow, meandering streets became less populated and more serene as we drew closer to the outskirts of the town. The fewer people we encountered, the faster and more boldly we walked, and the lighter our hearts grew. When we met up with our friends in the countryside, the town with the hostile people slipped behind the horizon, and I felt like I was entering a universe drenched in colors. The trees swayed calmly and motioned acceptance. Time stopped. All was safe, good, and trusting, just as I remembered it to be before the war.

Fredka and I let go of each other's arms to run with our friends on gusts of wind. We chased each other on green fields shimmering with wildflowers. We ran into wide-open horizons and let our voices reach the heavens; our laughter flowed freely like released tears.

The fields were wholly ours. The boys found patches of wild berry bushes where they had once picked currants and gooseberries with their lost siblings and friends, and where the best groves of cherry trees stood. Of course, there was no fruit on the trees yet, but budding blossoms floated above branches and made one think that the slightest puff of air would carry them off. The boys took us to pine groves where the ground was covered with thick brown needles and the tops of the trees stretched up tall into the sky. All was peaceful and safe, for the moment.

When the sun began to touch the notched lines of trees, our friends, Fredka, and I turned our backs on the wide meadows and groves and began to walk toward the town. We stepped with a bounce and renewed hope till the bucolic world began to converge into narrow, populated streets and we became self-conscious again. Our friends departed, Fredka and I clasped hands for security, and continued our walk home.

In no time we had returned to "our" street, entered Max and David's house, tiptoed softly up the dim stairs, entered the room, and shut the door. Being inside the room, behind the closed door, always brought a small relief, a feeling of seclusion and a suggestion of safety, like finding a foothold on a cliff. The room was quiet in the soft twilight. It felt familiar, even cozy, thanks to Mama's ceaseless efforts.

Mama rarely left the room. She bustled restlessly, like a caged bird fluttering above a thimble of water. Mama flitted about the tiny room trying to bring order, harmony, and meaning to our limited existence. She polished the few things we owned over and over again. She constantly rearranged the few movable objects for the best possible effect. She shined the window till not a speck could be seen. She washed and rewashed the few square feet of floor.

Of course, she also fussed with the food and tried hard to make something out of almost nothing. Mama thought big. She would get excited when my cousins brought a few eggs or a piece of meat. Actually, we all shared the excitement, but she was the only one who dreamed of what she could do with it to bring joy to Max, David, Fredka, and me. She would hold up each ingredient and make promises: "Oh, wait and you will see what I will make with it! It will be *comme il faut*," her favorite expression for very special.

When Mama ran out of things to do, she leaned her elbows on the windowsill and looked into the distance. She watched all that moved and swayed—people, clouds, creeping shadows, changing lights—and she dreamed. She loved the beauty and power of nature, and saw herself personified in natural things. I think the views from the window, and the unseen beyond the horizon, gave Mama hope—the kind of hope one gets from looking at the mailbox and dreaming of finding a special letter.

When Mama spotted Fredka and me returning from our outings, she rushed to meet us at the door. "Did you meet your friends? Where did you go? Oh, was it fun?" she would ask, relishing the thought that Fredka and I found safe places to frolic with friends.

After listening to our adventures, she would immediately show us what she had accomplished and wait to hear our praise. Unfortunately, we were too young and too self-absorbed to fully appreciate her loneliness and her need to be recognized for her efforts and love. The more she sought our praise, the harder it was to give it. The more she lived through us, the less comfortable we felt. We wished that Mama herself would reach out more to taste the flavors of freedom.

A minor incident has been bothering me all these years. It was an encounter that Max had with the silent woman who occupied his house. As Max was climbing up the steps one rainy day, he met her walking toward him carrying an umbrella—his mother's umbrella. He stopped and addressed the woman, "Excuse me, I recognize that this is my mother's umbrella. I do not like to trouble you, but it would mean a great deal to me to have it. I have nothing of my mother. I promise I will not ask for anything else, just this one remembrance."

The woman responded politely, "I will ask my sons if I can let you have it."

Pale with emotion, Max walked into the room and told us what had happened. A considerable time elapsed. Max passed the woman on the steps many times. Each time he looked at her hoping to hear her say, "Here is your mother's umbrella." But each time the woman slipped by him, she looked away and said nothing.

Max decided to remind her of her promise. The woman looked at him blankly and said, "Umbrella, what umbrella? I don't know what you are talking about."

20 *The Escape*

From the start we knew that our stay in Działoszyce would be limited. This was made especially clear after Max enquired at the district court about the deed to their house. Violent threats on his life followed immediately. A getaway had to be planned and carried out in utmost secrecy—an incredible challenge. My cousins had to figure out a way to remove the valuables still hidden throughout their house. They had to find a way to get out of the house and out of town without being stopped, find a place to escape to, and a way to get there. An Israel was dearly needed when our days in Działoszyce were done and we had no place to turn.

When our "hosts" left the house, Max and David browsed the stairways and corners to locate their hidden treasures, but they never ventured inside the rooms the people occupied. When they came back from these explorations, they told us that the house had been carefully ransacked and many items had been removed, but not all. Some things remained hidden and recoverable. Ironically, the major part lay hidden in the open-beamed attic, behind the trapdoor against which my cousins' bed leaned. I am sure that this helped them sleep a little better at night.

Anyone who looked at the nails and hooks that held up the knickknacks their mother had carefully selected saw only ordinary black nails bought in the hardware store. Only Max knew better. His father and he had shaped them from gold. They were so masterfully replicated that a person with the most discerning eye could not distinguish them from ordinary nails. I do not know what items my cousins collected during their explorations, or where they kept them. I remember them saying, "For the time being, it is best to leave most things where they are. Our room is not safe. The two sons could find them."

Sometimes, Max and David took clandestine trips out of town to make arrangements for our escape. They always departed before dawn, before the townspeople were up to spot them heading for the train station. They left without suitcases to avoid suspicion and stayed away only for a day or two.

When Max and David were gone, the three of us stayed in the room to guard their possessions and to make enough clamor to leave the impression that my cousins were home.

To protect us, my cousins told us very little about their getaway plans. They reassured us that our destination was a distant town where Max had worked before the outbreak of war, "far enough not to be pursued."

They cautioned, "We cannot tell you exactly when we will attempt our escape, but you have to be prepared to clear out of here fast. You will take only the things we will give you and hide them under your clothes or carry them discretely. We will have to sneak out during the night without making the slightest sound. If we are caught, that will be the end for us all."

When the crucial day arrived, Max and David announced, "We will leave tonight, near midnight when the whole town will be fast asleep. Till then, we must stay calm and maintain our old routine. Heaven help us if we raise the suspicion of the people in the house."

That evening, we ate our supper at the customary time. At the usual bedtime, we stretched out on the two cots fully dressed and listened to our pounding hearts. We stared into the dark emptiness and waited for it to grow even darker to give a better cover for our escape. We listened to the silence and waited until all we could hear was our own breathing.

When the town was so silent that we could hear the dogs barking in the next village, we rose from our beds, one at a time, took our assigned parcels, and tiptoed out of the room; we went down the stairs and past the doors where the house usurpers slept, opened the front door, and slipped into the deserted, moonlit street. David was first to leave, then the three of us followed, one at a time. Max was the last to slip out of the house.

We moved like shadows clinging to walls. Not to raise suspicion, we walked separately, a short distance from each other, and looked straight ahead. We hoped not to be noticed by insomniacs staring out of windows, or encounter lone drunks, or sleepwalkers. We were even afraid to be seen by the moon that seemed to roll down the rooftops and follow us. We walked in silence till we reached the train station. We stood on the platform and listened to the tracks for the thump of an oncoming train.

After a short wait, a train whistle broke the silence, the ground began to throb, and a bright headlight sped toward us. The engine puffed past us, then the train stopped, and a door opened. At long last!

We boarded, found seats, and David handed our tickets to the conductor. There was hardly anyone on the train to notice us. We sat and watched the train carry us through darkness into a rising new day and toward another strange town. Max and David had planned in advance every detailed step of this complicated escape. They had planned the time to leave. They knew the train schedule and bought the tickets ahead of time. They had a safe place waiting for us in Chorzów, a city in southern Poland, 120 kilometers west of Działoszyce. Chorzów had little meaning to me. All I knew was that we were getting away from immediate danger. It was not clear what to expect, but I hoped that we were getting nearer to salvation.

I think of our escape from Działoszyce both with triumph for having fooled fate, and with sadness for the less fortunate we had left behind. News of a pogrom in the town—that same dawn, just hours after we had left—reached us later. Jews were beaten and a few were killed. It is frightening to think how narrowly we had escaped. Max and David would have been the first to be robbed and killed by the two sons who surely were chief participants. What would they have done with the three of us? I am glad we were not doomed to find out.

Our friends who had survived the pogrom left their native town as soon as they could. Max and David managed to stay in touch with them, even as they moved from place to place till they found permanent homes. My contact with the friends I had made ended the night we fled. Occasionally, Max and David shared a bit of news about one or another. But I can barely remember their faces, except for my best friend Estusia and two other people.

The two people were a pair of young lovers, Marysia and her betrothed. The name of her betrothed left me long ago. Marysia was the one I admired. The two fell in love during the German occupation when they were both at the peak of health. Even though their love surmounted the most extreme adversities, it had little chance for joy. During the *akcja* (deportation raid), when Jews were driven out of their homes and carried away by the Germans, the two lovers ran for their lives and found cover in the countryside. Marysia's betrothed fell ill. To see a doctor was out of the question. It would give them away immediately. Only Jewish males were circumcised in Poland. As a result, his health continued to deteriorate, while Marysia remained robust, in spite of all her misfortunes. After the war, they returned to their hometown, Działoszyce, and found that no one else in their families had survived.

Marysia, about nineteen years old, with a doll-like face—big smiling eyes, sparkling white teeth, and thick, dark braids hanging down to her tiny waist—was the picture of health. She was small, vivacious, and beautiful.

Her betrothed was the opposite. He was bedridden and as dour as Marysia was cheerful. His body was wasted, his face was pale as death, and his eyes glowed with feverish despair. I rarely saw him in a good mood when I came to visit Marysia. He often chastised her, "Go away and leave me alone! I do not need your love. Go and save yourself! I am dead anyway. I don't want to be kept alive by you. I do not need you to prolong my suffering! Go away. Leave me alone!"

But Marysia never gave up. She tried to assure him that he was definitely getting better. She would turn to me and say, "He is so handsome! Look, he is getting better each day. Tell him. Isn't it so?" She brought milk, eggs, butter, and all kinds of nourishing foods to his bed and promised him that their love would overcome this "temporary" setback. "Didn't we survive the war?"

I wondered, *How could her love endure such punishment?*

I know that if there were the least chance of finding a safe place for her betrothed and herself anywhere on this planet, Marysia would have found it. What remains in the ruins of my memories is my admiration of Marysia's inexhaustible love, and the question, did they find a secure place to live?

21 *Another Strange Town*

H ow much time had passed from when we were liberated from the concentration camp in Częstochowa till we were on the train to our new destination, Chorzów? We were liberated in mid-January 1945. When we arrived in Działoszyce, the world was still under a crust of ice. Passover and spring followed soon and the fields miraculously turned green. We probably had arrived in Działoszyce in mid-March, approximately two months after liberation. When we left Działoszyce, it was summer. The sunflowers were showing their perfectly round faces atop their tall stalks, the air was warm, and the trees at the fringes of fields were dark and heavy with growth. It must have been late June 1945, five months after liberation.

We were again running from persecutors. Nevertheless, I took heart knowing that we had successfully crossed icy fields to find Max and David, and that we had escaped from the hooligans in Działoszyce. My inner voice told me, *Take nothing for granted, not even the rising sun.* I carried inside me the gifts I had recovered during the months in Działoszyce: laughter with friends and blissful moments in meadows where I had heard my own voice make the sky take note of me. In the concentration camps my screams had no sound, my fists and legs were held in check. There I wondered, *Where are the eyes and hearts of mankind and God? If they cannot be reached, how can I hope?*

* * *

Afraid to be recognized as Jews, we sat silently in a train compartment, our heads turned to the window. The four people whose knees were touching mine were my whole world. I know that my heart froze at the thought of how completely alone I would be without them.

The train dashed through country scenes as familiar to me as the faces of childhood friends. Running away from the land that had once been home left me feeling suspended between catastrophe and hope. I felt an emptiness of being without a country and fearful of our mysterious destination.

We got off in Chorzów and followed my cousins through a crowded train station into a modern city. The buildings were imposing, the traffic heavy, and the pedestrians indifferent. There was security in our anonymity, but I felt small and insignificant. My cousins navigated through a maze of streets with absolute confidence.

The big surprise came when Max and David stopped in front of a dignified three-story building on an elegant street in the center of town. They lowered their luggage to the sidewalk and pointed, "See this jewelry store with the large display widows? We are part owners. See the row of tall windows above the store? We have rooms in this apartment. This is where all of us will stay."

Mama, Fredka, and I were mystified. "What led you to this place? How did you manage to arrange this miracle?"

Max and David chose Chorzów for our escape because it was the only other town Max was familiar with. He had worked there before the war. Furthermore, it was closer to Germany. My cousins' plan was to cross the border and work our way to the American sector in Germany. Going to America, where Mama's siblings and their families lived, was our ultimate hope.

During their many secret absences from Działoszyce, Max and David had negotiated with two old friends: Mr. Rogal, Max's loyal Christian prewar friend from Działoszyce, and Walter, also a prewar acquaintance in Chorzów. The arrangements were an attempt to solve mutual problems, and the process was as bizarre as the times.

Chorzów was originally a German village, called Königshüte. After World War I, Chorzów passed from Germany to Poland. When Germany invaded Poland, Chorzów became a German city again. After the Russian liberation, Chorzów passed back to Poland. The German-speaking majority was expelled, and the town was resettled with Poles.

Walter was German—a persona non grata at that time—and went into hiding. He may have had other reasons for hiding from the new regime. We never found out if this was so. On the other hand, his wife, a Russian from Georgia, Stalin's birthplace, was a welcome citizen. However, she knew nothing about running their jewelry store. Therefore, Walter formed a partnership with Max, David, and Mr. Rogal, and the store was opened. Max and David ran the store, and Mr. Rogal, a Christian, provided legitimacy to the enterprise. Walter was a silent partner.

I never met Walter. I learned his name from his parrot. I am sure that Max and David never saw Walter, even while they were negotiating their partnership. The terms were discussed with his wife. Every time a decision had to be made, she said that she needed time to think and left the house. She always returned with a firm mind. Her husband's name or existence was never brought up.

The five of us lived with Walter's wife and the childless couple's parrot, which was as near human as you could possibly imagine. Their elegant apartment was located directly above the store and connected by a spiral staircase. Mama, Fredka, and I shared one bedroom with one bed, and Max and David shared another bedroom.

Walter's wife was tall, buxom, olive-skinned, and regal looking. Her dark eyes sparkled even when they were sad. She often left the house and stayed away long hours. When she came back, her steps were heavy and her face tight with melancholy. We believed that she was visiting with her husband.

I saw Walter's wife mostly in the kitchen when she and Mama cooked. The two women tasted each other's creations, talking guardedly about all sorts of generalities. Sometimes they burst into belly laughs about an observation they shared. Their comradeship made the air glow. They proved to me that spontaneous affection can break cultural barriers if given the chance. However, my pleasure was not free of anger. I resented the divide that set the two native Russian women apart from the very instant they were born. My bright and poetic mother never had the opportunities that were open to the other woman.

The living room was the most cheerful place in the house. It had tall windows with a splendid view of the main street. But the family parrot that held court in that room was the main attraction. Her tall cage stood near the door where she could greet all entrants and entertain them with a repertoire of cute antics.

The parrot woke up at sunrise and shouted her head off. "Walter! Walter! Come here, Walter! Walter!" The bird missed Walter who used to play with her as soon as he rose. When the calls were not answered, she called louder, cried, and moaned just like a human. Mama was always the first one to jump out of bed and hurry into the living room to console the parrot. At first, the bird turned her back and pretended to ignore Mama. Then, slowly, the parrot inched closer on the bar and leaned her head near Mama's face. Before you knew it, the two carried on like old friends. The parrot charmed Mama with her performances, and Mama delighted the bird with attention and approval. And, as she did with everyone she cared about, Mama brought her favorite treats. Sadly, that bird was Mama's only real friend in Chorzów.

Chorzów, a cosmopolitan city with streets that ran on forever, was much different from the small, out-of-the-way, rural Działoszyce. The buildings were imposing, and the streams of pedestrians walked with detached faces. I could not read their hearts as quickly as in Działoszyce, where people immediately recognized us as outsiders. We felt safer in our anonymity. We did not matter or exist to this town. We did not attract the sharp barbs of open prejudice as in Działoszyce. Still, we did not belong.

Our apartment, the store, and the scenes I watched from our windows represented nearly my entire universe. Besides Mr. Rogal and Walter's wife, the only people the three of us interacted with were those who dropped into the house or the store and left without a trace. Even that little bit was welcomed, because people cannot do without the company of people. Everyone deserves the pleasure of recognition.

Sometimes Fredka and I went on long walks, but they were without purpose or destination. We knew no one. There was no Jewish community to warm us. On a very few occasions, my cousins invited several business acquaintances to the house for *kolacja* (the evening meal). Sitting with guests around the table, looking at polite faces that expressed interest, validated me. I was proud of Max who tossed out ideas and kept the conversations interesting, and Mama who spiced the dialogue with poignant and strong comments. I enjoyed the modest but appetizingly prepared platters of cold cuts, cheese dishes, and salads that sat on the table.

There were no fields to run to in Chorzów. I often sat at the window and watched the passing stream of life, much as one looks at fish in an aquarium. I sat for hours, elbows resting on the wide parapet, chin cupped in my hands. My mind was a blank, just registering muffled bursts of laughter, oscillating blips of human voices, sounds of traffic, and horn-beeps filtering through the membrane of the windowpane.

People who passed my window interested me, particularly young people, and especially young couples who walked hand in hand and smiling into each other's eyes. I observed carefully what they wore, how they walked, how they tossed their heads flirtatiously, or flipped their gloves with studied elegance. They moved past my window like movie stars on a screen. I could hardly believe that I would ever be part of their world.

Sometimes I imagined, *What if I met a young man who could not live without me and I loved him? I would leave Mama and Fredka to be with my love and be happy ever after.* The punishing guilt of even thinking of deserting my mother and sister was as agonizing as the daydreams were sweet.

The scenes in front of my window changed as the sun crossed the sky and the shadows of buildings grew longer. When twilight began to fall, lovers parted and rushed away alone into the blue summer evening. People walked with hurried steps, clutching small packages of produce for evening meals, racing to beat the curfew.

At night, the empty streets were bathed in yellow streetlights and belonged only to armed Russian "protectors" who marched in small clusters, guns ready to make sure that all civilians were behind closed doors. The sounds and scenes of night were sporadic pounding military boots, clanging rifles, an occasional patter of running feet, and a shadow of a figure clinging to a wall or ducking in a dark doorway.

One night we heard a skirmish brewing right below our windows. Quickly, we turned off all lights and stooped under the windowsills, letting only our foreheads and eyes rise above the surface. With drumming hearts we sat curled up in darkness and watched a scene being acted out one tier below us. It was suited for the theater of the absurd.

Several armed Russian soldiers ran toward our building and shouted, "*Stoy!* [Halt], or we will shoot! Stoy!" A young man darted out from the shadow of a doorway and landed in the blocking arms of the soldiers who encircled him. An altercation followed.

The soldiers bellowed, "You don't appreciate our sacrifices to liberate you! We risked our lives; we left our homeland, our mothers, wives, and children to protect Poland!"

The young man said, "Thank you, but now you should go back home to your families who need you. We will take care of ourselves."

The soldiers felt offended. Voices rose and suddenly a shot was fired, the young man fell to the hard pavement, and a circle of blood formed below one leg. At that point we left the windows and waited for the echoes of war to stop. When we looked again, the scene was once more silent and empty.

Max and David were the unquestioned leaders of our family and made all important decisions. The three of us stayed in the background. Both brothers were resourceful and good businessmen, but Max, the older and more experienced of the two, was the head. In addition to being a skilled and talented jeweler, he had a circle of old acquaintances in town. He was well read, worldly, and controlling.

Mama too had a strong influence on us. She focused all her energy and love on looking after our needs, and gave a unique tone to the family. She enlivened and lifted our spirits with stimulating conversations about God, human nature, her philosophy of life, or anything that moved her at the moment. Max also liked to expound on ideas to make us think. The discussions brought relief from our nagging concerns, kept our ideals alive, and opened our minds to the possible, even if not probable.

Mama imbued us with courage. When Fredka and I despaired about our precarious existence, being beholden and totally dependent on our cousins, Mama would pull herself up to her full four feet and ten inches, and say forcefully, "You must not feel that way. You must feel yourselves worthy. We need Max and David, but they also need us. We look after their properties when they go out of town and we keep the house comfortable for them. We are family." Of course, they could have gotten along without us much more easily than we could survive without them. But what Mama said rang true and gave us heart.

The Store

Spacious dimensions gave the store an air of elegance in spite of dim lighting and sparse merchandise. A glass display counter curved along three walls and intersected at interesting angles. Two wide display windows with a few gold items caught the attention of passersby. The most beautiful pieces were the rings Max designed and crafted.

A wide archway in the main store opened to a smaller room with a third display window. This was the watchmaker's section and it belonged to Mr. Rogal. When I felt lonely for company, I liked to visit him. Mr. Rogal always greeted me with a wink that made me feel welcome and safe. His blue eyes smiled and his voice was always gentle and inviting, never resenting my interruptions. As I sat near him watching his busy fingers and listening to the familiar soft clangs of tools placed on a workbench, I felt the past touching me. Mr. Rogal and I exchanged few words. That was enough. His kindness filled a tiny corner in a vast void. I came to his room to feel Tata.

Max appreciated Fredka's poise and trained her to work in the store as a sales person. Fredka took this assignment very seriously. She sat upright on a stool behind the center of the counter directly opposite the door, with legs crossed and hands folded in her lap. Each time she saw a shadow nearing the store, she rose gracefully, ready to serve a customer. Few customers came into the store, and Fredka had little to do.

I missed Fredka's company. Fredka allowed me to sit on the top step of the spiral stairwell where I could quickly get out of sight if a customer entered. The stairwell connected the store to the apartment. During quiet moments, we invented games and giggled senselessly in spite of all our fears and worries.

Once, a swarm of Gypsies sashayed into the store. Smiling chattering faces, swinging hips in swirling skirts invaded the place. Max, David, Mr. Rogal, Mama, Fredka, and I followed the animated bunch to forestall a mishap. A beautiful young Gypsy stepped up to me. She took hold of my hand, held it gently and looked at it with the most heartfelt admiration. She said, "What lovely hands you have. Just look how gracefully shaped they are and so small, so beautiful!" I watched her, greatly surprised and pleased that there was something about me that was noteworthy. I knew that it was insincere, but the cheerful flattery from the pretty young Gypsy felt good, and I hoped that maybe she might be telling the truth. I almost felt sorry to see her leave. When the Gypsies entered the store, I feared they might cause damage. Instead, a lovely Gypsy left me with something wonderful and lasting.

Russian soldiers dropped in from time to time and most left without causing any commotion. There was one exception. Two soldiers swaggered into the store. They said they were shopping for bracelets. They pointed to one bracelet underneath the glass case and asked Fredka to place it on the counter. They examined it, and then asked to see a couple other bracelets. They shuffled the items around until one of the three bracelets disappeared in front of Fredka's eyes. She pointed to the spot and asked, "Where is the bracelet that was right here?" The soldiers puffed themselves up in indignation, fingered the triggers of their machine guns, and demanded, "What? Are you accusing us, the saviors of your country, of theft?"

Fredka stammered, "No, no. Of course not! I am not accusing, but, but where is the bracelet that was just here?" Max intervened immediately. He sent Fredka away and made an attempt to soothe the soldiers while appealing to them to help him find the lost item. It did not take long for Max to realize that the best he could do was to forget the loss and get rid of the soldiers before more serious damage followed. The soldiers let themselves be calmed, forgave the insult, and left well satisfied. We remained shaken.

Another Russian soldier with a handsome dark face came into the store repeatedly. He held his tall frame straight and walked silently around the store looking at displays, and then left without buying anything. Each time he returned, he tarried a bit longer, glancing at us furtively with his jet-black eyes as if trying to read our faces. We sensed in him a familiar call for help, for someone to trust. Max suggested that we all leave him alone with the soldier the next time the soldier came. Max soon learned that the soldier was Jewish and was not happy in Russia where he could not practice his faith. He wanted to escape and make his way to Palestine. He had a plan, but needed a place to change into civilian clothes, get rid of his gun and uniform, and leave at once to prevent danger to us. He said that he would understand if Max refused to help.

Max identified with the man's yearning for a place free of hatred of Jews. As he often did, without consideration of his own well-being, Max agreed to help. The soldier came into the store one more time and then disappeared. We hoped he would realize his dream.

Fredka's First Haircut

One bright day, Fredka sat in front of the mirror combing her hair. She ran the comb this way and that way, trying out different hairstyles. I am sure she enjoyed seeing the sun catch the gold highlights in her hair. She was struck by an idea. "I want to cut my hair!" she declared as she turned to face me. She described how great it would look and in-formed me that I would have to cut her hair because she had no other choice. We still had absolutely no money. We borrowed an old pair of scissors from Walter's wife. Fredka wrapped a towel around her shoulders, stared into the mirror and watched every motion I made. She cautioned me that I must pay close attention to her instructions since I had zero understanding of fashion. When I reminded her that it could not be all that serious—after all, hair grows—she raised her voice in alarm, "I knew you would not understand! I want it just right. Don't you dare to cut it too short!"

I truly tried my best. I liked to please my sister. I was aware of how much she had changed since her hair had grown back, and I took great pride in her attractiveness. I was as careful about following her directions as I was ignorant about how to achieve the best results. Her hair was thick and wavy, and it bounced down to her neck in uneven spirals. We did not know that wetting her hair would have made it easier to cut in an even line. I snipped here and there. I cut it again to get it even, until Fredka declared that I had cut her hair way too short and I had ruined her life. "Look what you have done to me! I look terrible! I cannot step out of the house this way! Why didn't you do as I told you?" She chased me through the house until Mama intervened. Eventually, Fredka sat down in a corner and cried a flood of tears. We were children again.

22 *Time to Leave Again*

The graying days of approaching fall deepened our isolation and loneliness. Max and David concluded that it was time to leave and find a friendlier country before winter arrived. There was one last thing we had to do before we left Poland forever. Mama pleaded, "We must go to Warsaw to make sure that we did not miss any survivors who might be looking for us, and to find out if we can recover any of the gold and jewelry we had buried in our bunker." Among the buried valuables were documents of a partnership in a sizable tract of land and a brick-making factory in Baniochy, a village near Warsaw.

Not all of us could go. Travel was still difficult, finding a place to stay in shattered Warsaw would be a problem, and someone had to remain to look after the store. It was decided that Fredka and Max would go: Max, because he was the elder brother and had the most experience in dealing with officialdom, and Fredka, because Mama turned to her and spoke with the voice of a true believer: "It would be useless for me to go. I am nothing. You must go. You will have a greater chance of breaking through bureaucracy. You are smart and beautiful. No one will turn you down."

Mama was pulling further away from outside confrontations. She remained as vigilant as ever in determining what had to be done to protect us, but she pushed us to carry out her ideas. She especially counted on Fredka's abilities and charm to make up for her own imagined shortcomings as she had once counted on Tata. That task weighed heavily on Fredka, but she never failed to meet Mama's expectations.

I, the younger and less diplomatic child, was not even considered for that trip, though I wished to go. I longed to see Warsaw one final time, even if it meant to look at the ashes of what was once my paradise and later my hell. I wanted to go to remember, as one goes to a cemetery.

Fredka and Max never found a trace of Warsaw. They told us that Warsaw was completely razed. Not a single habitable building survived the Warsaw Ghetto uprising of 1943 and the Aryan uprising of 1944. They walked on mounds of rubble that stretched as far as their eyes could see. Sharp angles of charred walls, propped up by piles of wreckage, gashed the desolate landscape. Heaps of broken brick and piping protruded from the ground here and there, like grotesque weeds. Warsaw was a cemetery.

Fredka and Max followed a maze of posted street signs to lead them to our street, Nowolipki Street. They said that the signs protruded from the destruction like grave markings. Fredka recognized the lone church spire precariously balanced atop the ruins of the church that once stood across the street from our house. It was the single identifiable fragment of architecture in this bleak landscape.

Stray dogs roamed the gloomy terrain and scratched in the rubble. Their barks broke the sepulchral quiet and scared Fredka. She wondered, "What are the dogs finding there?" She told me she was afraid that they were digging up the bones of our neighbors.

Fredka and Max returned with charred dust in their hair. Saddened and defeated, they shared with us the grim details of their experience. I had hoped, I had fantasized, to hear Fredka and Max tell us that something had escaped the cataclysm, something to return to, a few places to look for surviving family members and friends. Nothing was left.

Eventually, Warsaw was faithfully rebuilt, according to the original plans. "Warsaw is again exactly as it once was," people say to cheer me. I can imagine that if you had left Warsaw before 1939 and returned after the war, after reconstruction, you might say to yourself, "Same as it was." You would stroll in the same *Stare Miasto* (Old Town) and beautiful Łazienki Park. As before, if you were lucky to arrive at the park in the right season, you could sit on a bench among flowers and shrubbery, charmingly arranged in the French style, and listen to piano music floating from the tall windows of Chopin's palace. "Times have changed, but the city is the same," you would think.

But I know that this is not the same Warsaw. I would say, "You are standing on the ground under which the real Warsaw is buried, and lives that never reached their promise are buried with it. The real Warsaw is no more."

We decided to make preparations to leave our native land as soon as we could, and aim for the American Sector in Germany. Escaping the Iron Curtain would give us the opportunity to locate Mama's two sisters and brother in New York—if they were still alive.

The first step, leaving Poland, should have been easy. Seemingly, all we had to do was to apply for visas, cross the border to Czechoslovakia—only seventy kilometers away—and continue on to Western Germany. But exiting Poland was not at all simple then—ironically, not even for Jews who were unwanted. Bureaucracy insisted on passports, birth certificates, and an "acceptable" reason for leaving. We had none of the above. The only option left was the black market, the standard way of conducting business during the stormy times of war and postwar.

Fortunately for us, Max and David were more adaptable to the new order than the three of us. One ordinary, dull autumn day they came home and informed us, "We are now Austrian citizens, born in Innsbruck, and we are on our way to return to our homeland. We will soon have documents to prove that." They cautioned, "The names on your new documents are spelled in German, of course. Study it carefully and be mindful to sign your names correctly—just as it is printed on your new documents."

Shortly after this announcement, we left Chorzów and Poland forever. Our departure was as empty as our postwar existence in the only country we knew, and once loved, as our own. No tears were shed; no one lingered at the doorway looking with longing until we vanished into the distance. We carried what our cousins told us to carry, said good-bye to the parrot, and shook hands and hugged the two people we knew, Mr. Rogal and Walter's wife. We left them at the threshold of the apartment. Their eyes followed us sadly for the short distance to the bottom of the stairs, and we were gone. I left no friends behind and carried away nothing to hold close to my heart, except gratitude that we were no longer alone, cold, or hungry. In the shambles of my memories, Chorzów remains a time of waiting, waiting, while time fell like heavy drops of water from a leaky faucet. Mostly, I watched life passing by our windows and daydreamed. Yet, a degree of healing took place under the weight of loneliness. The passive existence in Chorzów gave us pause, a brief downtime after so many upheavals and wounds of war. It was much like the stupor of staring at a hospital ceiling while painful cuts mend.

With parcels dangling from our arms, we marched down to the train station to board yet another train to bring us closer to the Czech border, the shortest and fastest way to sneak out of Poland. I walked the last stretch of my homeland streets with the bitter taste of an outcast. I felt as if the sky were pulling away, abandoning me—as it always did when the world stopped being safe. The people striding past me reflected no common humanity. The real world was hiding from me.

We had no inkling of where we would stay once we crossed the border or how we would progress from there to West Germany. We hoped to blend in unnoticed among the German refugees flooding out of the eastern sector, and to rely on what we could learn on the way, plotting our progress from place to place.

To allay my fears, I conjured up pictures of aunts and uncles in faraway America who long ago wrote letters to us. I tried to imagine a place where concentration camps had never been heard of and where all children had a right to live. Above all, I reassured myself, *We are not alone. Max and David are with us. They have money and they are clever. They will protect us from hunger and will lead us to a brighter place.*

Katowice and Beyond

The first train took us to Katowice, about twenty kilometers away, to pick up our forged Austrian birth certificates and spend one night at the procurer's house.

On our arrival, Max and David rushed us though meandering streets; we got on and off crowded streetcars, feeling pressed to reach the smuggler's house without delay or complications. Still, I remember greedily snapping quick glances at the beautiful old city and imagining my aunt, uncle, and cousins who once lived there.

The overnight stay at the smuggler's house was a relief. Our host, a smart, friendly, vivacious young woman, entertained us in her cozy living room, talking with us late into the night. In her cheerful company, the dark city outside her windows seemed more remote, and thoughts of tomorrow less worrisome. She told us not to be afraid of border crossings: "Every day hoards of people cross into Czechoslovakia and from there to the American sector in Germany."

She encouraged us not to fret about the false certificates: "They are good. No one will know the difference." She instructed, "Just remember, say as little as possible. Stick to one single answer: you are going home to Austria."

"But we do not speak German. Won't that give us away?" we asked.

"No, no!" she waved away our concern. "No one will pay attention to you. The people you meet will have their own worries to think about."

* * *

It is strange how certain small occurrences stay with us forever because they betray something about ourselves. That evening, our hostess complained that she felt ashamed because of her flat chest. Mama responded that all her life she was embarrassed for the opposite reason. For those few seconds of conversation, time stopped and triggered in me a veiled fear that was not about hunger or the struggle for survival. I clasped my chest and prayed to be spared the fate of both women and to be a beautiful girl with perfect breasts.

The rest of the trip to the Czech border is now a blur of changing trains, towns and villages galloping backwards from train windows, and meeting uprooted people. Many Germans, expelled from Poland, sat on the trains with us. I thought with disbelief, *The masters of the universe are homeless now too.* We looked at each other, all of us dealing with painful memories and tormented feelings, not knowing what to say. In every face I saw trapped memories of war, guarded by a smile, shrouded in a frown.

At the Czech border, about sixty kilometers west of Katowice, the train came to an abrupt halt. We looked out the windows and saw armed soldiers posted at the border crossing. In an instant, they entered our car and hollered orders, "All passengers off the train and line up for a border search!"

I wondered, *Will they let us cross, or will they turn us back with our forged papers?*

The line of intimidated refugees shuffled past the checkpoint with stony, expressionless faces. The guards took their time looking at passports, searching bodies and parcels.

When my turn came, I stepped up to a guard. His flushed face and lecherous smile made me feel uneasy. Mama had passed the check and was waiting a short distance ahead. The guard's hand slipped under my skirt and his fingers moved up my thigh. "Stand still and nothing will happen," he commanded in a hoarse whisper while his fingers were groping. I stood frozen; death was touching me. Just at that moment Mama looked back and caught the sight of my panicked face. With lightning speed she barked at the soldier, "What are you doing?!" The brute at once let me pass.

Why had I remained rooted to the spot? Why did I not scream? I asked myself accusingly. *Mama did. I am no longer in a concentration camp*, I reminded myself.

A few more strides and we were on Czech soil. The guards treated us civilly, did not search us, asked few questions, and answered all inquiries with friendliness. Giddiness swept through the crowd. Faces relaxed and tongues loosened, and everyone babbled about their border crossing experience. The five of us looked at each other with renewed courage for the next step into the unknown.

We boarded another train and sped away. Our destination: Prague, the capital of Czechoslovakia, about 320 kilometers from the Polish border. From the window I watched the Polish soil pull away behind the caboose, converge into a thin dot, and vanish behind the horizon. Along with obvious relief that we had escaped safely out of Poland, I felt deep loss knowing that I might never again see the places where I first opened my eyes to love and beauty, nor ever return to resurrect memories that gave me strength to endure and hope.

I turned my head to the front of the train, toward the future, looking ahead with curiosity. The window framed new scenes that slipped swiftly out of sight. The world, fluid and unpredictable, brought fear and hope. Somewhere, beyond the new horizon, was home. But where?

People from all parts of Eastern Europe got on and off that train. Concentration camp survivors greeted one other like lost friends, shared rumors and observations, and discussed prospects. We communicated in familiar languages: Polish, Yiddish, German, and Russian. But Yiddish, the language that grew out of medieval High German with added vocabulary borrowed from numerous languages as Jews moved to other lands, was the most useful. All the while, we kept our eyes glued to the windows, anxious to reach Prague, the jump-off point to our future.

When I noticed a vast number of passengers sprinting from their seats and collecting their bundles, I knew that the train was pulling into the capital. We too jumped to attention and cautioned each other, "This is it, Prague! Stay alert and stay together."

23 *Prague*

The train slowed, breathed long, heavy puffs, let out its last huff of steam, and stopped. We pulled into a wide platform lined with tracks and teeming with passengers. Hurriedly, we collected our few belongings, got off the train, and paused in the middle of a rushing crowd to get the feel of our new surroundings. We looked at the passing faces the way children do when trying to discern the trustworthiness of strangers. "People look friendly!" we said hopefully as we observed cordial eyes. We listened attentively to fragments of conversations; it did not take long for us to recognize familiar Slavic roots in the language.

We followed the crowd out of the station and stepped into the center of Prague. We felt utterly lost. We stood in silence. Our eyes circled tall buildings, centuries-old domes, and steeples. We stared into the brisk traffic and found no hint of where to go in this city where we knew no one and did not speak the language. We each found courage somewhere within ourselves, and someone, most probably one of my cousins, said, "Let's go!"

Walking through the city, we talked to people, used bits of information we had picked up on the way, and landed at the door of a gray building with a sign: "KARITAS," the Czech acronym for the YMCA. We walked up a flight of stairs, and entered an airy dormitory room with long rows of neatly made beds lined against two opposite walls.

I felt comforted by the friendly atmosphere in the room. People sat on edges of tidy beds and carried on conversations in many languages. Others moved busily around, coming and going. The tone was civil and the faces of the people reflected a wide range of nationalities. Some people had recently been driven out of their homes by the changing of regimes, some were Jews who had come out of hiding, and others were concentration camp survivors. Recent history could be read in their gaunt figures and the shadows in their eyes. Many faces were veiled in secrecy.

Our entry did not cause much stir, nor did it require explanations. Faces turned to us with polite acknowledgment and mild curiosity. Someone walked up to greet us and show us five beds near each other. The beds were covered with fresh white linen. We immediately sat on them to confirm that they were really ours to use. We dropped our packages and looked around the sparsely furnished but immaculate dorm. Mama ignored her fatigue and began to arrange our few belongings.

For the next few weeks, this dormitory was home while we planned our next precarious step of crossing into West Germany. The place was our oasis. People warmed us with kindness, shared tidbits about their experiences, pondered where to go, and then they were gone and forgotten—except for one dark-eyed young man. I first noticed him when he walked by our corner and our eyes met for just a couple of blinks. In that instant I caught a gentle, almost imperceptible smile, and I became aware of a most pleasing face, a shock of black curls, and angular curves on a muscular figure. The impression never left me.

The young man occupied a corner bed on the opposite end of the hall. After that first meeting, he often stopped at our corner to say something to me. I liked his attention, but I felt shy and tongue-tied in his presence. Whenever I was in the dorm, my eyes darted to look for him. I hoped he would come to our corner to see me. He occupied my mind entirely and filled me with conflicting thoughts. He was the prince of my dreams. I imagined how wonderful it would be if I joined him forever. Then I was immediately seized by guilt and sorrow. My dream was impossible! I could never leave Mama and Fredka and go away to heaven knows where. I was embarrassed about my feelings and tried hard to keep my love secret. My feigned indifference did not escape Fredka, who startled me one day with the question, "You like him, don't you?"

I stuttered timidly, "He is not interested in me."

"Oh, yes, he likes you!" she assured. "He tries hard to get your attention. He always stops at our corner to speak to you. He likes you a lot!" I am not sure that I completely believed Fredka, but I was very grateful for her hopeful words.

Discovering love was one gift I found in Prague. The young man, whose name I no longer remember, remains an image of untarnished perfection, of young, untested love.

The city gave me other gifts. It let me stumble into a few ordinary experiences I had missed in all the war years. Every morning we left the dorm with our cousins or with new friends from our shelter to visit the city. Sightseeing in the midst of friendly crowds felt like waking up from a long, painful nightmare. We strolled through winding, narrow streets with small houses reminiscent of Stare Miasto in Warsaw. The rooftops were just as low—you could almost touch them with your fingertips—and the doors seemed too small for some people to walk through. The streets shimmered with motion and color. Sounds of lively conversations mingled with the din of traffic. Aromas of home cooking wafted in the air. We even stepped into restaurants, sat at tables, and ordered bowls of *barmborova polevka* (potato soup). This traditional dish was available in every restaurant that was open. It was a most special treat and brought back pleasures I had almost forgotten.

We crossed graceful old bridges and I watched the river reflect their golden lights. Sometimes we even joined long lines of people to buy bread. I remember the specialness I felt when we visited the temple where a clay figure represents the Golem of Prague, an inanimate figure created by a rabbi and endowed with special powers to defend the Prague ghetto from anti-Semitic attacks. I was deeply moved by this preserved link to Jewish folklore. It was the first Jewish landmark I had seen since leaving Warsaw. In Poland, even the Jewish cemeteries had not escaped desecration.

But sadness veiled the beautiful city. It was apparent in the mostly dark and empty store windows, the bread lines, and the presence of Soviet tanks rolling down the streets, along with marching armed soldiers.

The long walks in Prague tied a lost world to new beginnings. They touched in me the pain of mourning and the joy of greeting a new free day. I was reminded of bright, green days in prewar Warsaw and Saturday strolls with Tata. Of course, the walks in Prague did not match my lost prewar paradise. But they touched an inner core of soft feelings. They woke me up to a fuller spectrum of color, the vibrancy of freedom, and the riches of simple moments that I once took for granted and still hoped to rediscover.

24 *Hof*

We left the shelter in Prague to continue on our journey to West Germany with the ultimate hope of reaching America. We had 180 more kilometers to travel by train and one more border to cross to reach the American zone. We had no reliable information about the West zone because the communist government slanted the news.

The train carried us through remote places to an unknown destination. I wondered, *How will I face the German people and how we will be treated there?* Beyond that, I wondered, *Will we ever find our American family? Will we ever reach that land?* And what was America really like? I imagined places where prairies and mountains ran into an endless beyond, like in pictures I had seen in children's cowboy movies long ago. I imagined New York City the way I had heard about it in songs and stories: a city of skyscrapers that blocked the heaven and dissected the earth into a maze of narrow canyons.

When we neared the border crossing and Russian soldiers stomped into the train to check documents, I went stiff with fear. I swallowed my breath, clutched my forged birth certificate tightly in my clammy palm and concentrated on not saying anything that might betray us.

Was it a gloomy fall afternoon when we crossed into the western sector of Germany, or was it my worries that hung like a gray mist over the rust-tinged landscape? The sight of armed Russian soldiers guarding the border added a precarious eeriness to the bucolic landscape. What lay ahead of us, beyond the lush green and persimmon-colored horizon, remained a mystery.

What do we do now? Get off the train in Hof, a city close to the Russian border, or continue deeper into the western sector where we might be safer? We still could not believe our good fortune and remained concerned that we might never find security and true freedom. Too tired and too confused, we decided to look for a place to spend the night in Hof, and then decide what to do next.

Hof, on the Saale River, a significant border checkpoint between the Soviet and the western sectors in 1945, is an old industrial city in picturesque Bavaria. It is a small city with simple houses and churches with pointed steeples. Thousands of German refugees expelled from territories reclaimed by Poland and Czechoslovakia, and those fleeing from other communist regions, poured into Hof. Some refugees stayed, others just passed through on the way to other destinations. All needed shelter.

We found temporary housing at Der Weisse Hahn (The White Rooster), a hostel for refugees, located on the ground floor of a building near the center of the city. The hostel consisted of one large dormitory with a single large window, and about twenty-five wrought-iron beds lined in straight rows along two parallel walls. Our beds were near the entrance and directly across from a window. Max, David, and Fredka each had their own beds; I slept with Mama. A large family of Gypsies occupied a cluster of beds on the opposite far corner. The others were mostly German refugees. Every day new people came to replace those who left.

We took our meals in a restaurant in the center of Hof, where most refugees ate. I looked forward to the meals at small tables and to meeting people. Local Jews, who stopped in to look for lost relatives and to greet newcomers, interested me most.

I still remember Herr Müller, a short, plump man with round eyes who left the hostel every morning in a Tyrol hat, a cotton bag slung over his shoulder. He returned in the evening, often with wild flowers in his hand. He never missed saying, *"Grüss Gott"* (good day) and doffing his hat respectfully. He was German. The Nazi government put him into a concentration camp because he was "mentally inferior." I remember him for his gentleness, innocence, and sadness, and for the wrong done to him.

And I remember the Gypsies for their lightheartedness and for being less inhibited than the rest of us. Sometimes, in the middle of the night, I was awakened by their laughter and the unfamiliar sounds of lovemaking that came from a bed in their corner. To protect me from those sounds, Mama drew me close to her and whispered, "Sleep. It's nothing. Don't pay attention. Sleep."

Speaking of love, there was Paul, a lone survivor whom Fredka met at the restaurant where we took our meals. He swept Fredka off her feet with his good looks and spirit of a romantic hero. Paul also made a favorable impression on Mama and me when he climbed out of the blue evening twilight through the open window and landed on the floor of Der Weisse Hahn to see Fredka. He bowed politely to our corner, explaining that the door was locked. Indeed it was, but the evening was young, times were strange, and one did strange things. Mama and I fully understood. Fredka blushed with embarrassment and pleasure. Mama and I chuckled with amusement, pride, and happiness for Fredka. She was now as beautiful as we remembered her to be before our time in the concentration camps, and she attracted attention. During the months after liberation, from winter till fall, she had been transformed from a ghostly skeleton, with frightened eyes peering out of sunken hollows, to a beautiful girl with rounded curves, plump cheeks, and bright blue eyes. Gone was the bristly stubble that covered the top of her head like quills. Thick waves of light brown hair bounced down to her shoulders. Above all, she no longer wrapped bony hands around a hunched torso to calm despair; her limbs flowed with freedom and grace. My sister was returned to herself, and to us. Not yet in full safety, but much revived and enabled.

The offender and the victim are forever linked by the same event, and are condemned to relive the shared past a thousand times; one to soothe his conscience, the other to soothe his pain. Our German neighbors at Der Weisse Hahn occupied many of my thoughts. I did not trust them when they told me they had been against the Nazi regime and knew nothing of Nazi atrocities. I understood that not everyone was a demon, but it was hard to tell people apart. All Germans were friendly and polite now, the flip side of the savage invaders.

I was on guard and I agonized: Who were the Germans who had tortured us and destroyed nearly everyone and everything that counted in my life, who had gassed my father and millions of my people? How could I look at my German neighbors and not wonder? How could I live without speaking out for those who did not make it out of the pits of hell? I had to tell those who were responsible that they were devils.

Questions screamed in my head. Where were their eyes and hearts when their Jewish friends and neighbors were driven out of their homes, marched through their streets in broad daylight, clutching the small hands of children? Did they still believe in "Jewish greed" when they plundered Jewish homes and businesses? Who were the millions saluting and shouting, "Sieg Heil!" at Hitler's rallies?

I agonized and listened with deep anger as well as desperate hope to recognize the good people who had refused to coexist with evil.

Our cousins: *left*, David; *right*, Max, in Hof.

Before long, my clever two cousins rented two furnished rooms in a spacious apartment in a central location. Frau and Herr Schultz, a German couple with a brood of well-behaved children, were the proprietors. Herr Schultz, with stringy dark hair, tall, thin, and quiet, sat mostly at the kitchen table near the window, listening to the news on the radio and watching Frau Schultz attending to chores. He rarely left the house. We sometimes wondered if he was avoiding being seen.

Frau Schultz, a thin, careworn woman with pale blue eyes and faded blond hair, was full of energy and good will. She took care of everything and everyone. She ran errands, cooked, cleaned, sent the children off to school, and showered her husband with attention and endearing names: "Schatzi" and "Liebling." She rented the rooms to us, collected the rent, made sure we were comfortable, and told us all the gossip of the neighborhood. She pointed out the neighbors who were Nazis and the neighbors who were unfaithful to their wives. She shared with us the reason that she and others had many children: "The government rewarded large families with big apartments and other privileges."

Our two adjoining rooms, with tall windows facing the street, were bright and cheerful. One room was very large and served as a combination living room, dining room, workroom, and bedroom for Max and David. They slept on two single beds, which we used for sitting space during the day. Mama, Fredka, and I shared the smaller room with a bay window and double bed.

We stayed in Hof approximately two years. It was the longest we had stayed in any one place since our release. I remained a member of a rootless minority in a foreign country that I feared and distrusted, and my future remained uncertain. Yet my heart leaped with freedom and I felt painfully alive when I walked arm-in-arm with Fredka and friends on streets that ran farther than my eyes could see. My heart opened as wide as the horizon when I climbed to the crests of country hills, and the world shone with promise when I looked into fields shimmering with life. People who think that sorrow stops you from living know little about life.

We fared better in the American sector than we had in Poland under Russian protection. Life was better for everyone. The Americans were generous and caring occupiers. Friendly soldiers passed out candy bars to children and assisted in rebuilding the country that had left a major part of the continent in ruins. They established Displaced Persons (DP) camps to provide shelter, food, and medical assistance to survivors who needed help. If it were not for Max and David, I am sure that the three of us would have been grateful to stay in a DP camp. However, it is questionable whether we would have ever gotten that far without my cousins.

Thanks to the American CARE (Cooperative for American Remittances to Eurpoe) packages we received monthly, we felt less dependent on Max and David. The packages were valuable in the turmoil of postwar Germany, where commerce and industry were crippled, and everything was in short supply. Basic food items such as sugar and butter were scarce, and candy bars were a luxury beyond most people's reach. So were nylon stockings. The CARE packages included lard, Spam, a large slab of chocolate, and nylons. It was possible to go into any bakery, butcher, or dairy store and trade these luxury items for bread, butter, cold cuts, meat, or other staples.

We were less isolated in Hof than we had been in Działoszyce or Chorzów. Hof quickly lost the "cleansed," pure German characteristics that had existed under the Nazi regime. The city was teaming with refugees yanked from many regions of Europe. We did not stand out in the crowd. Many Germans felt a bit contrite and made an effort to recover from the bigotry of the Third Reich. People were generally friendly, even helpful.

There was a tiny Jewish community and a two-room community center on the ground floor of a building in the city. On warm days, young Jews clustered in front of the entrance and greeted one another with bright smiles. The place always felt cheerful and welcoming. Fredka and I often walked there to meet friends and to hear people discuss current events. We never missed Friday evening dances to recorded music. At such moments with friends, I abandoned my worries and felt lighthearted and playful—a sensation I had missed for so long.

Counting on my fingers, I come up with twenty-three Jewish Hof inhabitants who still roam in my mind, like friendly ghosts. I am sure that I have forgotten some. Maybe twice that number of Jews—fifty—lived in Hof at that time. Most were young and in their twenties. One child, a beautiful eight-year-old girl with enormous brown eyes, lived among us. She survived the war in hiding with her mother. There were two Jewish mothers, the little girl's mother and Mama. That put Fredka and me in a very enviable category.

Mania Kostman was Fredka's and my best friend. She was seventeen years old—half a year younger than Fredka, and a year older than I. Her friendliness and love of life sparkled in every aspect of her person. It shined in her large blue eyes, rang in her friendly voice, and danced in her gait. One would never have guessed that this beautiful, healthy girl had lost everyone in her family except for her older sister's husband, Hupert, who acted as her surrogate parent. His infant child had been killed along with his wife and the rest of his family, except one sister and her husband, Dr. Gingold, and his nephew, Jurek. They all lived together as one family.

Mania, Fredka, and I bloomed in each other's company. We traded wartime delicacies from CARE packages to buy tickets to every operetta performed in the town, as well as every movie and play. We saw Franz Lehar's operettas over and over, until we knew every song by heart. We sang the arias all the way to and from the theater. We sang them to each other in our house while Mama cheered us on, glad to see us happy. When our voices ran dry from singing, laughing, and talking, we joined Mama in a game of cards.

I do not remember ever seeing Mama playing cards at home in Warsaw. I remember her being busy running the house, looking out for everyone's well-being, visiting with her sisters, reading when she found a spare moment, and on special occasions going to the opera with Father.

In contrast, in Hof she rarely stepped out of the house and often filled her spare time by playing gin rummy with Herr Schultz at the kitchen table. Herr Schultz sat with a somber face, eyes glued to his cards, and said little; Mama, on the other hand, divided her attention between guarding her hand and talking. She did not like losing and could not tolerate silence for long. Herr Schultz was the best listener in the house and he must have heard an earful from Mama. However, it was hard even for Herr Schultz to remain silent

Seated, Mama; *right*,
Fredka; *left*, me, 1946.
We have "fattened up"
considerably.

in Mama's company. Their conversations were friendly, usually brief, and sometimes oblique. One exchange flashes across my mind. This time Herr Shultz broke the silence with this comment: "You know, the Germans were not the only ones in history to destroy Jewish people. In biblical times, they put Jewish infant boys into baskets and set them on the river to die."

Mama snapped back, "Yes, that is true. And you know what happened to them. They too ended in ruins."

When I think of Mama during the war, I see a figure with boundless courage. It is hard to imagine the incredible valor and energy my emaciated mother was able to summon for our sake. Vigilance burned in her eyes, guarding against the unexpected. If she spotted potential danger, she moved with speed and daring to steer us out of harm's way. Mama's drive kept us alive. She ran, cajoled, begged, pushed, and gave up her portion of bread when Fredka was sick, in spite of her own hunger pangs—anything to keep us alive. And now, after the war, her intrepid strength was waning. She remained driven and alert, made important decisions to keep us moving toward a secure place and a normal life, but she now relied on Fredka and me to carry out her plans. That put unfamiliar burdens on us. Such responsibilities are not normally expected of people as young as we were. But, in retrospect, it was not all bad. Her new helplessness, as well as her trust in us, made us responsible and self-reliant beyond our years.

Sadly, Mama grew more and more self-conscious. Her world was shattered—her family, friends, home, and standing in a community were gone. The challenge of finding a new life overwhelmed her. Perhaps she felt guilty about going on without the people who had meant so much to her. Maybe, with the gas chambers out of sight, she needed time to grieve—time to sit quietly, to say good-bye to the people whose ashes were flying in the wind.

Mama undertook one last bold act to set us on the path of independence. She let Max know that she wished to take charge of our own CARE packages. Some of the CARE items—chocolate, nylons, and lard—were tradable in stores for meat, bread, other staples, and clothes. Max took Mama's request as a sign of lack of appreciation and understanding of his and David's efforts. "You would have been lost without us," he reminded Mama.

Still, Mama did not like to have to ask my cousins for every little thing we needed. She began to contemplate separating from them and shared that thought with Fredka and me. We were alarmed. "How will we survive without them?"

She persisted, "Don't be scared. You have not lived life yet. Sometimes you must take a chance. You must trust your own abilities. We owe Max and David much. However, we also contribute a great deal to our joint survival. That is as it should be, but it is time for us to be on our own. With the CARE packages we will manage. We will be no worse off." Mama's daring frightened us. We too did not like being beholden; still we pleaded with her to be patient.

One day, Fredka and I came home and found Mama alone in our room. She looked up at us and spoke in a grave tone, "It is over. I had a spat with Max. I told Max that we will no longer count on them for our support and we will manage our own CARE packages."

Fredka and I complained, "How will we manage to survive on CARE packages as our sole source? How will we find our way out of here on our own? Who knows what problems we might have to face alone? You did not have to be so hasty."

Mama raised her shoulders like a warrior, puffed out her chest as she always did in a crisis, and spoke with force, "Don't be afraid. We are not helpless. Besides, we have family in America and we will find them." Fredka and I had our doubts.

Her face was taut, her brows pulled tight with determination, but I saw a shadow of fear hiding in her bold blue eyes.

Getting Along on Our Own and Paving Our Way to America

We still shared the rooms in the rented apartment with my cousins and continued to care about each other. However, everything in our lives changed. We shouldered the full responsibility for our own support and arranging for our emigration.

Mama took charge of the first task: solving the food problem. She turned to Fredka and me and said, "We have to trade the luxury items in the CARE packages for staples available in stores. You will carry it out far better than I ever would be able to. You will have to do it."

The idea of bartering in stores sounds preposterous now, but that was what people did then, when currency had little value, unemployment was high, and there was a scarcity of everything.

Fredka and I were afraid of the task. We felt timid, embarrassed, and self-conscious. We did not speak German well. It mortified us to try to negotiate with the storekeepers. But Mama stressed the urgency, listing her inadequacies and our attributes. We accepted the responsibility that Mama placed on us with resentment and resignation. We wanted to please her, so we did as we were told.

At first, Fredka and I entered the stores with sinking hearts and trembling legs. We always went together to give each other courage. The endeavor was so distasteful to us that we worked out an equitable system, taking turns to enter the store first and state that we wanted to trade: chocolate, or sugar, or nylons, or whatever, for bread, or meat, and so on. This arrangement between us worked well most of the time. But I am ashamed to admit that sometimes I turned Fredka's tendency for correctness into a game, especially when she acted the part of big sister, or little mother, and instructed me on proper comportment.

When it was my turn to go in first and speak to the storekeeper, I stepped forward, held the door open, and waited for Fredka to walk in. I knew that she would never take a chance to appear foolish standing there. To avoid embarrassment, Fredka stepped up to the counter and chirped out shyly what we had come for. Afterwards, she would be furious with me. She chastised me and threatened she would not go into another store even if we starved to death. I felt both guilty and amused that my trick never failed. I apologized with true sincerity and promised never to do it again. I hate to remember that I did a lot of promising.

With time and success, we got somewhat used to the repugnant task of trading. The storekeepers often responded cheerfully, but not always. We got to know some store owners, and I did not even mind too much going by myself, if I had to. Distasteful as they were, the shopping expeditions pushed us into the world, tipped us toward self-reliance, and helped us learn the language quickly.

In spite of our resolve not to learn German—our act of revenge—Fredka and I picked it up quickly. Our alert young minds soaked up the language from daily interactions, from the books on the Schultz's shelves—the only books available to us—from theaters, and from movies. We learned the language to communicate, participate, and survive.

In addition to solving daily survival problems, we had to find a way out of a hostile Europe. Many of our friends had plans to go to Palestine. We too often talked about going there to find a home to protect us from being chased and persecuted again, as Jews had been for centuries in spite of our allegiance to the countries of our birth. However, that choice had many risks. It involved illegal entry and possible incarceration by the British authorities, who sent Jewish newcomers to prison in Cyprus if they caught them. There was also the risk of being slaughtered by Arabs who wanted the land for themselves.

My best friend, Lolek, went there to seek this dream. He was a year or two older than I, tall and lanky. I liked his pale blue eyes and his wavy blond hair that glowed in the sun. Lolek and I took free piano lessons together from his sister-in-law, Ruth. He lived with Ruth and his older brother, Heniek, with whom he had survived the Holocaust. We took long walks together to the outskirts of Hof, where we sat on hillcrests and watched the wispy fog drifting over jade peaks and valleys. We talked a lot, laughed a lot, and shared our fears and hopes. One day, he said good-bye to me and left to fulfill his destiny. I never heard from him again. People who did not want him there killed him. The news reached me through Heniek, his brother. A new hole pierced my heart.

Although we felt a strong tug to go to Palestine, Mama was not prepared to endanger our lives after bringing us out of the Holocaust. "We must try first to go to America where we have family and where many persecuted people have found a home." She decided to focus on finding her two sisters and brother in New York—a daunting task. We did not have their addresses, they were older than Mama, and we could not be sure they were still alive.

We started with the United States telephone books that Fredka had located at the DP Camp where she worked for a short time. My uncle and aunts had common surnames:

Shapiro, Epstein, and Szenkin. We sent out many letters, counted the days, and waited. Then, one day a long letter in Yiddish from Mama's eldest sister, Aunt Riva, arrived from New York. It said, "The whole family is happy to hear from you, and happy that you are alive." The horizon seemed to be opening.

Mama wrote back. She informed them about the tragic deaths of my father and all our family members who had lived in Poland. She named each one separately to resurrect them in memory: "Dudek and Josek, both geniuses, fled to Communist Russia to seek safety. They were killed. Aunt Malka, Aunt Hannah and their husbands and children, Lolek and Moniek, all were exterminated in concentration camps; Uncle Kagan, who lived in Baniochy, near Warsaw, with his extensive family, not one survived." She wrote them how lost and helpless she felt. Fredka and I told Mama that her letters were too long. Mama kept writing and assuring us, "They are my sisters and brother. They will understand our plight perfectly."

Letters, stained with tears, went both ways across the Atlantic. We learned that Mama's brother, Abe, had suffered a stroke and could not write. My two aunts wrote us about their children and grandchildren. They promised to help us come to New York, but were not sure how long the process might take.

My hopes took wing, and so did my apprehensions. I did not know my two elderly aunts and uncle, or my cousins, who were all adults. I fretted, *How would we be received? We had no money and did not know a word of English. Would we overwhelm our relatives with our needs? How would we find work and a place to live?*

To prepare for my new life, I made up my mind to learn a skill, typing. I thought it was dignified and could be acquired quickly. This choice was partly influenced by my envy of the pretty and efficient-looking young women in government offices who bossed us around. I found a tutor and dipped into our CARE packages for payment. I borrowed a typewriter, set it on a small table under the window in our room, borrowed a German book, and copied pages without looking at the keyboard. The results, when I looked up, often made me despair, but I did not give up. The lessons lasted for several months and were of benefit to me later.

It is mostly fortunate that what is sown in childhood is harvested throughout life. It is equally fortunate that people who die do not vanish from our lives and often continue to point the way. Tata left us with this important message: "Education is the most formidable weapon. What you learn and store in your mind, no force can wrest from you. Material things can be replaced if you use your mind." So, to arm ourselves to face new challenges, homeless and penniless in a new land, Fredka and I turned to the books again.

Together we found an English tutor, a distinguished-looking, middle-aged German professor of languages who had been expelled from Czechoslovakia. We paid him with *brötchen* (small bread rolls) that Fredka and I obtained in trade for large squares of American chocolate. We took our lessons seriously, worked hard, and had great fun stringing together English words to greet our tutor, or report an event. He chuckled with delight when we showed off our skills.

Our instructor, whom I grew to love, lent us old British books with short stories and pictures that were not particularly relevant to the world we lived in. Nevertheless, we memorized every phrase on every page and thus learned grammatical patterns.

Sometimes our tutor stayed after the lessons to chat with Mama. Their short and guarded conversations interested me greatly. I understood that both tried to work out in their own minds the madness of the war, their personal losses, and how to deal with the burdens of the aftermath. Sometimes their conversations got a touch intense, but never unfriendly. Once, our tutor pointed out that the Allies dropped bombs on German cities too, and that German civilians also suffered.

Mama reminded him, "There is a vast difference. The Allies are Europe's saviors," she said with passion. "They bombed cities to stop Hitler's thirst for carnage. They dropped bombs to end the war. In contrast, the Germans bombed to occupy, plunder, and methodically kill innocent civilians. If Hitler had stopped his madness, there would have been no bombing."

These conversations lingered in my mind because I too did not know how to go on with life after the irrevocable losses. I listened to find answers, and I listened because I genuinely liked my tutor and wanted to trust him, but I was afraid.

The English lessons brought a quick payoff. Before long, Fredka and I composed English letters and sent them to our family in America. Our cousins, Martha and Joe, the first to write back, praised us for our efforts. We were overjoyed with our success. Along with the letters from America came packages with food, and used clothes in good condition. These packages brought us additional capital to trade for everyday needs. We accepted these gifts with gratitude and sadness—thankful that our family cared, and embarrassed to be needy.

With the CARE packages, parcels from family in America, and moral support from the Jewish community, we managed. Fredka and I had crisp new dirndls that smelled of new fabric. Fredka looked wonderful in the full skirt tucked in her at her small waist. She even had an old rabbit fur coat she wore with pride. Most of the available Jewish bachelors wooed Fredka. She stayed aloof, committed to no one, and cheerfully flirtatious.

Life taught us to leave absolutely nothing to luck or chance. "We must take charge of our immigration to America, or we might never make it," Mama prodded. We soon learned that the Russian quota was wide open. No wonder: the Russian government did not permit anyone to leave. That presented an opening for us. Mama was born in Ciasnik, a shtetl in Byelorussia, and had lived there until she was chased out along with other Jews during the pogroms after World War I.

Mama said, "We must not waste a single instant." She sent Fredka and me to the American Consulate in Munich. She insisted, "You must go. You are bright. You are beautiful. No one will turn you down." Neither Fredka nor I had the confidence my mother projected. We did not feel beautiful, nor did we believe that we were better able to move officialdom to act in our favor. We were afraid of take the train to Munich alone. We needed her to take charge, but we recognized that she was building an immovable wall around herself. We could no longer fully count on her.

Just before we started our trips to Munich, Max found two cousins who had survived the war and lived in West Germany: Natka, in Bamberg, and Fishel, in Munich. That meant that at least one member of each of Tata's brothers' families had survived the war. Not a single one from Mama's side of the family had made it. We immediately got in touch with them and saw them from time to time. When we went to the American Consulate in Munich, we stayed with cousin Fishel and his new wife, Stefka. We felt very fortunate.

The first trip Fredka and I took to Munich made me feel uneasy for a number of reasons. The city was vast, chaotic, and devastated by war. Here and there, well-maintained residential buildings stood isolated by hills of rubble that were blocks long. The absence of young men in the crowd was glaring. It chilled me to see people turn away from me to hide grotesquely maimed faces, or to notice empty sleeves hanging down from men's shoulders and empty pant legs. In addition, I felt unsafe among the large numbers of strangers whose attitudes I did not trust.

Streetcar traffic was frantic. Few tracks were in working condition, few cars ran, and large crowds waited at the stops. When a streetcar arrived, the crowd shoved to get on and continued pushing even as the car was pulling away from the stop. People rode standing on the steps and hanging on the sides.

The shattered city brought back frightening memories and puzzling thoughts. Seeing a German city so full of suffering surprised me. I was baffled at the price the German people had been willing to pay to dominate others. *What frightening madness*, I thought.

To compound our discomfort, waiting at a streetcar stop, Fredka and I noticed people rudely turning their backs on two men dressed in traditional Jewish clothes. We assumed that the two men were asking directions and no one wanted to help. We quickly stepped up to the two Jews to show solidarity and offer assistance. We talked to them briefly, and then they left. We remained standing at the stop feeling isolated and scared.

When our streetcar arrived, I held on to Fredka's hand and pushed with the crowd into the car. Suddenly, an elderly woman who was almost on top of me screamed, "Oh, my chest! My chest! She hit me in my chest!" Then I heard her hurl shocking words at us: "*Verfluchte Ausländer!*" (Accursed foreigners). An alarm went off in my mind—she must mean me. My elbow was touching her chest. We were so tightly squeezed that everyone had an arm or a leg pressed against someone. I looked up at the old woman and saw a wrinkled face, a grandmother's face. But not her eyes! Her eyes glared at me with frightening hatred.

"*Raus Ausländer! Raus Ausländer!*" (Foreigners out!), echoed the crowd. A hate-fired mob against the two of us and we could not get off and escape.

Fight back! a voice in me ordered. I stared back into the hard faces and I heard my own voice rise above the mob, "Look out the windows! Look at the ruins you have brought on your cities! Have you not caused enough destruction to the whole world, and to yourselves? Have you not learned anything?" Silence fell. People turned their faces away from us. I glared at any face that dared to look up. I glared like a trapped animal trying to scare off attackers.

A young man who caught my combatant stare said meekly, "Fraülein, why are you looking at me so angrily? You should see what we did to London. It is in worse ruins."

I shot back at him, "London is in ruins, all of Europe is in ruins, you are in ruins, countless millions are dead, and you caused it. You alone will have to live with this shame. How can you be proud of that?"

We got off at the proper stop and rushed to my cousins' flat and let ourselves be soothed. Fishel and Stefka lived in a rented furnished room in an apartment belonging to a thin, elfish-looking, middle-aged German bachelor with eager eyes and an anxious demeanor. My cousins had shared use of the kitchen, dining room, and bathroom. Their landlord, friendly and accommodating, allowed my cousins to invite us to the house and let us sleep on one of the two single beds in their room. I felt awkward sharing the bedroom with the newlyweds.

The landlord was peculiar and pedantic. As soon as you left the bathroom, he followed, wearing white gloves, checking to see that all was left as spotless as before. If a smudge from the bathtub appeared on his glove, he bolted to speak to Stefka. "Look what I found! The tub was left dirty." Stefka always listened sympathetically, corrected the omission, and things went on smilingly.

During our visit, the man's cleanliness obsession got him in trouble with a fly that sneaked into the apartment. He chased it through the house. Each time he closed in, it got away. Finally it landed on the crystal chandelier in the dining room, and waited there as if to say, "Catch me!" The man raised his bony thumb, drew back his arm, and aimed at the fly with full force. It flew away again and the chandelier exploded with the tinkling sounds. The man was rushed to the hospital with a broken thumb.

Back from the hospital, feeling cheated by the fly that got away just as he was about to nail it, the landlord went straight to Stefka for sympathy. The lines on his face swam with animated indignation as he told his side of the story. Stefka smiled, secretly amused, and listened with sympathy.

The homey and humane atmosphere in my cousins' house lifted my spirits. I enjoyed the hospitality and cheerfulness. I remember with fondness the pleasure I got from reading the thin paperbound opera librettos I found on a small bookshelf in their room. Fishel and Stefka did not let us get too discouraged by the streetcar incident and helped us move past it. They showed us around the city and introduced us to the Jewish Community Center.

Somewhat restored, Fredka and I continued with our mission. We moved around the city without further unpleasantness. We picked up immigration forms and took a train back home feeling a bit worldlier. The ugly incident on the streetcar was frightening, but it underlined an important message: I had faced a threatening mob, not gun barrels, and I was now able to fight back by speaking up.

The red tape involved in coming to America took time, patience, and repeated trips to Munich. Every few weeks Mama said, "Maybe it is time to speak to someone in authority in Munich? They might forget about us." Her fear was understandable to us. We were the forgotten. Sometimes only Fredka and I went. If it were absolutely necessary, all three of us went. Whenever possible, Mama declined to go, making excuses for herself and showering us with compliments. "Youth is an adornment. Attractive people have friends for gratis; old and ugly people have undeserved enemies." We were annoyed with Mama's generalities. Her flattery made us doubt ourselves and feel angry. We also knew that Mama was persuasive and not easily turned down by anyone. There was no use arguing.

Most often, Mama sent Fredka alone to Munich. She was the older sibling and it was more economical if only one of us went. Above all, Mama was absolutely convinced that Fredka's attractive appearance and gentle demeanor appealed to the best instincts in others and that she could move the heart of the devil himself. The more trust Mama put in her, the more afraid Fredka was of failing us. But, like most things in life, adversity has its paradoxes. Despite strong fears and resentment, Fredka went whenever Mama pressed, and she grew with each new challenge. I felt left out and missed my sister. Furthermore, I did not like having to go to the store by myself to barter for basic food.

Before long, Fredka learned her way around Munich and the labyrinthine immigration system. Mania, our best friend, also applied for immigration to America and joined Fredka on the Munich trips. They met wonderful young people at the Jewish Community Center who took them into their circle. Together, they went to theaters, concerts, and dances at the center.

When Fredka and Mania returned from their Munich trips, they talked incessantly about their new friends: attractive and flirtatious Janka with flowing blond hair, Zyga who was crazy in love with pretty and capricious Halina, and the three lovely young sisters and their brother, Ignac, who had miraculously survived the war together. I felt that I knew them long before I met them.

Fredka's eyes lit up when she described Sol, who had survived alone as a partisan in the Wilno (Vilnius) forest and showed special interest in her. "He is very cute," she assured me. "He is lanky, has smiling blue eyes, and thick, wavy blond hair slicked back like a tango dancer." Then she listed all his attributes in a dreamy voice. "He is quite engaging. He knows all the popular songs and has a nice voice; he likes to recite Yiddish poetry, and he is a good dancer. Mania swooned when she talked about Kuba, a violin student who played for her with heartfelt seriousness. Of course, I felt left out having to stay in Hof while they were meeting interesting people in the big city.

Later, I had my turn, and Fredka's new friends in Munich became my friends too. I met Sol, who wooed Fredka with song, sweet talk, and fancy footsteps on the dance floor. I met Kuba, who showed interest in Mania. My heart trembled when I met Ignac, the one who survived the war with his three sisters. He was tall and sinewy, with a sweep of tight chestnut curls, and he hardly took note of me. I have not forgotten the enchantment I felt when my friends took me to see Mozart's *Die Zauberflöte* (*The Magic Flute*), and the excitement I felt when I saw *Das Buntes Vierfel*, a political satire. I went to dances with my friends at the Jewish Community Center and learned to open my heart a little wider and to laugh with greater abandon.

I doubt that I fully appreciated how special my survivor friends were. With very few exceptions, all were alone in the world, all were victims of terrible injustice, and all lived with deep sorrow. Yet they were full of vigor, amazingly self-sufficient, friendly, and well mannered. With their benevolence and joy, they were resurrecting the quality of life as it used to be when life was good. Love remained their guide.

However, that was not always simple. An unforgettable example of conflict between the impulses for revenge and compassion comes to my mind. A friend in Hof told me about two lone Jewish young men, about eighteen years old, who set out to kill a few Germans to avenge the murders of all their family members—to set the accounts right. When they pointed their guns and saw the helplessness and fear in the faces of the people they were about to kill, they saw the faces of their own mothers, fathers, and sisters, and threw the guns away.

That incident haunted me and made me think of the fury I felt. The struggle to hold on to my humanity had been a concern for me ever since Nazi boots stepped on our streets and began to trample on our lives. How do you keep your faith in love and trust when your people are being shoved, by your fellow men, into gas chambers and crematoria? With bitter hatred, I often vowed to wreak vengeance upon the barbarians. Yet, if hate was all I was left with, I would be defeated. I would become like the Nazis. That was not acceptable! The more we were tortured, the more we clung to memories of what was good and right. That was our way of holding on to meaning. When we were in the darkest pits of hell, Mama's whispers never ceased to drone in my ears, "They are shaming humanity! You are good and innocent."

I pondered, as many of my friends did, *How do I live with my anger? How do I stand up for the wronged and remain fair, humane, and reasonable?* I had to believe that all people are capable of contrition. I had to believe that those who had brought so much pain to the world would open new doors to a saner world. How else was humanity to survive? But I was not sure that goodness and reason would prevail.

Months flew by, seasons changed, and we remained in Hof until the spring of 1947, close to two years after liberation. Much revived, but not yet completely rescued, we waited for a letter to tell us we could go to the land of our hopes, America.

In late spring the long-awaited letter arrived with instructions to report in four weeks for an interview with an American official in Munich—a hint of light at the end of a tunnel. Wide-eyed with excitement and worries, the three of us calculated our chances. One moment we imagined scenarios of crossing the ocean and falling into the arms of our relatives awaiting us at the shore in New York. The next moment we imagined being turned away and remaining stateless, homeless, abandoned.

"Mama, how in the world will we ever be able to convince the American authorities that you were born in Ciasnik?" Fredka and I worried. "We have no proof, no documents."

Mama kept up her optimism. "They will have to believe us. We will make them understand. None of the remaining Jews have documents. They must know that. They will recognize that we are honest."

We rehearsed what we would say and how we would conduct ourselves to make a favorable impression. Mama wrung her memory for details and dates of when she was driven out of Russia during pogroms. We picked the clothes we were going to wear, and Mama baked cookies for the road. She always baked up a storm and packed little bundles of food when she felt threatened by the outside world. Everything, our whole future, depended on one interview that would last minutes.

We left for Munich with a dozen bags of food dangling from Mama's arms. Fredka and I refused to carry any of it. To soothe us during excruciating moments of waiting and uncertainty, she always reached into a bag and said, "A cookie? Just one. Eat. You will be hungry. You'll need the energy."

Fredka and I took a perverse satisfaction in turning her down at such tense moments. "Mother, leave me alone. I am not hungry. My stomach is in knots. Stop nagging."

The deciding day of the interview remains vivid in my mind. I remember every detail and every word uttered as clearly as if it had happened only yesterday. I remember the long train ride filled with premonitions of possible failure, and the long wait in the waiting room to be called in to see the official who would decide our destiny.

When our turn came, we entered a bright office and faced a tall, blond Aryan-looking man behind a wide desk. His face was pink and wholesome, like the faces that triggered fear in me. *Can we trust him?* I wondered. The man must have sensed our fear. He bowed his head to us politely, reached out his arm to greet us, and led us to the three chairs facing his desk.

Before proceeding with the interview, the official assured us that he understood our circumstances and unease. He explained that he had to ask all the questions listed on the form spread out on his big desk. "You might find some of the questions embarrassing. I am sorry, but I cannot avoid it," he apologized. Touched by this courtesy, Mama thanked him profusely and offered a few brief explanations about our unfortunate circumstances.

The interview was conducted in German. Mama carried on with confidence and answered every question precisely. The questions seemed to me endless and tormenting. They all centered on Mama's claim that she was born in Russia and was therefore qualified to enter on that country's quota. "How is it that your children were born in Poland? Did you return to Russia? Can you explain why your children were born in a different country?"

What if he finds Mama's explanations insufficiently convincing? What will happen to us? Where will we go then? I blurted out, "It would not be practical for my mother to go to Poland to give birth and then return to Russia, then back to Poland."

He smiled and said, "Quite right."

When the interviewer asked Fredka if she ever gave birth to a child, Fredka got flustered and responded with utter seriousness, "No, but my mother did."

The man and Mama chuckled softly and Mama said, "She is a child, after all." That pretty much ended the interview.

We fumbled at the door, desperate to know if we had passed muster and when we could go to America. The man was reassuring, but noncommittal. "You will hear from the American immigration office soon," he told us. "It is not up to me, but do not worry," were his last words. I learned later that this nice official was a CIA agent.

Over the next few months, one by one, many of our friends departed for new worlds: Palestine, America, Australia. We hugged our best friend Mania and cried when she left for America. Sol, Fredka's friend in Munich, left too, and wrote long letters to Fredka from New York. We waited and time dragged.

We went to Munich several more times. The trips were stressful and bittersweet. I loved seeing my cousins and friends. The city was interesting and fun, but not always safe. On our last visit my eyelid puffed up with a huge sty. My cousins' landlord recommended an ophthalmologist. Mama sent Fredka to go with me. It turned out that the ophthalmologist was more interested in our imperfect German than my inflamed, half-closed eye. The stupid doctor made us repeat sentences and broke out in laughter. The harder he laughed, the more awkward our sentences sounded. He called in a couple of doctor friends from adjacent rooms to hear the funny accents of the two Jewish girls. They chuckled in chorus and made what they thought were amusing remarks about us. When the ophthalmologist finally decided to examine my eye, I was afraid of him and did not want him near me. I could not wait to leave and I threw away the medicine he gave me.

It is too bad that this is the last memory of my Munich visits. On balance, I found room to grow in the twenty-one postwar months in Germany. I lived freely in streets with wide-open horizons, among hills and meadows I could not outrun, and I met faces that often, though not always, smiled back. Still, my heart remained caged.

25 *Voyage to America*

n mid-July 1947, we finally gathered our few belongings and said good-bye to Max and David. They too had applied to go to America and awaited their turn. We were glad that they would follow us. We hugged and parted with our friends. Most of them I never saw again. We left and took a train to Munich and from there to the pre-embarkation camp in Bremerhaven.

We stayed with Stefka and Fishel in Munich for one week. We spent a great deal of time at the American Immigration Office being processed for the voyage to America, and saying good-bye to our friends. We were inoculated, photographed, and given stamped identity cards printed in English. They were in fact issued by the Hebrew Immigration Society, but I did not know the difference. When I held my new ID, I felt strangely validated: I was "somebody" again.

I possessed two other documents I had acquired during our stay in Hof that acknowledged my existence: a registration issued by the German police office, dated October 10, 1945, and a red cardboard ID with a stamped photograph and my fingerprint, dated April 1946. I guarded the red cardboard ID with utmost care. I thought that without it no one would believe that I was myself. At the same time, I felt diminished by it. It says in bold

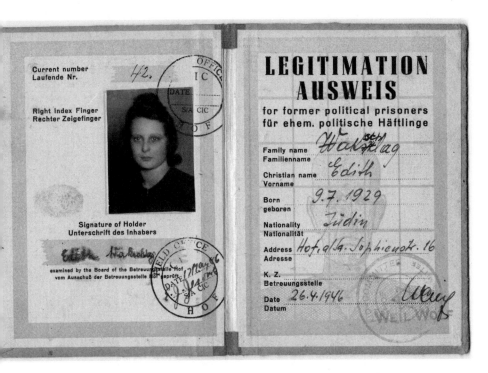

 note: the following handwritten fields appear on the card:

LEGITIMATION AUSWEIS
for former political prisoners
für ehem. politische Häftlinge

Current number / Laufende Nr.

Right Index Finger / Rechter Zeigefinger

Signature of Holder / Unterschrift des Inhabers

examined by the Board of the Betreuungsstelle Hof
vom Ausschuß der Betreuungsstelle Hof geprüft.

Family name / Familienname

Christian name / Vorname

Born / geboren

Nationality / Nationalität

Address / Adresse

K. Z. / Betreuungsstelle

Date / Datum

My documentation card classifying me as a "former political prisoner," 1946.
Courtesy United States Holocaust Memorial Museum.

print, in English and German: "Legitimation for former political prisoners." I was not a political prisoner! I had no political views. I had only hope—I was a child. I was a Jewish child with a missing identity, missing address of origin, and missing citizenship. In addition, my name is carelessly written on this red ID card.

I do not like to look at the police residence registration. It reminds me that I was "*Staatenlos*" (stateless), without legal protections and entitlements. Still, I guarded these documents with great care until I donated them to the US Holocaust Memorial Museum in Washington, DC, with the assurance that they would be well protected. That happened after I had been an American citizen of long standing, with full and deeply appreciated privileges.

On the day of our departure from Munich, we collected our cardboard suitcases. Stefka and Fishel escorted us through the city to a train depot designated for refugees heading for Bremerhaven, six hundred kilometers away. It was a large, fenced-in camp, cluttered

Für amtliche Vermerke

Zweitschrift

Anmeldung bei der polizeilichen Meldebehörde 14. Juni 1947

Am _____ 1.10.45 194__ ist / sind für dauernd — vorübergehend***) zugezogen (Nichtzutreffendes streichen)

nach _____ Hof/Saale _____ Kreis _____ Hof/Saale _____
Vorder-/Rück-
Seiten-/Mittel- gebäude, als Mieter — Untermieter — Schlafstelle — Dienst — Besuch bei _____ Greim Elise _____

Letzte*) Wohnung: KZ-Meidanek _____ Kreis _____ Lublin/Polen _____

Lfd. Nr.	Familienname (bei Frauen auch Geburtsname und gegebenenfalls Name aus der letzten früheren Ehe	Vornamen (sämtliche, Rufname unterstreichen)	Familienstand (led., verh., verw., gesch.), b) bescheid. Ehe; verh. seit	Beruf (genaue Bezeichnung der Berufstätigkeit und Angabe, ob selbständig oder Angestellter, Arbeiter usw.)	Geburts- Tag	Geburts- Mon	Geburts- Jahr	a) Geburtsort b) Kreis c) Provinz/Land d) Staat (wenn Ausland)
1	Wakschlak	Michaela	verw.	ohne	9.	12.	97	Uzasznik
2	geb. Schenkin							
3	Wakschlag	Frieda	led.	ohne	4.	1.	28	Warschau
4	Wakschlag	Edith	led.	Bürohilfe	9.	7.	29	Warschau
5								
6								
7								

Lfd. Nr.	Religion	Staats- u. Landes- angehörigkeit**)	Wohnort und Wohnung a) Bei den letzten Personen- standsaufnahme bzw. am letzten 10. Oktober/Ort, Kreis, Straße, Hausnummer b) Vor Kriegsausbruch, d. h. vor dem 1. 9. 1939 (ständiger Wohnsitz: Ort, Kreis, Provinz bzw. Land)	Bei Zuzug von auswärts: a) Haben Sie schon früher in der hiesig. Gemeinde ge- wohnt? Bejahendenfalls wann und wo?	b) Für den Fall, daß vor- übergehend: Zweck u. voraus- sichtlich. Dauer d. Aufenthalts in der hiesigen Gemeinde?
1	jüdisch	Staatenlos Fr. Polen	Polen		
2					
3					
4					
5					
6					
7					

G. R. Nr. 2012

Kova-Druck 781/3. 0 (11547) Bayer. Kommunalschriften-Druckerei, München 34, Bayer. Straße 22

Wenden!

Documentation reporting our arrival, Hof, 1947.

with people, luggage, and friendly orderlies who calmed the tumult and directed people to assigned assembly points and then to the trains.

Again we boarded a freight train that was not meant for human transport, which carried frightening associations. But this freight train ride, though not worry free, remains in my memory as a flight to freedom, entirely unlike the rides in those other freight trains that sped furiously into the end of life.

Saying good-bye to our cousins, Stefka and Fishel, Munich, 1947.
Next stop: Bremerhaven and then America!

We spent, roughly, one bewildering week at the Bremerhaven pre-embarkation camp, a wide-open field with lines of barracks and an encircling wire fence. It had likely been a German military base during the war. We had no routine to follow, except to wait for daily directions. We were housed in barracks with strangers from all over Europe and shared with them a fevered excitement and concern whether we would find America as we hoped or pictured it to be. We took our meals in a common dining hall and watched movies shown for our entertainment.

To overcome loneliness, groups with common backgrounds clustered under shady trees to share the latest gossip. I liked to observe the vivacious German GI brides who sat together and giggled with joy as they talked about their bridegrooms waiting for them. Their long, mascara-coated eyelashes, their attractive clothes, and the lightness in their laughter fascinated me.

While we were in Bremerhaven waiting for our ship to come, someone from HAIAS

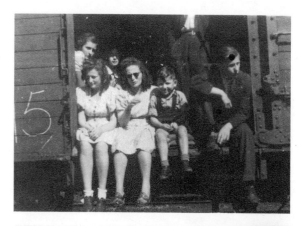

On the train to Bremerhaven and
our new life.

(the Hebrew Immigrant Aid Society) came to visit us and gave us ten dollars. I don't remember whether the gift was ten dollars for all three of us, or ten dollars each. That was
all the money we had to take with us to America. A lump swells in my throat when I
think of that visit, just as it did long ago when the money was handed to us. I was moved
that people in America bothered to think of us and send us money. But the gift was char-
ity. It stung me and set me apart. I remember the HAIAS woman's kind voice saying, "I
understand perfectly how you feel." *How can she?* I wondered.

The *SS Marine Flasher*, a broad-beamed World War II US military transport ship, painted blue-gray to blend with the shades of the ocean, resembled a giant floating warehouse.
Anchored at Bremerhaven, the ship's towering height was impressive, but I found it hard
to trust that it could stay afloat on the immense, churning ocean.

On July 24, 1947, I stepped up to the ship and the whole world hid behind its enormous side. I fell in line with the other passengers to climb up the gangplank, feeling small

and scared. Mama and Fredka too felt intimidated. For reassurance, we stayed close to survivor friends we had met in Bremerhaven. I held on to my mother and sister for fear that they might be blown off the deck.

When we reached the main deck, we listened to safety instructions and the daily routines, then followed a steward through a maze of narrow aisles, up and down flights of metal steps, and into a large, windowless dorm packed with rows of stacked hammocks. Bare bulbs swung from a low ceiling and everything rocked back and forth. My legs felt rubbery as I swayed with the room. Awkwardly, we moved forward to claim three hammocks that were close together and near people we knew. We deposited our few belongings in a designated space, tried out our hammocks, and then followed the crowd to the open deck. There we basked in the profusion of sunlight flooding from the sky, and we began our vigil of staring into the endless horizon so that we could be the first to see the shores of America come into sight.

The voyage to America took eleven days. Few passengers stayed in their swinging hammocks through the night. One by one we staggered to the open deck, spread our blankets near friends, and stared into an ink-black sky incrusted with a universe of shimmering stars. We chattered about dreams and fears.

Oftentimes, Fredka cautioned, "We must not set ourselves up for hurt and disappointment. We must expect absolutely nothing and be grateful for anything we find." Of course, Mama and I agreed. And so we floated in limbo, too frightened to hope, too timid to expect or wish, but humble and prepared to accept our fate. We talked in whispers till sleep overtook us.

Sometimes I drifted away from my mother, sister, and friends and leaned on the railing. The moonlight lay scattered on the ocean like knife points. I listened to the wailing chorus of breaking waves until every last thought was driven from my mind. Then, I went back to rest my head in Mama's lap and let sleep swallow me.

When the sun's disk had barely touched the eastern rim of the horizon, everyone on the deck was up to watch the layers of red morning light spreading over the world. Then, slowly, we staggered down into the dim interior to wash the sleep from our faces and to eat breakfast.

The meals rarely stayed long in my stomach. The *Marine Flasher* wallowed on the surface, rising and falling with the waves, like a roller coaster. After every meal I leaned over the ship's sides, and let the undigested food ooze out from my mouth. Snatched from my lips by the wind, it sailed out in long, thick threads.

*   *   *

We counted each sunrise, watched waves flow from form to form and waited for land to appear. On the eleventh day of constant vigil, I heard a rumor, "At any hour, the figure of the Statue of Liberty will rise on the horizon to greet us."

"What does she look like?" people asked one another as we squinted into the mist to find her.

Suddenly, I saw fingers pointing. "There, there she is! Can you see? Can you see?"

I looked into the distance and could not tell if I saw a faint outline of the Statue of Liberty or another cloud hanging down to the ocean. Gradually, the curves of the statue emerged from the haze, floated toward the ship, and grew bigger and sharper. I noticed the torch in her hand high above her crowned head and I knew that we were about to touch shore. I continued to stare into the fog to see beyond her, until the perspective broadened and a long slice of land came into clear view. Too overwhelmed with the importance of the moment, I gaped like a creature watching her own birth. Filled with the vigor of one new to the world, I was ready to fight for a fresh chance at life, but I was also afraid.

The line of land floated closer to the ship. Silhouettes of buildings began to fill the horizon. In no time New York was on top of us, fizzing with energy and glittering with lights. Giant buildings rose like mountains to push the sky aside, and a new world opened before me.

Part III: A New Dawn

26 *America at Last*

O ne is born more than once. One is born each time one defeats death, transcends unbearable loss, discovers a new truth, or reaches a shore to reclaim one's inalienable rights to be free and to belong.

We disembarked the SS *Marine Flasher* at the New York Port Authority on a muggy third of August in 1947. We crossed an arched gateway at Pier 59 and entered a cavernous hall teeming with bewildered immigrants. We were herded through customs, and then informed, "You are free to go as you please." We lifted our cardboard valises, inched forward, and then stopped. *Where do we go?*

At the far end of the hall, behind a low barrier leading to the exit, we spotted a group of well-dressed people holding up signs, calling out names and scanning the faces of the newcomers. *These must be American hosts,* we realized.

We moved close to the barrier and stuck our heads into the throng of greeters to look for Sol, Fredka's friend from Munich, who promised to greet us on arrival. Of course, we had high hopes to find our relatives standing next to him. No sign of Sol. We scanned the faces for features that might resemble dead uncles or cousins, but recognized none. I began to fret. *Dates got mixed up. They forgot. What will we do?*

Suddenly, a familiar voice blared out, "Fredka! Fredka! " We turned our heads and saw Sol waving his hands wildly and screaming, "Here! Here!"

Thank God!

As we elbowed our way through the crowd toward Sol, I noticed a beautiful young woman with silky brown hair tied back with a ribbon standing next to him and staring at us. Her wide smile and tear-filled hazel eyes recalled cousins I had lost. It took only seconds for her to be at our side hugging us and introducing herself, "I am Martha, Abe's daughter." I felt enormous gratitude and cautious hope, as well as sadness.

Wishing to make the right impression on my American cousin, I held back my tears. I scrutinized her and took note of her fashionable clothes: a pastel dress hugging her tiny waist and flaring out into a circle at her calves. The equally chic wedge sandals did not escape my notice. Her white smile glowed with confidence and ease. I wondered, *Will I ever look as beautiful and self-assured?*

For a few long seconds Martha stared at us as though we had just risen out of the earth. Then, a smile lit up her face and she said, "You don't look like I imagined. You are beautiful!"

"Sank, you," Fredka and I responded.

Martha chuckled, "I am so happy to see you. You must be tired. You came such a long way and you have been through so much." She articulated each word in slow motion as if we were hearing impaired.

"We are happy to see you. We are not tired. We are happy to be in America," Fredka and I replied, showing off the bit of English we had studied so assiduously and learned just before leaving Germany.

Martha giggled with approval. "You speak English! That's wonderful!"

Mama could hardly contain herself. She tried the fragments of all the languages she had learned during her two exiles—a little Polish, a little Russian, and German—to help her tell Martha how moved she was to finally be in America; how she longed to see her two sisters and her brother Abe. "Where are they? Aren't they here?" She pleaded. "Are they all right?"

Martha recognized Mama's agitation but did not understand a word Mama uttered. Sol stepped in to let us know that only Martha and he had come to greet us. "The others are at Uncle Abe's house waiting to meet you," he explained. "Martha will drive us there." We followed our two hosts out of Pier 59 into the new world.

Stepping into a street whirling with rushing New Yorkers in wide-shouldered zoot suits, women in ankle-length skirts, ponytails, and platform shoes was a dizzying introduction.

We climbed into Martha's car, and scenes rolled into focus like fragments in a dream—at once familiar and strange. The tall buildings appeared out of proportion. They meandered at sharp angles as far as the eye could see, and stood packed so close together that they seemed to squeeze the air out of the city. We drove on amazing overpasses that coiled above streets. The stream of whizzing cars and trucks, the rasping sounds of tires, giant billboards on rooftops, blinking signs—all the clutter and buzz made the city spin and glitter. Martha and Sol cheerfully explained the passing scenes to us. Sol called out points of interest and prepared us for new surprises along the way.

The ride was exhilarating, but I was impatient to reach my uncle's house and meet our American family. Beneath the thrill of a realized dream—being in America—brewed concerns about our homelessness and the abhorrence of being a burden to a family that we had never met. *Will our aunts, uncles, and cousins love us nearly as much as the ones in Warsaw?* I tried to imagine how we might be greeted, and rehearsed how I might respond.

Sol interrupted my brooding with an announcement and a pointing finger, "This is Brooklyn. This is where your Uncle Abe lives. This is where rich people live in privately owned houses with green lawns. We are almost there."

Martha pulled up to the curb, stopped the car, and declared, "We are here." My heart lurched. She led us up stone steps, across a wide porch, and opened a handsome wooden door. We entered an impressively furnished, sun-bathed room. People I had never seen before sat in a circle on softly upholstered couches. They immediately turned their faces to greet us. Two small, demure ladies with down-white hair jumped to their feet and rushed to embrace us. Mama called out, "*Riva! Sonia!*" (Mama's two sisters.) Uncle Abe remained seated in a large armchair. His arms shook uncontrollably and his legs dangled lifelessly from the chair. He tried to speak to us, but his stutter broke with emotion. Tears streaked down his furrowed cheeks; and eyes—as blue and expressive as Mama's—peered out of puffed sockets and spoke with feeling. Mama rushed to hug him and tell him in Yiddish how much this moment meant to her. "We lost everyone. I waited so long for this moment!"

Aunt Lilly, Uncle Abe's wife, and two more uncles greeted us next. Joe, Martha's brother, enveloped me in his massive arms and held me close to his burly chest. His smile was as wide and generous as his sister's. We were greeted by Martha's handsome husband, Alvin, and his parents. Mama looked around the room and asked, "Where are all your children? And grandchildren? I so hoped to see them."

"They live far from here and they lead very busy lives. You will meet them soon."

* * *

We spent the afternoon talking and getting acquainted. My Yiddish-speaking aunts served as interpreters. The conversations were emotional and complicated. Language and background experiences separated us from the others.

We had dinner in a gracious, traditional dining room. More conversation followed. Most questions were left unanswered; tears and painful memories remained hidden, pushed down like silenced screams. Mama attempted to tell about the murders of our family, how much she missed them, and the tortures we had endured.

They listened for a while, then redirected the subject. "Americans too have suffered," they informed Mama. "There was scarcity of many things—nylons, for example—and many American soldiers died."

Mama stopped talking. She leaned back in her chair and looked bewildered as if her hopes were plunging into an abyss. From the first day that letters began to arrive from the United States, Mama promised us, and herself, "Wait until we go to America and tell our family what happened here. They will understand."

I do not doubt that they cared and wanted to comfort us. But how do you describe the color of the sky to a person who is blind, or a city to one who lives in a desert?

I listened to the oscillating drone of voices with a heavy heart and wondered, *How do I measure the Americans' war costs against the utter starvation, incarceration, and rivers of blood that were our daily experience? Will I ever be able to close the chasm that separates me from those who did not lose civilized existence and their childhood to war?*

Soon twilight glowed softly. The company left. We visited with Aunt Lilly and Uncle Abe till dark. I felt exhausted from trying to absorb all that had happened on this first day of our new life. Then Aunt Lilly led us upstairs to our bedroom. The room felt cozy and secure. I gladly slipped into the soft bed and drifted off to sleep while my mind whirled with new impressions and concerns. Still, there was a song in my heart. I was young. I could scarcely imagine how Mama felt.

We stayed in Uncle Abe's house for two weeks waiting for our new life to unfold. Fredka and I kept our ears open to catch new English words and guess their meanings. We studiously watched lips stretch and contract to form vowels and diphthongs, and tips of tongues placed between teeth to produce the unfamiliar "th" sound. Then we listened critically to our own reproductions, sometimes tearfully and at times with pride. We started the habit of memorizing songs and pages from books to help us increase our vocabulary.

Immediately, the two of us learned to use the subway. We traveled to neighboring boroughs to enquire about employment and to visit old friends from Europe. Mama remained bewildered. She could not get around by herself to see her beloved sisters: Aunt Riva who lived a few stations away in Brooklyn, and Aunt Sonia who lived in the Bronx. The subway confused her to no end. Fredka and I had to hold her hand and coax her, like a child, to set foot on the escalator. The trains and the rushing passengers made her head spin. Above all, she was in a panic that we might get on the wrong train—as if our lives could come to an end.

"Ask. Please ask. Maybe it is the wrong train. Who knows where we might end up?" She would tug at us and plead as we pushed her onto the train before the door closed.

Mama's apprehensions frustrated us. The more she pleaded, "Ask, ask. Do it for me," the more we insisted on her trust. "Mother, we know what we are doing. Please stop confusing us. We have not gotten lost yet."

That much was true. On our own, we reached our destinations without fail. When Mama was with us and we tried to prove our competence to her, we often made mistakes. In the end we had to ask for directions, and Mama felt justified. "See, it's always good to ask. What does it hurt?"

Mama, so strong and resourceful in the darkest times, was now so utterly lost!

One bright day, Martha said to my sister and me, "You are making great strides learning English and adjusting. We must do something about your names." She turned to me and noted, "No one here could possibly pronounce Estusia (my name). I think you should change it to Estelle. That name fits you perfectly." I eagerly agreed and immediately felt a little more American. We jointly decided to call my sister Frieda. I think Fredka was less happy with the change.

Transfer

After two weeks in the USA, it was decided that it would be best for ailing Uncle Abe if we stayed with Aunt Sonia. One nondescript morning, Joe, Uncle Abe's eldest son and my most caring cousin, arrived in his car to takes us to our new destination. We stepped into the car, holding on to our meager possessions: a cardboard valise packed with faded underwear and a few dirndls I could not wait to pitch out of sight.

After a long ride, we arrived at a red brick high-rise at the Amalgamated Union Housing Complex in the Bronx. A door on the ground floor opened, and Aunt Sonia, Uncle Sam, and their daughter, Frieda, welcomed us warmly into their modest apartment. Joe helped us unload our bundles, hugged us, promised to come to see us soon, and left.

As Aunt Sonia led us through her apartment, I tried to guess at her life. I took note of the smallness and tidiness of her home and how much it reflected my aunt. She too was petite, careworn, and neat. Fine worry lines were scribbled in corners of her face, kindness glowed in her dark eyes, and a puff of white hair, like a cumulous cloud, crowned her gentle face.

Uncle Sam and my cousin Frieda too were generous with smiles for us as I looked at them, juxtaposed against old images floating in my head. Mama's childhood story whispered in my ears: "My two sisters—much older than I—loved me and babied me when I was little. Sonia was the most affectionate. She used to tie ribbons to my hair and carry me in her arms."

"What happened to her, Mama?" I could hear my childhood voice float in a distant time warp.

"Uncle Sam fell in love with Sonia's beauty and wit. They married and went to America where Uncle Sam hoped to find success."

The story continued like new chapters each time a letter arrived from America. In time, I learned that two sons and a daughter were born. The story stopped abruptly with the outbreak of war. Now, after a long period of darkness, the people in the ancient story came to life at the threshold of their home. The young man who swept my aunt off her feet to carry her off to a life rich with promise had turned into a retired old man. He had not found the streets lined with gold, but he remained in love with Aunt Sonia—that was obvious.

Frieda was no longer the dark-haired little princess of her family. She was a tall shapely brunette, with jet-black eyes, frizzy hair, and an angular face that evoked little notice. She was in her late thirties and unmarried—a grave concern to my aunt.

We settled in our little room, appreciating the kind hospitality of our hosts, and watched time tick tediously by without making noticeable progress toward independence. One lonesome day, I decided to make an unannounced visit to Uncle Abe in Brooklyn. This visit should have been long forgotten, but it still festers like a wound that refuses to heal.

On the long subway ride I conjured up a fantasy that the cousins I had not yet met might drop in, by coincidence, at that precise hour. When I arrived I only found Uncle Abe drooping sadly in his armchair and Aunt Lilly and Martha sitting beside him. All three were surprised to see me, but welcomed me graciously. Aunt Lilly embraced me and asked in amazement, "How did you find your way here by yourself?"

The highlight of the visit came when Martha invited me to her room to spend time with me alone. We chatted like friends who want to get to know each other better. I was curious to learn about her growing up in freedom. I listened breathlessly to hear about college life and her degree in teaching art; and how she met Alvin, her husband. We talked and smiled at each other, and all the while I was thinking, *I am sitting here with my American cousin.*

When it was time for me to leave, Martha walked me to the door and told me that she loved my visit. As I was turning to step across the threshold, she leaned toward me and started to say something. I looked at her expectantly, hoping that she would invite me to visit again. But she stopped in mid-sentence and I left the house trying to read her mind: *She wants to invite me, but she is afraid that it might commit her to more than a mere visit.*

When I was one block away, I heard her call, "Estelle, Estelle, wait!" She ran up to me, reached out for my hand and said again, "I loved seeing you." She hesitated, and then pressed a folded bill into my hand. "Please, buy something pretty for yourself."

I felt stung. "No, no." I protested. "I don't want that. That is not why I came to see you." She wrapped my fingers over the money and insisted, "Please, keep it."

The money sealed my isolation.

27 *A Place of Our Own*

Our family found a two-bedroom apartment for us in a middle-class, residential area on Bronx Park South, across the street from the Bronx Zoo. It was a walk-up flat on the fifth floor with an expansive view of dense greenery behind the zoo's fence. I awoke each morning to the roar of lions and wild shrieks of birds, and I loved it. The building was neat, the neighbors friendly, and the rooms bright and airy. In addition, our family outfitted the flat with bedroom, living room, and kitchen furniture, dishes, and cooking utensils. We were deeply grateful.

Mama immediately began to make plans for us. She declared, "We are on our own now. You two will find work and I will stay home and take care of you, as a mother should. I will have delicious food waiting for you when you will come home hungry and tired from work. I will keep the house sparkling and cozy for you."

Of course, Fredka and I would have much preferred if Mama went to work and we could go to school, like most American young people our age. But that was beyond our hopes.

We rarely saw our American family. Aunt Sonia and Aunt Riva were too old to travel far and Uncle Abe was too ill. Mama spent hours on the phone with her two sisters, pouring her heart out, and they listened lovingly. We hardly ever heard from our cousins. Perhaps we should have done more to extend invitations and encourage contact, but we were too timid and awkward to take the initiative.

Belsey's Shop

Fredka and I found work at Belsey's ladies' cloaks and suits shop, located in a skyscraper on Seventh Avenue in Manhattan. Fredka hand-sewed hems in garments and I sat next to her sewing buttons.

Our shop, on the thirty-fifth floor, had huge plateglass windows with spectacular views of Manhattan. We could see the lofty spire of the Empire State Building whenever we glanced up from our work. On occasion, we were distracted from the otherwise dull hours by window washers standing on the narrow ledges—way above the ground— swishing their squeegees across the outside panes. Watching them nonchalantly unhook and rehook their safety straps and slide from window to window made me gasp with fear for their lives.

Fredka and I sat at a small table with three other women, all past middle age. Tillie and Rose were petite women with curly graying hair who never married and calculated that they did not miss much. The third, Gussy, was an opinionated widow with a calling to correct all social ills. The three good women took it upon themselves to take care of us—the two "Greenas." To teach us English, they made us repeat after them, "Oines" and "toid." For the longest time I thought that Ernest and Oines were different names, and I had trouble finding Thirty-First Street because I was sure it was not the same as "Toidy-Foist Street."

Working with old immigrants was not our first choice, but we learned a great deal from them. Most of the people in the shop were Jews and Italians who immigrated to the United States after World War I, and many were ardent socialists. They often talked about their past sacrifices to build the union, current events, and important figures on the national scene: Paul Robeson, Henry Wallace, Harry Truman, Thomas Dewey, and the charismatic Vito Markantonio, who ran for mayor of New York. Their voices mingled pleasantly with the hum of sewing machines and the hiss of steam irons, and kept our minds awake.

Considering our circumstances, Fredka and I felt fortunate to have found employment at Belsey's. Not many garment shops in New York were located in new buildings with large windows admitting streams of sunlight. Not all shops guaranteed union wages, employee-elected shop stewards, and grievance committees to assure that fair labor practices were observed. With the assistance of my Uncle Sam's neighbor, we became full-fledged members of Local 9 of the International Ladies Garment Workers Union (ILGWU).

Abe Cohen was the shop foreman. He made sure that people did not dillydally and he kept an unofficial count of the work we turned in. He also kept a vigilant eye on the bathroom door and knocked if he thought you lingered too long. Still, he was well liked. When his wife died, the men in the shop decided to help him find a new wife: me. I do not know what Abe thought of this, but he suddenly appeared at my side often and smiled at me a lot. I felt greatly embarrassed and pretended not to notice.

The kind women at my table urged, "It's a great opportunity, Estelle. He is good-looking, he has a good income, and he is in good health. You will be set for life."

"Yes, but he is old and has more gray hair than my father would have had if he had not been killed. I am not interested. I have other plans."

"What plans do you have?" They pressed. "You are young and pretty—true. But, let's face it, you are a Greena. You might end up sewing buttons the rest of your life, like we do. We too were once young and pretty."

I had no set plans. Like all young people, I saw promise waiting for me somewhere in the future, even if I did not yet know how to find it. I knew that I wanted to catch up with my American peers whose upbringing I could barely understand. I had to learn to talk easily with them, and above all, I had to understand the lightness in their laughter and their ability to take so many important things for granted—especially their parents.

While Fredka and I were at work, Mama would put on a smock, brush her dark-tinted hair out her way, and rush about trying to create a home atmosphere resembling her stolen paradise in Warsaw. She opened windows to invite fresh air and sunlight. She dusted, and polished, and punched pillows with her fists to fluff them up.

When she was done with sprucing up the house, she would slip out of her grungy smock, stuff her plump body into a stiff corset (she never gave up wearing one), and pull the laces tight to achieve the right body shape—ignoring the discomfort it caused. She would put on a fresh dress, stockings, and pumps to match. She would step in front of a mirror to powder her flat nose to make it seem less wide, put a smudge of rouge on her creamy cheeks, raise her head high to compensate for her short neck, step back to take a final glance at herself—and her sardonic eyes would smile back at her. She would tap out of the house, her heels clapping briskly, her dress swaying in the breeze. I would have been proud to walk with her arm-in-arm.

Me, 1948.

Mama was off on her daily walk to Tremont Avenue, shopping for dinner for us. Mama loved people and loved the outdoors. I am sure she did not miss a thing on her way—the beautiful and the ugly, the kind and the hostile. And she never failed to report it all to us as soon as we came home from work, including editorial comments. Indifference was foreign to Mama.

Mama must have been listening for our footsteps to come home at the end of the day. Before we would reach the last flight of stairs, she would fling the door open and call down to us, "Fredziuchna? Estusiuchna? Is that you? Oh, I have been waiting all day for this moment."

She would give us time to wash up, and then the three of us would sit down at the kitchen table. She would bubble and fuss, "*Kinderlech* [dear children], you are tired and famished." She would place the food in front of us and say, "Eat, eat. It is comme il faut!"

Paradoxically, the harder she tried to please us, and the more she depended on our approval, the harder we found it to show our appreciation. "The food is okay, Mama. I am not very hungry," we would say heartlessly, feeling guilty at the same time.

Still, she would light up the evenings, bringing to life her half-empty days. "You know, some storekeepers speak Yiddish," she would announce. "Imagine, some ask me, 'Why didn't you fight back? Why did you go like sheep to slaughter?'"

"It upsets me and I tell them, 'We did not march like a stupid horde of sheep, or a swarm of people with dead souls. We were individuals with wants and dreams, and names: Samek, Malka, Hannah. We were mothers and fathers who held hands of frightened children we wanted to take home and tuck safely into their beds. And there were people who carried guns less than an hour before we were escorted by a war machine that took our breath away. It's easy for you to speak. America got rich from the war.'"

Then, she would inhale sharply and try to lighten the mood. "But the people here are nice and friendly to me. The butcher always takes time to cut up the chicken for me, perfectly, better than I could do it myself."

She would quickly invite Fredka and me to talk about the hours we were away from her. "How did your day go? Are the people nice to you? You are so clever, they must be very happy with your work!"

Too tired and too uncertain to share our true feelings and doubts lest we let Mama down, our answers were short and unrevealing.

Americanization

Did you ever try to glue together a broken vase when pieces are missing? This is how it felt trying to fall in step with the new world. All the doors were open to us—figuratively—

and we lived in the friendliest country we had known since the Nazis cast us out from the human community. Still, we remained out of context. To fit in, I took careful note of the clothes young women wore when I walked to and from work. I did not miss the pearl earrings dangling from their ears, the dark stockings with still darker seams running down the middle of their calves, the bobbing hair tied back with silk bows, the swirling skirts. And I imagined myself in the prettiest outfits.

Some weekends after we had caught up with our sleep—often not before one in the afternoon—Fredka and I would go to the Grand Concourse to pick out a special dress and accessories from fashion stores. Mama took delight in our frivolities and praised our purchases.

In the evening, we would put on our favorite outfits and beautiful suede high heels—disregarding any discomfort—and meet with old friends from Munich: Sol, Janka, Halina, Kuba, Ziga, Riszek, and Mania, who one by one immigrated to New York. All survived alone. The lucky ones lived with nice—and some not so nice—aunts and uncles. The less fortunate lived alone in rented rooms. But all were bursting with determination to start life anew. Some found jobs in stores selling shoes or clothing, and dreamed of establishing their own businesses. A couple of young men worked in garment shops preparing to become fashion designers. Sol, Fredka's admirer, was one of the striving future designers. He called frequently at our house to take Fredka out on dates.

When Fredka went out on a date, Mama glued herself to the window like a sentry, and waited for her to come home. As soon as Fredka opened the door, Mama pounced on her lamenting, "Where were you so long? I did not know what might have happened to you! Why didn't you call? I was worried out of my mind. Why do you do this to me?"

"Mama," Fredka pleaded in utter frustration, "I was not gone long. I am an adult; I can take care of myself. I don't want you to stay up waiting for me."

"But how did I know? You could have been killed. Why didn't you call?"

"I did not think of calling you. Where was I going to find a telephone? For God's sake! Please let me be, Mama. Quit worrying so much."

Several nice young men courted my sister, but they distanced themselves as soon as they realized that Fredka felt duty bound not to let Mama live separately from her.

"I am nothing without you. For me life is over," Mama would often repeat to us. The war was over, but perhaps not for my mother. Neither Fredka nor I knew how to convince her that it was time to quit making us her sole reason for living and free us from unnecessary guilt.

Sol was an exception among the young men who showed a serious interest in Fredka. He appreciated what Mama meant to her. Not a single member of his large family survived the Nazi slaughter, not even a distant cousin. His fellow Wilno (Vilnius) partisan survivors remained a sustaining force in his life. There was the Golomb family with two children who treated him as their own. And there was Leon, also a lone partisan survivor, a darkly handsome, conniving, enterprising, completely free spirit who had become Sol's surrogate brother.

Thus it was ordained, though not entirely by the divine, that Fredka would marry Sol and we would all live together.

With Sol on the scene, I had to give up part of my sister. I felt abandoned, shut out. There was no one left to stand beside me. *How will I meet people and go places all alone without Fredka?* I felt happy for my sister and sad for myself.

Sad or not, I found new attachments, none like my sister, but nonetheless precious. I met Reginka (Regina) Akerman, a pretty and wise lone survivor, who lived with her aunt, uncle, and two cousins a few short blocks from us. She was equally at a loss to make friends with the young people we encountered daily. Neither one of us knew how to view life from their vantage point. Nor did our American peers know what to make of us.

I considered Reginka's two cousins, Naomi and Beth, both close to our age, prototypes of American youth: friendly, easygoing, and demanding. I watched them, with great interest, put on globs of makeup before they went out for the evening. I learned from them how very important it was to have a date every weekend, and that it was proper to kiss your date after he walked you home.

In the world Reginka and I grew up in, young people customarily met in groups to go to dances, to movies, to the theater, or to sit around a circle and discuss things in general. We flirted a great deal, but having a date every weekend was not essential. Furthermore, where we came from, kissing was considered serious. You only kissed a very special boy. That took more than one or two dates to decide. There was no way that Reginka and I were ready for this.

28 *Wedding Bells*

Fredka and Sol wed in a small temple on March 7, 1948, seven months after we stepped off the SS *Marine Flasher*. A kind, grandfatherly rabbi conducted the ceremony. A small group of spirited survivor friends joined in the celebration. Only a few members of our American family attended. After the ceremony, the Rosses, our wonderful neighbors, invited the entire party to their house for a joyful reception.

As soon as Sol moved in with us, Mama began to find faults with him. "I think we made a big mistake. Fredka is far too good for him."

Mama didn't bother to hide her scorn for Sol. I cursed the demons that had caused her love to twist.

Before Mama had a chance to adjust to Sol, another young man, Henry, entered our existence. I met Henry at a political rally I attended with friends. I noticed him standing with a friend at a distance and looking at me. In no time, he was at my side and engrossed me in a conversation on a topic I have since forgotten.

When we left the rally, Henry held in his hand a slip of paper with my telephone

Left to right: me, Sol, Fredka, and Mama at Fredka and Sol's wedding, 1948.

number. I carried away a picture in my head of a thin, boyish-looking young man with huge, intelligent brown eyes, and a fashionable wave in his slick hair.

The following weekend, Henry came to our house to take me out to dinner to Howard Johnson's, on Jerome Avenue. We talked and listened to each other with rapt attention.

That evening, Henry began to share with me his heroic story of being left alone in Berlin, Germany, while his beloved older brother, Eddy, fled from the Nazis to South America, and his parents escaped to China. Henry, thirteen years old then, remained under the guardianship of an uncaring uncle to await a scheduled departure on the Kinder Transport to England.

A twist of fate changed this plan. Henry came down with scarlet fever. His uncle brought him to a hospital and never returned. A kindly man, Dr. Krohn, nursed Henry to health, then took him to his house to join other children who lived with him as his own.

One day, a hoard of Nazis stormed to their door and roared, "*Aufmachen! Aufmachen! Verfluchte Hunde! Juden!*" (Open! Open! Accursed Dogs! Jews!).

Dr. Krohn bolted the door shut, gathered his children close to him, the youngest (two years old) in his arms, and countered the savage pounding of boots and rifle butts with silence. Later, when the barbarians miraculously gave up and left, he soothed the children's anguish with unbounded love and beautiful recorded classical music.

Henry and me, 1948.

Shortly after this, Henry's parents managed to send him a visa to join them in China. That was still during the Hitler-Stalin pact, and Henry was able to reach Shanghai via Russia, traveling on a trans-Siberian train. Parting with his beloved Dr. Krohn and the children in the orphanage left Henry scarred with guilt and armed with love for music and books.

Dr. Krohn's love left an indelible imprint on Henry, as it did on me—the listener of his story.

Henry and his parents spent the rest of the dismal war years in China. After the war, his brother, Eddie, brought them to New York.

Henry's story soon became part of my story. Every evening after work as a waiter in Manhattan, he dashed to the subway station to grab a train to the Bronx to be with me. One special evening, sitting close at a corner table in a Manhattan nightclub bathed in dim purple lights, Henry looked tenderly into my eyes and said, "I love you. Will you marry me?" He added quickly, "I know I have a miserable job, and I make very little money, but I promise to try to do better."

"I am not worried. You are smart and this is America—anything is possible. I love you and I will marry you." Henry took me into his arms and we kissed as if no one else were present.

We parted that evening fortified by love and the naive optimism of the young. I entered my house on feet barely touching the floor, peered into the dim nocturnal serenity, and tiptoed to my bed.

The next morning I shared the news with my family. Mama approved, but with some reservation. "*Zol zein mit mazel* [may luck be with you]. I am happy for you. I am also concerned. Will he be able to support a family? But I remain hopeful. He is a bright young man."

Fredka assured me, "You can always count on my support, Estelle." But I could read concern on her face.

Sol opposed. "Marry Harold," he said. "He is settled and prosperous. He loves you and will treat you well. I am not so sure about Henry."

Their acceptance of my decision came with the understanding that Henry would move in with us until we could afford a place of our own—a serious concern to all of us. Henry's father, Max, and step-mother, Alice, took me into their family with love. Eddy, his older brother by five years, remained arrogant and aloof.

Our wedding in May 1949 was a simple affair, and the planning much less intimidating than Fredka and Sol's had been. It took place at the same temple, and the same kindly rabbi performed the ceremony. I wore a pretty, taupe-colored lace dress and short veil that Fredka had helped me select. Mama, my sister, and Sol stood by my side with much love and hope for my happiness, keeping their fingers crossed that Henry would soon find a job that would pay well enough for us to move out.

Sometimes, wish fulfillments come from the most unexpected places. I read in my union newspaper that the ILGWU was opening a school for union organizers. All graduates would be hired at the end of one year's study of labor law, labor history, and labor relations. Knowing how much Henry hated waiting on tables, how hopelessly bad he was at it, and how much he would love the opportunity to study, I rushed home to share the news with him. We stayed up half that night wracking our brains: "Can we get along an entire year on one income? Will it put an unreasonable burden on Sol, Fredka, and Mama?" At the end of our wrangling we concluded, "This is our best hope."

I talked the matter over with Mama, Fredka, and Sol. They listened with concern, weighed my options, and then promised to be supportive. Henry applied, passed all the interviews and entrance exams, and was accepted.

The year passed, but not easily. Money was a constant issue. Henry studied hard but was often moody about the lack of privacy. Sol resented Henry's moodiness and could not wait for him to graduate and move out. Mama tried harder than ever to please everyone with her cooking. Fredka and I found ourselves caught in the impossible trap of feeling responsible for everyone's happiness.

Yet a special light entered our existence that year. Fredka gave birth to Fern. Of course, everyone feels close to the miracle of life when a new baby is born. But when you carry in the wreckage of your memories the disappearance of all the children you had known and loved, your heart nearly breaks with joy and hope. When I beheld that little bundle of existence—so tiny I could nestle her in the palms of my hands—I felt that I was holding a salvaged spark of my father and my people, a miracle with infinite prisms of renewal.

Mama immediately had a new mission in her life. I too assumed that my role as the baby's sole living aunt made special demands on me—all much welcomed. We surrounded the new life with attention and love. We jumped to her side at the least sound of complaint, stuffed food into her mouth each time she opened it, and went gaga when she did something new. With so many female protectors, Sol had little room to express his opinion about raising the baby. He went his own quiet way of a traditional father: the provider.

Fredka, the happiest and proudest of mothers, had the wisdom to draw limits for Mama and me, in the best interests of the baby. We respected her role and admired her good judgment and firmness.

Cleveland, Ohio

At the end of that school year, Henry and I moved to Cleveland, Ohio, where Henry assumed his position as an organizer for the International Ladies Garment Workers Union. I did not leave Mama and Fredka with ease. Nor was I free of fear of a strange city where I knew no one.

We moved into a tiny, sublet room in a private home owned by a meddling elderly couple. I soon found work in a friendly office and made new acquaintances. Life ebbed and flowed uneventfully, until one autumn day in 1951 when we learned that I was going to have a baby. The news filled us with new dreams, hopes, and a flood of energy. We rushed out to find an airy four-room flat to welcome our baby. We hunted in furniture stores for sale items, painted our new home, and took pride in the results.

Motherhood and Finding a Special Path of My Own

Our son was born on Mother's Day, and the anniversary of Victory Day, May 8, 1952. We named our baby Steven (*Symche*, joy, which was my father's Yiddish name). With Symche at my breast, I felt my heart expand with love. I never tired of watching him and marveling at how quickly his eyes grew wide with wonder. At night, the softest smack of his lips had me up and at his side in a flash, while the loudest clamor from elsewhere left me sound asleep.

I cherished the gift of motherhood, but joy begs to be shared. I missed Mama and Fredka. I longed for their support and advice. I wanted to show off to them Steve's amazing accomplishments. I missed Sol's direct comments and hilarious jokes. Above all, I missed little Fern. On Passover, we loaded our car, folded back the rear seat to make a sleeping area for the baby, and drove through the night to New York. Steve stayed awake most of the exhausting trip, turning and tossing to follow with his eyes the lights of cars passing from opposite directions.

The reunion was a great comfort, but unsatiatingly brief. We talked and hugged a lot, and it was time to leave. Few visits followed. They were made more special when we got to see my cousins Max and David, who had immigrated to America and went on to raise families.

Three years had passed since Steve's birth, too fast to fully appreciate its lasting impacts. Steve remained the center of my universe as I watched him grow into a bright little boy with a crown of straw-colored hair and eyes wide with curiosity. During the month of Steve's third birthday, May 1955, another beautiful, bouncy boy entered our family constellation and lit up every corner of our existence. We named him Andy.

With the two exuberant boys in my life, I felt richer than ever. Still, there were moments of unanswered cravings, of emptiness that begged to be filled. I missed family, old friends, and a community with a common history.

You never know when an opportunity will open a new path; nor can you tell if you will find the courage to exploit it. In my case, a whimsy of fate set me on a special journey. My children and two extraordinary people pointed the way.

It all began when we enrolled Steven in a nursery school at the Jewish Community Center. To my delight, mothers took turns, once a week, to assist the hired teacher. Just as all mothers do, I looked forward to seeing my child interact with his classmates. I did not take particular note of how Steve's little friends responded to me. But their teacher did, and she tried to convince me, "You have a special gift with children. No other mother evokes the responses from them that you do. You must go to school and get a degree in education."

"Do you realize what you are suggesting?" I asked. "I have only completed three years of formal elementary school and I never went to high school. I am not qualified to go to college. Furthermore, English is not my native language. Thank you, but I cannot even think about such grandiose dreams."

She pressed, "Western Reserve University is here in town. Go there and speak to someone at the School of Education. See what they think."

So one day I left Andy with a friend. I plopped Steven into the car, gave him his favorite satin-rimmed blanket-rag, and a few Tinkertoy cars, and I drove to the School of Education at Western Reserve University. I knocked on the door of the dean's office. I had no idea what a dean of a college was. If I had known, I would have been scared. I asked the secretary if I could see someone in charge of education. A few seconds passed, then the dean stepped into the office and introduced himself. I told him briefly about the nursery school teacher's recommendation, about my background and lack of education, and I asked if there was a training program for nursery school assistant teachers.

To my great surprise, the kind man did not send me on my way. Instead, he invited me into his office and engaged me in a long conversation on a variety of topics. His comments and queries put me completely at ease. We talked until dusk began to fall. Fortunately for me, Steven played quietly with his toy cars, soothed by the low tone of conversation, his blanket, and his thumb.

At the end of the meeting, the nice man said, "Young lady, you will not be a teacher's assistant, you will be a teacher. First, you will have to take a college entrance exam. I do not doubt that you will pass. Furthermore, you will receive a grant in aid to make it possible for you to pursue your education; and you can attend evening classes to accommodate your children's needs."

I was as fear struck as I was complimented by this response. I protested, "The last time I was in a formal classroom, I was nine years old. Maybe it would be best if I only took courses to qualify for an assistant teacher?"

"Not to worry," he said. "Why do you think I spent all this time talking with you? Why do you think I asked you so many questions? You proved to me that you will do fine."

He set up an appointment for my college entrance exam. I passed and continued to chase dreams—an endowment from my father who had a French teacher for Fredka and me in the bunker when the last remnant of the Warsaw Ghetto was going up in flames. Paradoxically, my brightest inspirations have been born in the darkest places.

I never weighed the price I would have to pay for my undertaking, nor would I let anything stand in my path. It was as if an invisible hand took over my destiny.

Necessity creates solutions, and my schedule quickly fell into place. A babysitter took care of the children on the evenings I had to attend classes and Henry was out of town. When everyone was fast asleep, and the night so silent that you could hear a mouse stir, I tiptoed out of bed and into the kitchen, pulled up a chair to the table, and sat down to delve into my schoolwork and into a space of my very own. Sometimes, I studied until I became aware of the rising orange tinge of the sun, and I quickly jumped into bed to catch a few nods of sleep.

At first, my classes were excruciatingly difficult, but the rewards sufficed. I enjoyed the people I met in my classes and loved studying with them for tests. I made friends with admirable women who started college after they had families. My life took on a precarious pace of meeting deadlines and keeping up with daily chores. I was determined not to let my personal pursuit deprive my children of their deserved attention. And I felt that I must not neglect Henry—a product of prewar German upbringing who held firmly to the conviction that a male does not help with household chores. Still, I felt more alive.

Mama's Visit

To my great dismay, Mama strongly opposed my college classes and would go to any extreme to stop me. "One does not go to school when one is married and has children," she would lecture when she came to visit. When Henry worked late and she saw me near the door to go to class, she would suddenly announce, "I just decided, I am going out too. You will have to stay with the children."

"I will not stay. I will find a babysitter and be late for my class. But I am going!" Furious and guilt-ridden, I would holler at her, "I am only taking two classes. Why don't you see that the children are not deprived in any way? Why don't you want to recognize that when I better myself, I better their lives? How I wish you would do good things for yourself. Go places. Meet people. Have a life!"

There were also wonderful moments during Mama's visits. On scenic car rides, or when we listened to music together, her face would light up with enchantment and she would say, "This moment should last forever! It should never end! It is so beautiful!" Not a shimmer, or phantasmal shadow, or a note would escape her rapt attention.

Or when she played with the children and made funny faces at them to make them laugh. She looked at them with awe. "They are so beautiful, so exceptionally bright. Steven will be a composer or a philosopher," she would predict with absolute conviction.

I treasured these moments when Mama returned to me as I remembered her to be. But her contentment was easily shattered: "Henry is too demanding; I am not treated with deserved respect." When she raced to pile up bread on her plate, before anyone touched the breadbasket, she complained, "I don't think you all wash your hands well enough."

All smiles would vanish from the children's faces; Henry would grow somber and irritable, and I would be forced into the role of an arbitrator.

I grieved. *Why can't Henry be more understanding? Why can't Mama see that her capriciousness robs her of her grandchildren's affection?* I so hoped that one day they would be able to imagine her the way she had been, a true hero, and that one day they would understand that not all Holocaust survivors are able to start over again.

"In the concentration camps, finding the will to fight was easy; it was a basic instinct; you must live. But in the United States the will to fight was more complicated; it was finding happiness and meaning for existence," my grandson Matthew observed in a high school paper. He wrote that years after Mama died, but memory is not linear.

Indeed, finding meaning and contentment after the war was a greater challenge for Mama than for Fredka and me—we were young and life was starting for us.

Mama looked back. She rarely ventured far from her street. Television became as real to her as life. When Liberace appeared on the screen, it was as if a special guest entered the room. She returned his theatrical greeting and his saccharine smile with a nod of her head and a gracious grin. She listened to each schmaltzy note as if it he were in the room playing for her.

Her most independent undertaking was walking to a neighborhood school for a preparatory course for American citizenship. When the sessions were over, she was the proudest new American imaginable, finally officially stamped and validated. No longer "stateless"—a soul without rights.

Fredka

Neither the long miles between New York and Cleveland nor the flux of time eroded the quality of attachment between my sister and me. "Estelle, I am so proud of you!" she cheered me on the phone when I was accepted at Western Reserve University. "I know how Mama feels about it. Don't let her deter you. It is good to be selfish. Imagine how guilt-free we would be if Mama did nice things for herself."

I knew she was right. I knew that it was good for my children to have a self-sufficient mother, and it was good for me.

How do you get rid of deathly fears that have no place in a free land? You call your sister, of course.

"Are you still as afraid of dogs as I am?" Fredka's voice would ring in my ear across the miles of telephone wire.

"What do you think? Of course."

"We must get rid of this nonsense. Our children will learn from us to be afraid," she would say.

I would eagerly agree, "You are right. Really, it's stupid. After all, the dogs here are not Nazi-bred. These dogs are cute. Our children say so." But in my head I would see dogs, no matter how small, wrap their sharp, bloodstained fangs around my throat.

It took years of mutual encouragement before we stopped turning catatonic when a dog crossed our path and Fredka could boast to me, "I was so brave today, I petted a dog! Of course, Fern kissed the dog on the mouth. I trembled, but I managed to fake a smile."

Eventually my children had their own dog, Mutley, in the house. Guess who took care of it? And I gained enough confidence to stroke him, especially when my children coaxed, "Pet the dog, Mommy. Why are you so scared? The dog likes you." My children taught me courage, and more.

Shortly after I started college, Fredka applied and was accepted at the Brooklyn College Special Baccalaureate Program. With this, she stepped up the first rung toward a career as an educator and writer.

29 West Virginia and Beyond

I had barely shaped my life in Cleveland when Henry was transferred to Huntington, West Virginia, to open a regional ILGWU local. He was happy with his new assignment. I fretted. *Will I be a complete outsider in this town at the hem of the world?*

Huntington was a serene town at the terminus of the Chesapeake and Ohio Rivers. It had small homes with wide front porches and sweet-smelling honeysuckle hanging from trellises. There was no match there to the Cleveland Playhouse Theater, or the Severance Hall Symphony, but I learned quickly that one's soul does not have to starve if there are books and record stores and interesting people. Actually, the town had much more than that. It was encircled by roads that took you up dizzying, green mountain ledges. I loved that! So did Mama when she came for a visit. It did not take me long to appreciate the quiet, matter-of-fact town and my gentle neighbors.

My boys owned the town and safely explored all its corners. Best of all by far, Bobby, my third son, was born in Huntington. He uttered his first words with a melodious West Virginia twang and kept it as long as we lived there. His brothers were his role models, and it did not take him long to become clever and self-sufficient.

The boys bloomed, and the hours of the day flew by as quickly as thoughts. Then night descended—the children were fast asleep, Henry was attending meetings with union members or political groups, and an acute longing would gnaw at me. I missed my family and my community of friends more than ever. To fill a corner in this void, I enrolled at Marshall University for evening courses and continued my studies.

One special visit to New York, when Fredka gave birth to Stephanie, came and went as quick as a cat's leap. I rocked the new baby in my arms, let her steal my heart, and then flew away.

Curtain Fall in Huntington

Was I the last to learn that Henry had had an affair? Who could tell? One day, he simply confessed. In one instant, my world shattered. The man I loved became unreal, a stranger in some deep impenetrable way. I listened to him in silence and horror as he made it clear that I could no longer count on him. I wanted to howl and scratch and bite and shriek. Instead, I sat like a wooden figure, too ashamed of ordinary anger.

The children! How will I support my boys? Who can I turn to for advice?

Calling Mama or Fredka was out of the question. An immutable pact we had formed in the concentration camps would not allow me: we must bear our own pain in silence to spare the other. "I am fine; I can take the cold, the hunger, the fear. Please don't worry about me," we would say.

I discretely called the doctor for a miracle medicine. The doctor prescribed pills. Of course, they did not solve my distress, but they numbed my senses.

The phone rang one morning. I lifted the receiver and I heard my voice speak to Fredka in slow motion and with fake cheer, "I am almost completely well. You have no cause to worry about me."

"What? You were sick? How could you not tell me? We must stop this nonsense. The war is over. You worry me more by trying to protect me from the truth." Her voice dropped, and she cooed a few soothing words before we hang up.

That same evening I heard a soft tap on my front door. I looked up and heard Fredka's voice through a door crack, "Estusiuchna, it's me, Fredka." The door opened ever so slowly, her face leaned toward me. "I left the girls with Mama and grabbed the earliest plane I could catch to be with you."

There are angels in this world!

After Fredka left, Henry's friend, Miles Stanley, convinced us to seek professional counseling. Our marriage was saved, my festering wounds bandaged over.

Soon after, Kennedy was elected president and Henry was rewarded for campaigning with him in West Virginia. Henry got a new job, for which he was well qualified, with the Economic Development Administration, Department of Commerce, in Washington, DC. We moved again.

It took Henry no time to find a charming small house in Chevy Chase. I cannot forget that Sol and Fredka generously lent us the money for a down payment. We enrolled the children in a neighborhood school, and I signed up at the University of Maryland to complete my degree in education and gain greater independence.

Just as Bobby turned five and started kindergarten, I graduated and found a teaching position in a public school near our house. In the morning, my boys were off to Rolling-wood Elementary School and I to Rock Creek Forest, ten minutes away, to teach sixth graders. My work recalled the wonderfulness of childhood that I had missed. I treasured my students' drive to challenge the status quo, their curiosity, and their capacity to experience the pure joy of being.

After eight years of teaching at one school, I earned a master's degree from George Washington University and a new position as a reading teacher. I made new young friends who taught me to appreciate their tenacity and exuberance.

Fredka too was making up for lost time. She was among the first to join the Women's Strike for Peace. I am awed remembering that my sister was invited to go with Coretta Scott King and the Women's Strike for Peace to the seventeen-nation disarmament conference in Geneva in 1962, and that she spoke on global peace in the House of Commons in London. Who could have imagined that my sister, a person who once lived under a regime that took away all her rights, even her right to live, would one day stand in this venerable place and have the ear of esteemed public servants dedicated to upholding the noblest ideals of government: freedom, security, and equal rights for all people?

How gratified Tata would have been to know that his two daughters transcended hell and continued to reach. "Girls must never fall short of their dreams and potential. Girls must never take a back seat to boys," were among the first values he taught us.

How proud he would have been to see Fredka earn a PhD degree from the City University of New York Graduate Center—as if there had never been a Holocaust to block her path.

Above all, he would have cherished, as much as I do, the book Fredka wrote: *Bearing the Unbearable, Yiddish and Polish Poetry in the Ghettos and Concentration Camps*, published by SUNY Albany Press.

Glaser family, 1968.

Fredka, 1962.

Mama's Last Struggle

Mama too was proud of us, but never ceased to measure our achievements against a dream lost. "Just think what our lives would have been if there had not been a Hitler. And Fredka would surely have married a more interesting man than Sol." Till her dying day, Mama continued to agitate and hope that Fredka would find a more "suitable" man.

Eventually, Fredka found a small apartment for Mama a few blocks from her house in Belle Harbor, New York. She was not happy to live alone, but Fredka's house was tranquil and Mama adjusted—reluctantly but with dignity. She spruced up her small flat and took pride in its appearance. She took short walks to Jacob Riis Park to meet with a friend, and remained a close part of Fredka's family life.

That precarious harmony lasted for nearly two decades. Then, we began to notice a change in Mama. At first it was subtle. The bright twinkle in her eyes gradually dimmed; she became confused, suspicious, and agitated. We soon had to face the shocking fact that our mother was suffering from Alzheimer's disease. Before long, she could not look after herself, and we had to place her in a nursing home.

Mama quickly shriveled to a miniature self, delicate and brittle as old lace. Her skin remained luminous. Her eyes stayed sky blue as ever, but she was so utterly lost! She no longer nagged and was easier to love. I did not want to let go of the feisty mother I knew.

I sat at her side, pleading, "Mama, say something to me, just one thing? Do you know who I am? I am Estusia. I love you."

She stared into me, as if I were a fragment of memory, and remained mute. Her silence screamed in my head. Sometimes, I spoke for her—imagining reading her mind—and wrote it down in my diary to give it an illusion of permanence.

A Diary Entry During a Visit with Mama

Windows hermetically sealed. Not a crack to admit a wisp of wind or a sound into my room. Nothing glides, nor caresses, nor sways here. No shadows or glimmers dance. I press my face to the windowpane and watch the mute animation outside, like watching fish in an aquarium.

What good are your visits? You come for just a blink of time. Then, you leave me among strangers. So I sit and wait for death to come. I am not angry, just helpless, cut off. I miss the warmth and nearness of your children, the sounds of home. I don't entertain dreams or fantasies any longer. They are too sharp a contrast to my present reality.

There is mercy in nature. Death dims life slowly. I cooperate. Make no mistake, I am a survivor. This time to survive is to surrender.

My heart still pulsates with a subconscious force. Who planted this in me, nature? Or someone, long ago, wanted me to live?

I am bobbing like a crippled fish between waves. See me in the chair? I hang on one side. The aide you hired props me up with a pillow, and I bob to the other side, and hang. I absorb the food they pump into me. It isn't that I want it, and it isn't that I don't want it. Live or die? I don't contemplate. I just breathe.

I don't complain or rejoice—except an occasional flash of recognition returns. I do little or nothing to kindle it.

I am in a fog of nothingness. My surroundings and sounds—be they your cooing and pleading, or the feeble mumblings of my neighbors—all fuse into a meaningless hum. Your arrivals and departures, all that goes on around me, is a haze. I float in a cloud of ether. I am in a place inside me I have never been before.

A Final Breakup

It did not take me half as long this time to figure out the cause of Henry's absentmindedness and self-absorption. He had a new fling. It was time to call our marriage quits.

For thirty years, Henry and I had been one in the eyes of all who knew us and in the way we shared our lives: the heartbreaks and the joys. How does one suddenly rise one morning as a half-person? How does one live alone? How does one shop and cook for oneself only? How host a dinner party?

Again, I searched for chinks of light to find heart. I reminded myself that I was in a stronger position the second time around: the boys were grown and I had a job I loved. Steve and Andy had graduated from college, and Bob was a student at Tulane University. I was angry enough to accept a new identity: single.

With great trepidation, I took a first bold step and went to a meeting of Parents Without Partners, held in a private home in my neighborhood. Afraid to enter, I caught sight of a woman who looked as timid as I felt heading toward the dreaded door. I approached her and asked, "Are you going there? She nodded, "Do you mind if we go in together? I don't know anyone there. I am a little scared."

"That would be nice. I am Helen Lessin. I don't know anyone there either."

Meeting Helen and Halina Yasharoff, another divorcee, was a Godsend. We immediately became family and remain that way to this day. We planned joint holiday dinners with our children, went to concerts and plays together, and supported one another unselfishly.

One year later, Helen married Donald Shaw, Halina married Richard Peabody, and I met Charles (Chuck) Laughlin.

Chuck, a pleasant-looking man with smiling brown eyes, receding hairline, and a firm body frame was born in Davenport, Iowa. Chuck loved nature and hiking; so did I. We often trampled together on the Appalachian Trail, getting to know each other, letting the sounds of our voices and the metronome of our footbeats soothe our anxious hearts. Chuck too was recently divorced.

I quickly learned to admire Chuck's analytical mind, his depth of knowledge, and his accomplishments. He was an electrical engineer at NASA's Goddard Space Flight Station, had been the project manager of the Hubble Telescope, and one of his inventions, the Nimbus Weather Satellite, still orbits the earth. Above all, Chuck won my affection with his love, thoughtfulness, loyalty, and complete dependability. He was as steady as an oak tree.

Thankfully, my sons worked through the family breakup thoughtfully, listening, observing, and being supportive to each other, to me, and to Henry.

30 *Farewell to Mama (1981)*

Just a phone call and the world lost a tone of luster. Fredka was sobbing, "Estusiuchna, Mama just died."

We knew that moment was coming. And we knew that death at this point would be liberating. Still, people you love never grow old in your mind, and you cannot imagine the world without them.

When she was lowered into her grave, my family stood in a tight circle, and friends were near, reverently honoring the passing of a life. How different this first natural loss felt from the countless deaths I had witnessed before. I felt agony and gratitude.

"I love you, I love you," I whispered. *You will live, you will live,* my heart screamed. *You will live in every cloud configuration you taught me to see, in every spring flower and sparrow's song. You will live in each grass blade and newborn dawn, in the love and generosity you have in your progeny sown. Mama, how I lament your torments.*

When I was a child, I knew little about my mother, the person. She was my mother and that encompassed all. I knew that mothers could see into every corner of their child's soul, guess every whim, soothe every fear, and protect from every wrong, even the child's own folly. I liked Mama best when she was indiscriminately sympathetic to my point of view, and I judged her harshly when she was less than omniscient. I confess that I scrutinized Mama with the selfish heart of a child, even when I was no longer a child. There is so little I know about her inner self. All I have now of Mama is abstraction.

Mama was born in a remote shtetl called Ciasnik, in the province of Vitebsk, in western Byelorussia. Based on family accounts, my ancestors were always on the march. A country that welcomed them one year chased them out the next. One day a person was rich, the next day homeless. I loved to listen to Mama's stories about Ciasnik. They sounded like tales from a storybook, a real storybook—my storybook about the world before my world. I still remember asking, "Mama, why did you leave your shtetl?"

"We were chased out by hooligans," she replied with few words.

"Where were the policemen? Did you go to them for help?"

"The Russian authorities did not care about Jews being beaten, robbed, or chased. They helped."

Aghast, I asked, "Where did you go?"

"We packed up what we could carry on our backs and left the shtetl with the wild Cossacks chasing after us."

I pictured her running from the hooligans. My mind froze on her words.

"That was terrible. What did you do?"

"We were very hungry," she said softly as she busied herself with small chores. Her words mingled with cinnamon smells of just-baked cookies.

"How hungry?"

"Well, so hungry that we ate potato peels."

"Oh, my gosh!" My heart sank to hear that my loving mother had suffered such unheard-of starvation. The world suddenly felt less safe.

Mama's anecdotes of Ciasnik were not only of sadness. She spoke with love of the people who worked hard to care for family and community, and to serve their God. She brought to life weddings, babies being born, and holidays celebrated between disasters. She recalled golden fields at harvest time and hauntingly dazzling peasant songs filling the autumn sky like winds.

Mama lulled us to sleep with traditional Yiddish and Russian lullabies with themes of love, longing, and meadows blue with forget-me-nots.

Mama rose from a history of persecution with the heart of a hero. Ciasnik remained for Mama what Warsaw represents to me—a place where dreams and love thrived, despite human cruelty.

31 A New Leaf

Chuck and I married in January 1986, five years after we had met. A few months later, Chuck retired from NASA and accepted a one-year position with the Italian aerospace agency, Aeritalia, located in Turin, Italy. I took a one-year leave of absence from my teaching position to join him.

Living in Turin was a glorious way to start life together. The windows of our tenth-floor apartment, on Corso Monte Cucco, looked out on a ring of mountain peaks, and at its feet sprawled a panorama of Baroque rooftops, church spires, and a scatter of green slopes climbing toward the mountain crests. Our lives were rich with adventures: traveling, meeting people, hiking down the slopes of Mont Blanc, Monte Rosa, and more.

Chuck's most valued accomplishment during our stay was writing a winning proposal for Aeritalia to be prime building contractor for the inter-European X-Ray Astronomy Satellite (SAX). This was the first inter-European competitive bid that the agency had won. As a result, Chuck's contract with Aeritalia was extended for two more years. The SAX satellite was launched from Cape Canaveral a year after we returned home.

What special gift, besides stunning memories, did I bring back from Italy? Without doubt, it was attending an Italian history and language class given by an extraordinary

Chuck and me, Italy, 1986.

woman and polyglot, Mara Moscca. Two mornings each week, I joined a small circle of French and British women (wives of professionals working in Turin) in Mara's living room to listen to her Italian history lectures and to discuss novels she selected for us to read. We read nearly all the novels by Natalia Ginsburg and a few by other popular Italian writers. The class was challenging, but I quickly learned to communicate with people in their native language and to appreciate their culture.

Like cut flowers, our Italian adventure decorated the moment and then left a void. Nonetheless, we were happy to be back with family and old friends.

The good years with Chuck rolled on swiftly and with few complications. Children married. Their wives—first Cena, then Jenni and Chris—entered our lives and made us love them. Grandchildren were born, and we found new happiness in watching them grow up and fly off to become more fully themselves. But God caresses with one hand and punishes with the other (Mama's saying).

Learning Again to Accept Loss

In mid-1990, we began to notice changes in Fredka: her reasoning was not as sharp as we expected of her, her patience was growing short, and she suffered frequent physical pain.

"All my aches and stress, my throbbing head, my aching back, my forgetfulness stem from Brigitte's beating in Majdanek. Remember how her whip came down on me like a gate of hell? You remember it, don't you?"

"Yes, I remember."

Sadly, Fredka was frequently haunted by her Holocaust experiences, in spite of her many interests, accomplishments, and the passage of time. Her joys often touched the edge of suffering. "Because I love my children so much, I feel all the more the horror of the slaughter of children in the Holocaust. Don't you sometimes feel that way?"

Of course I do. Still, I think that I was better at staying grounded in the present. Perhaps that is why I live longer. The past weighed on her and came back to haunt her at the very time when she was most vulnerable—when she was diagnosed with Alzheimer's disease.

As her illness progressed, she became artful in disguising her forgetfulness with a quip and a chuckle. She was just as quick to accept the bitter truths. She climbed down every humiliating step of her illness with inspiring courage.

Because of a mix-up, we saw together the movie *Elegy for Iris*, an account of Iris Murdoch's encounter with Alzheimer's, written by her husband, John Bailey. The scenes were

My granddaughter Lauren's wedding, Chicago, September 2010. All three of my sons and their families are in this picture. Courtesy Lauren and Jason Cutler.

Fredka's daughter Stephanie and her family. *Far left:* Stephanie's husband, Barry; *far right:* Stephanie; *middle:* their children, Michelle and Brian, August 2010. Courtesy L. James Miller.

frightening. I pleaded with Fredka, "Let's leave. We saw enough. Why do we have to see it to the end? Please." No entreaty would get her out of her seat.

When the film ended and we stepped out into the fresh air, I felt guilt-ridden and frightened for my sister. Fredka surprised me again: "I am glad we did not leave," she declared with a sober face and composed voice. "I had to see all of it. In a way it was cathartic. I must face what is happening to me. Iris lived with it."

The time soon came when Fredka's surroundings grew foreign and menacing to her, and she had to swallow ever more potent medications to give her peace. She spent hours drowsing in her armchair, her back reclining for support, shoulders drooping, arms folded in front of her like tucked wings of a dove. "I am fine," she would murmur when we tried to comfort her. "I am just so tired."

On May 31, 2005, my sister shuffled out of her chair to lie down in her bed. Without disturbing a soul, she let her last breath expire. Irena, her wonderful caregiver, came into her room to check on her only minutes later.

Fredka stayed in her home throughout her illness. Sol; her two daughters, Fern and Stephanie; sons-in-law, David and Barry; and her grandchildren, Noah, Michelle, Adam, and Brian—the loves and pride of her life—all shared her ordeal.

Fern's voice on the phone, hoarse with pain, whispered the shattering words to me that my sister was no more. I remained standing, planted to the floor as if I had been transported to a dark planet! My heart had died and the world was empty: could such emptiness ever be filled?

How will I live without my first playmate, my bossy big sister/little mother with whom I practiced to hold my anger, manage my jealousy, and count on love? Will I ever laugh as heartily, as senselessly as I did with her? And who will help me remember that love, and decency, and a child's heart can survive even crematoria and gallows? Will I be able to go the rest of the road without her to give me heart to face new challenges?

Four years into Fredka's illness, Chuck was diagnosed with multiple myeloma. He too faced his tribulations with courage and humility. He rarely complained and continued to look after the people he loved, even while life was slowly seeping out of him. At first I could not face the seriousness of his illness. I hung on to every hope that the next new drug would perform a miracle and he would remain part of me as long as I lived. Neither my love, nor the dedicated efforts of Doctor Boccia could stop the progress of his illness. Chuck died in June 2008, at home with family and friends at his side.

I roamed silent rooms, finding scraps of comfort in the traces Chuck left, touching the objects he touched, resting my head on his pillow. Sometimes, I felt his presence, light as air, or I heard his breath next to me, real as life. I would turn to him, and he would melt like an apparition.

Sol died in August of the same year. Another light went out, another segment of shared history ended. Memories stay: his patience to put up with Mama's erratic behavior in his house, his humanism, his heroic stories of partisan existence in the Vilnius forest, and the wonderful jokes he always came up with to loosen a tight moment.

Life Flows Again

I felt abandoned. Afraid. would this emptiness left by the three deaths ever end? And then life slowly started to flow again. I took long walks in Rock Creek Park. I drank in the forest mist, and I walked to the song of the rushing creek. In the silence of nature, I felt moved by memories, by my life, by my death. By contrast, the fact of what I had took on a glorious splendor. More than ever, I felt the nearness of my grandchildren: Lauren, Nina, Emmarose, Eric, Matthew, Alex, Twain, and Jeremie; my children; Fredka's family; and my friends.

They, and my optimistic nature, and my memories of the ordinary people who paid the supreme price to live according to the dictates of their conscience, are the source of my renewal. They—and all children—are the reason why, after eighty-two years of climbing in and out of darkness, I still believe that the source of joy is inexhaustible. And I still believe, as firmly as ever, that there will always be among us Lamed Vav Zaddikim, thirty-six righteous people, to perform Tikkun Olam, the healing of the world. I am convinced that any one of us may be one of them. After all, they go unnoticed because of their humble nature.

In loss and grief, I collect all that cannot be lost, or shattered, or separated—eternity of moments and unity of universes.

Fredka's grandson's wedding. *Left to right:* David, Fern, Krystyn, Noah (the groom), Jillian, and Adam (Fern's youngest), August 2010. Courtesy Krystyn and Noah Zagor.